The Poet's Work

The Poet's Work:

29 Masters of 20th Century Poetry
on the Origins and Practice
of Their Art

Edited by Reginald Gibbons

Houghton Mifflin Company Boston

Library of Congress Cataloging in Publication Data
Main entry under title:
The poet's work.

    Bibliography: p.
    1. Poetry—Addresses, essays, lectures.
2. Poetics—Addresses, essays, lectures.
I. Gibbons, Reginald.
PN1064.P6   808.1   79-10673
ISBN 0-395-27616-0
ISBN 0-395-28057-5 pbk.

Printed in the United States of America
v 10 9 8 7 6 5 4 3 2

Grateful acknowledgment is made for permission to reprint the following:

"Writing," from *The Dyer's Hand and Other Essays,* by W. H. Auden. Copyright
© 1972 by W. H. Auden. Reprinted by permission of Random House, Inc.
    "The Specialization of Poetry," by Wendell Berry, reprinted from *The Hudson
Review.* Copyright © 1975 by Wendell Berry. Reprinted by permission of the au-
thor.
    "The Pleasures of Formal Poetry," from *A Poet's Alphabet,* by Louise Bogan.
Originally from the symposium entitled "Experimental and Formal Verse," includ-
ing contributions by William Carlos Williams and Richard Wilbur, in *The Quar-
terly Review of Literature, Thirtieth Anniversary Poetry Retrospective,* vol. XIX,
Nos. 1–2 (1974). Copyright © 1954 by the *Quarterly Review of Literature.* Re-
printed by permission of the publisher.
    "Words Before a Reading," from *Poesía y literatura I y II,* by Luis Cernuda.

How the feminine silver burns
That's struggled against oxide and alloy,
And quiet work silvers
The iron plough and the poet's voice.

— *Osip Mandelstam*
(Translated by Kenneth Irby)

The friends that have it I do wrong
When ever I remake a song,
Should know what issue is at stake:
It is myself that I remake.

— *William Butler Yeats*

Preface

WHETHER IT IS TO describe his or her own work — its sources, themes, models, or its place in the world — or to recount the steps, both intuitive and reasoned, by which it came into being, a poet's thoughts about his poetry, and about poetry in general, have a special claim on our attention. But not every poet wants to write down such thoughts, nor is every poet capable of doing so. And if a desire to write of the vocation or craft of poetry does make itself felt, many poets will resist it, preferring out of superstition or modesty to keep what they know to themselves. Thus, the first thing to be noted about this kind of writing is that historically it is relatively scarce, and for the most part has occupied the minds of poets only in occasional essays, letters, or digressions from other subjects of inquiry.

Until our century, comparatively few poets have bothered to leave any account at all of their own writing. The self-consciousness of the poet, however, appears to have increased markedly in the modern era, and in our own time there has been a prodigious outpouring of documents recording the attitudes, or perhaps we may call them the beliefs, of poets in many languages. Poetic self-scrutiny has become a frequent and expected adjunct to the writing of poems, most recently in the form of the interview.

If such writings are rare in some languages, this fact must have causes of great complexity; these would have to do not only with the intrinsic nature of poetry in those languages but also with the varying expectations, from nation to nation, that a modern poet feels are laid upon him both by the tradition of poetry — including his fellow poets — and by the larger society in which he works. (Of course, larger influences do finally influence the "intrinsic" nature of poetry.) These expectations may not always extend to a desire to hear a poet speak openly and in prose about his own work. That modern poetry is often considered obscure, however, may have impelled more poets in our time to speak of it in prose, and it seems that this impulse has been felt more keenly by poets writing in English. Indeed, it seems true that we as readers, insofar as we can influence the poetry of our own time, have done so partly by our interest in such writings in English, thus at least influencing poets if not poems.

The curious reader who has glanced ahead at the table of contents will have noted already, then, the absence of several great modern poets who wrote trenchant and compelling essays on poetry, among them Yeats, Eliot, and Pound. Their prose and poems are so universally available that it seemed wiser to use the limited space of this volume to collect more out-of-the-way pieces. But it goes without saying that a collection such as this, however much space it might save by eliminating what is elsewhere easily accessible, must remain incomplete. The list of other writers, both English-speaking and foreign, who might have found a place here is very, very long.

In order to remedy the deficiencies of this volume, in part at least, I have appended A Very Selective Reading List, where, in addition to historical sources and the basic prose of Yeats, Eliot, and Pound, the reader will find mention of interviews, essays, books, and so on, by other poets not included in this volume. Moreover, the Notes on the Poets and Selections contain references to further works by those poets who *are* included here. (The sources of the selections themselves, in many cases worth study in their entirety, can be found on the copyright page.)

The selections, representing a wide variety of poetic traditions and approaches, are divided into two sections and appear chronologically ordered in each. In the first section, the poet's sense of his vocation and his understanding of why he writes are uppermost. These two concerns take several forms. For some poets (like Pessoa, Cernuda, or Montale) the question of poetic vocation is understood as a question about the self and the origins of poetic intelligence. For others (like Mandelstam, Schwartz, or Shapiro) it is more a question of how the poet lives in the larger culture around him. The one is an introspective investigation; the other looks outward. The question of *why* one writes may elicit many different sorts of answers, but despite the apparent differences between the works by Stevens, Seferis, and Kunert, for example, it is this one question that interests them all. Since every poet is a unique figure, his sense of poetic vocation may also be singular, and in several of these pieces (especially Char's, Lorca's, and Pasternak's) we encounter an inquiry, however oblique, that leads back through the individual poet's sense of his own art to the nature of poetry itself.

In the second section, the poets are primarily occupied with craft and with the welter of decisions, dogmas, beliefs, and methods that come into play as a poem takes shape. Some poets have approached this topic fragmentarily — Valéry, Machado, and Auden, for example. Others have soberly taken stock of their own powers and necessities, as have Crane, Thomas, and Levertov. Williams and Heaney, especially, strive to relate their sense of craft to their sense of place. In a few cases, we have more formal essays, like Moore's and Bogan's.

Taken together, these pieces will, I hope, feed the appetites of young poets and creative-writing students for thought about the craft they are learning. For there is much to be gained in a testing of one's own seriousness against that of great poets. And to begin to find one's own way through the poetry of the past, even the recent past, is to find some of the unacknowledged (because as yet unrecognized) sources of one's own poetic intelligence.

A token of the shared solicitude for poetry, among poets, has been the hoard of welcome suggestions I have received from poets and friends as I compiled this book. For the possibility of having overlooked some things (and I am sadly certain that I missed many) I take all responsibility, even as I thank those who helped me to find what is here. I especially thank Jonathan Galassi whose careful editorial hand gave shape to the final manuscript.

Reginald Gibbons
Princeton, New Jersey, 1978

Contents

II. PRACTICE: The Poet's Work

Marianne Moore, Poetry   159

I. ORIGINS: The Sources and Motives of Poetry

Czeslaw Milosz

Ars Poetica?

I have always aspired to a more spacious form
that would be free from the claims of poetry or prose
and would let us understand each other without exposing
the author or reader to sublime agonies.

In the very essence of poetry there is something indecent:
a thing is brought forth which we didn't know we had in us,
so we blink our eyes, as if a tiger had sprung out
and stood in the light, lashing his tail.

That's why poetry is rightly said to be dictated by a daimonion,
though it's an exaggeration to maintain that he must be an angel.
It's hard to guess where that pride of poets comes from,
when so often they're put to shame by the disclosure of their
   frailty.

What reasonable man would like to be a city of demons,
who behave as if they were at home, speak in many tongues,
and who, not satisfied with stealing his lips or hand,
work at changing his destiny for their convenience?

It's true that what is morbid is highly valued today,
and so you may think that I am only joking

or that I've devised just one more means
of praising Art with the help of irony.

There was a time when only wise books were read
helping us to bear our pain and misery.
This, after all, is not quite the same
as leafing through a thousand works fresh from psychiatric clinics.

And yet the world is different from what it seems to be
and we are other than how we see ourselves in our ravings.
People therefore preserve silent integrity
thus earning the respect of their relatives and neighbors.

The purpose of poetry is to remind us
how difficult it is to remain just one person,
for our house is open, there are no keys in the doors,
and invisible guests come in and out at will.

What I'm saying here is not, I agree, poetry,
as poems should be written rarely and reluctantly,
under unbearable duress and only with the hope
that good spirits, not evil ones, choose us for their instrument.

Translated from the Polish
by the author and Lillian Vallee

Fernando Pessoa

Toward Explaining Heteronymy

1

(Manuscript, 1915?)

I DO NOT KNOW who I am, what soul I have.

When I speak with sincerity, I do not know what sincerity I am speaking with. I am varyingly someone other than an "I" of whom I do not know if he exists (if he is those others).

I feel beliefs which I do not hold. I am ravished by passions I repudiate. My constant study of myself is constantly pointing out to me breaches of faith by my soul toward some character which perhaps I never had nor does it think I do have.

I feel multiple. I am like a room with innumerable fantastic mirrors that distort by false reflections one single pre-existing reality which is not there in any of them and is there in them all.

As the pantheist feels he is tree [?] and even the blossom, I feel myself as different beings. I feel myself living alien lives, in me, incompletely, as though my soul shared in all human beings, incompletely, through a sum of non-"I"s synthesized in an afterthought "I."

2

(Manuscript, n.d.)

Be plural like the universe!

3

(Typescript, n.d.)

Since we are Portuguese, one should know what we are.

A. Adaptability, which in the mind leads to instability, is therefore the diversification of the individual within himself. A good Portuguese is different persons.

B. The predominance of emotion over passion. We are tender-hearted and not very intense, unlike Spaniards — our absolute opposites — who are passionate and cold.

I never feel so Portuguesely myself as when I am feeling different from myself — Alberto Caeiro, Ricardo Reis, Alvaro de Campos, Fernando Pessoa, and as many others as there have been or will be.

4

Aspects (Preface for the projected edition of his works)
(Typescript, 1930?)

The complex *oeuvre*, whose first volume this is, is in substance dramatic, though in form various — in this case, passages of prose; in other books, poems or philosophies.

Whether the mental constitution which has produced it is a privilege or a sickness, I do not know. What is certain, however, is that the author of these lines — I am not sure if he is the author of these books — never had one personality only, and never thought, or felt, except dramatically — that is to say, in an imagined person, or personality, who could have those feelings more properly than he himself could

There are authors who write plays and novels, and in those plays and those novels they attribute feelings and ideas to the characters inhabiting them, and are often indignant when these are taken as their own feelings or their own ideas. Here the substance is the same, though the form be different.

To each relatively permanent personality that the author of these books has succeeded in living within himself he has given an expressive temperament, and has made of this personality an author, with a book or books with whose ideas, emotions, and art he, the real author (or perhaps apparent, since we do not know what reality may be) has nothing to do, except that he has been, in writing this down, the "medium" of characters he himself created.

Neither this work nor any to follow have anything to do with who wrote them. He neither agrees with what gets written in them nor disagrees. He writes as though to dictation, and, as though the dictating were being done by someone who might be a friend and therefore with reason be asking him to write what he dictated, he finds interesting—perhaps only out of friendship—what, at dictation, he is writing.

The human author of these books does not recognize in himself any personality. When by chance he feels a personality emerging within himself, he soon sees that it is a creature different from what he is, even though similar; a mental son, perhaps, and with inherited qualities, but the differences that come of being someone else.

That this quality in the writer may be a form of hysteria, or of so-called dissociation of personality, the author of these books neither contests nor upholds. Slave as he is of the multiplicity of himself, it would not help him at all to agree with this or that theory about the writings which have resulted from that multiplicity.

That this way of producing art should cause wonder does not surprise him; what does surprise him is that there should be anything that does not cause wonder.

Certain theories which the author does at present hold have been inspired by one or other of those personalities that have, for a moment, for an hour, now and then, passed consubstantially through his own personality, if this exists.

To assert that these men, all different, all well defined, who have passed bodily through his soul, do not exist—the author of these books cannot do that, because he does not know what existing is, nor which—Hamlet or Shakespeare—is the more real, or indeed is real.

These books will be the following, for the time being: first, this volume, *Book of Unrest*,* written by one who says he is called Vicente Guedes, next, *The Keeper of Sheep*† and other poems and fragments by (the likewise deceased) Alberto Caeiro, who was born near Lisbon, in 1889, and died where he was born, in 1915. If I am told that it is absurd to speak like this about someone who never existed, my answer is that I also have no proofs that Lisbon has ever existed, or I who am writing, or anything whatever.

This Alberto Caeiro had two disciples and a philosopher-contin-

* *Livro do Desassossego.*
† *O Guardador de Rebanhos.*

uer. The two disciples, Ricardo Reis and Alvaro de Campos, followed different paths, the former having intensified the paganism discovered by Caeiro and made it artistically orthodox, and the second, basing himself on another part of Caeiro's work, having evolved an entirely different system, one based entirely on sensations. The philosopher-continuer, António Mora (the names are as inevitable—as much imposed from outside—as the personalities are), has one or two books that he is writing, by which he will completely prove the truth, metaphysical and practical, of paganism. A second philosopher of this pagan school, whose name, however, has not yet appeared in my inner vision or hearing, will give a defense of paganism based entirely on other arguments.

It is possible that later more individuals of this same class of genuine reality may appear. I do not know, but they will always be welcome to my inner life, where they are better at living with me than I am at living with external reality. I need not say that I agree with part of their theories and do not agree with other parts. This is neither here nor there. If they write beautiful things, these are beautiful, independent of any metaphysical considerations about their "real" authors. If, in their philosophies, they say any truths—if there are truths in a world that consists of there being none—those things are true independent of the intention or "reality" of whoever says them. By becoming like this—at worst a high-sounding lunatic; at best not just one writer but a whole literature—while I may not have done much toward amusing myself (which to me was already a sufficient aim), I do perhaps help to aggrandize the universe, since whoever, when he dies, leaves on paper a beautiful line of poetry has left the heavens richer and the earth too, and more movingly mysterious the reason for there being stars and people.

With such a deficiency of literature as there is today, what can a man of genius do but convert himself, on his own, into a literature? With such a deficiency of coexistible people as there is today, what can a man of sensibility do but invent his own friends, or at least his intellectual companions?

I thought at first of publishing these works anonymously as far as I am concerned—and, for example, establishing a Portuguese neopaganism with various authors, all different, collaborating in it and spreading it. But, besides the fact that the Portuguese intellectual milieu is too small to allow one (even without breaches of confidence) to keep up the mask, the mental effort necessary for keeping it up was futile.

In my vision, which I call inner simply because I call the determinate "world" outer, I hold steady, clear, recognized, and distinct the physiognomy, the traits of character, the life, the ancestry, in some cases the death, of these personages. Some of them know some of the others; others do not. As for me personally, none of them knew me, except Alvaro de Campos. But if, some day, traveling in America, I were suddenly to meet the physical person of Ricardo Reis, who (as I see it) lives there, not a single movement of surprise would pass from my soul to my body. It was all certain — but, before this, already certain. Which is life?

5

Aspects

(Manuscript, 1930?)

The series, or collection, of books, whose publication begins with these, represents not a process new in literature but a new way of employing an already time-honored process.

*

I desire to be a creator of myths, which is the highest mystery that any human being can perform.

*

The concocting of these works does not represent any metaphysical position whatever. I mean, in writing down these "aspects" of reality, totalized into persons supposed to hold them, I am not laying claim to some philosophy which insinuates that the only thing real is the existence of aspects of some reality that is either elusive or nonexistent. I do not hold that philosophical belief nor the contrary philosophical belief. In my craft, which is literary, I am a professional, in the highest sense of the term; that is, I am a scientific worker who does not allow himself to hold opinions foreign to the literary specialization to which he devotes himself. And my not holding either this or that philosophical opinion with regard to the concocting of these person-books must, equally, not lead anyone to believe I am a skeptic. The matter in hand is on a plane where metaphysical speculation, because it does not legitimately come in, has no need to have any particular characteristic. Just as the physicist holds no metaphysics in his laboratory, and the doctor holds none in the diagnoses he makes [?] not because he cannot, but because (...) so my metaphysical problem does not exist, since it cannot, nor should it, exist within the pages of these, my other-men's-books.

6

Draft of a letter to Adolfo Casais Monteiro*

(Manuscript, 1935)

I have always, since a child, had the compulsion to augment the world with fictitious personalities, dreams of mine rigorously constructed, visualized with photographic clarity, understood right into their souls. I was only five years old when already, as an isolated child who wanted only to be so, I used to take as my companions various figures from my dreaming—one Captain Thibeaut, one Chevalier de Pas—and others whom I have now forgotten, whose forgetting, like my imperfect recollection of those two, is one of the great regrets of my life.

This looks like simply the kind of childish imagination which amuses itself by attributing life to dolls. But it was more: I did not need any dolls to help me conceive those figures intensely. Clear and visible in my constant dreaming, realities precisely human to me—any doll, being unreal, would have spoiled them. They were people.

What is more, this tendency did not go away with childhood. It developed in adolescence, took root as that grew, became finally the natural form of my spirit. Today I have no personality: all that is human in me I have divided among the various authors of whose work I have been the executant. I am today the point of reunion of a small humanity which is only mine.

It is, however, simply a case of the dramatist's temperament raised to the maximum—writing, instead of dramas in acts and action, dramas in souls. This phenomenon, apparently so confused, is in substance as simple as that.

I don't deny, though—I favor, even—the psychiatric explana-

---

* See *Páginas de Doutrina Estética,* 1946; p. 261 ff.

tion, but it must be understood that all the higher activity of the spirit, because it is abnormal, is equally susceptible to psychiatric interpretation. I do not mind admitting I may be crazy, but I insist it should be understood that I am not crazy differently from Shakespeare, whatever the relative value of the by-products of our craziness may be.

As a "medium," in this way, nevertheless, I subsist. I am, however, less real than the others, less coherent, less personal, eminently open to influence by all of them. I am also a disciple of Caeiro, and I even remember the day — March 13, 1914* — when, having "heard for the first time" (that is, having finished writing, in one single gulp of the spirit) a large number of the first poems of the *Keeper of Sheep*, I immediately wrote, straight on, the six intersection-poems which make up *Slanting Rain*† (*Orpheu* 2), a manifest and logical influence of Caeiro on the temperament of Fernando Pessoa.

7

(n.d.)

Some persons I put into stories, or into subtitles of books, and sign what they say with my own name; others, I project absolutely and do not sign except with the statement that it is I who wrote things down. The types of person are distinguished as follows: with the ones that I detach absolutely, the very style is foreign to me and, if the character asks for this, even contrary to mine; with the figures that I countersign, there is no difference from my own style, except in the inevitable details without which they would not be distinct from each other.

I will compare some of these persons, to show by way of example what these differences are. Bernardo Soares, the assistant librarian, and Barón de Teive — both of them persons I regard as foreign — write with the same stylistic substance, the same grammar, and the same kind of taste. In fact, they write in the style which, good or bad, is mine. I cite these two because they are cases of the same phenomenon: lack of adaptation to the reality of life and, what is more, lack of adaptation for the same motives and reasons.

---

* Translator's note: this date is given as March 8, 1914 in the letter of January 13, 1935, to Adolfo Casais Monteiro.
† *Chuva Obliqua.*

But while it is the same Portuguese in Baron de Teive and in Bernardo Soares, the style does differ in that the nobleman's is intellectual, stripped of images, rather — how shall I put it? — stiff and restricted; that of the bourgeois writer is fluid, of the nature of music and painting, not very architectural. The nobleman thinks clearly, writes clearly, dominates his emotions, though not his sentiments; the librarian dominates neither emotions nor sentiments, and when he thinks it is in a manner subsidiary to feeling.

There are, besides, notable similarities between Bernardo Soares and Alvaro de Campos. But at once there arises in Alvaro de Campos the negligence of his Portuguese, the looseness of his images, more intimate and less deliberate than with Soares.

Sometimes to distinguish between them lays great burdens on my power of spiritual discernment; for instance, to distinguish some melodious composition of Bernardo Soares from a composition of the same gist which is mine.

There are moments when I do it suddenly, with a perfection that leaves me amazed; and my amazement implies no conceit, for, not believing in even a fragment of human liberty, I am amazed at what happens in me, just as I would be at what might happen in other people — in two strangers.

Only a strong intuition could be a compass in the wildernesses of the soul; only by means of a feeling which uses the intelligence yet does not get assimilated to it, even though fused with it for the moment, is it possible to distinguish these dream persons, in their reality, from each other.

*

In these proliferations of personality or, rather, inventions of different personalities, there are two grades, or types, which will be revealed to the reader, if he has observed them, by distinct characteristics. In the first grade, the personality shows up by means of ideas and sentiments of its own, distinct from mine, just as, on a lower level than that grade, it shows up by ideas offered in the course of reasoning or argument, which are not mine — or, if they are, I am not aware of it. The *Anarchist Banker* is an example of this inferior grade; the *Book of Unrest* and the figure of Bernardo Soares are of the higher grade.

The reader must have been surprised that, though I publish the *Book of Unrest* (or it is published) as being by a man called Bernardo Soares, an assistant librarian in the city of Lisbon, I have nonetheless not included it in the *Ficções do Interlúdio.** It is because Bernardo Soares, while distinguishing himself from me by his ideas, his sentiments, his ways of seeing and of understanding, does not distinguish himself from me by his style of expression. I present that different personality through the style which is natural to me, there being only, to distinguish him, the inevitable special tone which the speciality of his emotions itself necessarily projects.

In the authors of the *Ficções do Interlúdio* not only the ideas and the sentiments are distinct from mine: the very technique of composition, the very style, is different. There, each personage is created different through and through, and not just differently thought out. That is why verse predominates in the *Ficções do Interlúdio.* Othering oneself is more difficult in prose.

*

Aristotle divided poetry into lyric, elegiac, epic, and dramatic. Like all well-conceived classifications, this one is useful and clear; like all classifications, it is false. The genres do not separate out with such essential facility, and, if we closely analyze what they are made of, we shall find that from lyric poetry to dramatic there is one continuous gradation. In effect, and going right to the origins of dramatic poetry — Aeschylus, for instance — it will be nearer the truth to say that what we encounter is lyric poetry put into the mouths of different characters.

The first degree of lyric poetry is the one where the poet, focused on his sentiment, expresses that sentiment. Should he, though, be a creature of variable and varied sentiments, he will express something like a multiplicity of personages unified only by a temperament and a style. One step farther up the poetic ladder, and we have the poet who is a creature of various and fictitious sentiments, with more in him of imagination than of sentiment, and living each state of soul through intelligence rather than through emotion. This poet will express himself as a multiplicity of personages unified not now by temperament and style, since temperament has been replaced by imagination and sentiment by

---

* Translator's note: the title Pessoa was reserving for the poems of the three heteronyms, Caeiro, Reis and Campos.

intelligence, but only by style, pure and simple. Another step up the same ladder of depersonalization, or perhaps imagination, and we have the poet who, as each of his various mental states appears, integrates with it in such a way that he completely depersonalizes himself, so that, living that state of soul analytically, he makes of it something like the expression of another person, and, this being so, the style itself tends to vary. Now take the final step, and we shall have a poet who may be various poets — a dramatic poet writing in lyric poetry. Each group of states of soul relatively close to one another will become a personage, with his own style, with sentiments perhaps different from, even opposed to, those typical of the poet in his real-life person. And so lyric poetry — or some literary form analogous in its substance to lyric poetry — will have raised itself to dramatic poetry, yet without giving itself the form of drama, either explicitly or implicitly.

Let us suppose that a supreme depersonalized writer like Shakespeare, instead of creating the character of Hamlet as part of a play, created it as simply a character, without a play. He would have written, so to speak, a play with only one character, a prolonged and analytical monologue. It would not be legitimate to go hunting, in that character, for some definition of the sentiments and thoughts of Shakespeare, unless the character were faulty, because it is the bad dramatist who reveals himself.

For some temperamental motive which I do not propose to analyze, and it is not important that I should, I have constructed within myself various characters, distinct from each other and from me, those characters to which I have attributed various poems I do not know how, in my own sentiments and ideas, I would have written.

That is how these poems of Caeiro, those of Ricardo Reis, and those of Alvaro de Campos must be considered. It is no good searching in any of them for ideas or sentiments of mine because many of those poems express ideas I do not accept, sentiments I never had. They must simply be read as they are — which is indeed the way one should read.

An example: I wrote with alarm and repugnance the eighth poem of the *Keeper of Sheep*, with its childish blasphemy and its absolute antispiritual attitude. In my own and apparently real person, with which I live socially and objectively, I neither use blasphemy nor am I antispiritual. But Alberto Caeiro, as I conceive him, is so. Therefore, he must write so, whether I wish it or not, whether I think like him or not. To deny me the right to do this would be the same as denying Shakespeare the right to give expression to the soul of Lady Macbeth, on the grounds that he, the poet, was not a woman nor, as far as one knows, hysterico-epileptic — or attributing to him a tendency to hallucinations and an ambition which does not recoil before crime. If it is so with the imaginary characters of a play, it is equally legitimate in the case of imaginary characters without a play, for it is legitimate because they are imaginary and not because they are in a play.

It seems unnecessary to explain a thing that is so simple and intuitively comprehensible. But it happens that human stupidity is great, and that human good will is not conspicuous.

8

Preface to Ficções do Interlúdio

(Typescript, 1916?)

Astrologers refer the effects to be found in all things to the operation of four elements: fire, water, air, and earth. This perception will enable us to understand the operation of influences. Some act on men as earth does, burying them and abolishing them, and those are the governors of the world. Some act on men as the air does, enveloping them and concealing them from one another, and those are the governors of the beyond-world. Some act on men as water does, which soaks and converts them into its own substance, and those are the ideologues and the philosophers, who diffuse through other people the energies of their own soul. Some act on men as fire does, which burns in them everything accidental, and leaves them naked and real, individual and truthful — and those are the liberators. Caeiro is of that race. Caeiro had that force. What does it matter that Caeiro be of me if Caeiro is like that?

So, operating on Reis, who had as yet not written anything, he made come to birth in him a form of his own and an aesthetic persona. So, operating on myself, he has delivered me from shadows and letters, has given more inspiration to my inspiration and more soul to my soul. After this, so prodigiously achieved, who will ask whether Caeiro existed?

Translated by Jonathan Griffin

Osip Mandelstam

The Word & Culture

THERE IS GRASS in the streets of Petersburg, the first runner-sprouts of the virgin forest that will cover the space of contemporary cities. This bright, tender greenery, with its astonishing freshness, belongs to a new, inspired nature. Petersburg is really the most advanced city in the world. The race to modernity isn't measured by subways or skyscrapers, but by the speed with which the sprightly grass pushes its way out from under the city stones.

Our blood, our music, our political life—all this will find its continuity in the tender being of a new nature, a nature-Psyche. In this kingdom of the spirit without man every tree will be a dryad, and every phenomenon will speak of its own metamorphosis.

Bring it to a stop? But why? Who will stop the sun as he sweeps in summer harness to his paternal home, seized by a passion for returning? Rather than beg alms from him, isn't it better to favor him with a dithyramb?

> He understood nothing
> And he was weak and shy as children are,
> Strangers trapped wild animals
> And caught fish for him . . .[1]

Thanks to you, "strangers," for such touching concern, for such tender care of the old world, which is no longer "of this world," which has withdrawn into itself in expectation of and preparation for the coming metamorphosis:

> Cum subit illius tristissima noctis imago,
> Qua mihi supremum tempus in urbe fuit,
> Cum repeto noctem, qua tot mihi cara reliqui,
> Labitur ex oculis nunc quoque gutta meis.[2]

Yes, the old world is "not of this world," yet it is more alive than it has ever been. Culture has become the Church. There has been a separation of Church (i.e., culture) and State. Secular life no longer concerns us; we no longer eat a meal, we take a sacrament; we do not live in a room but a cell; we do not dress, we attire ourselves in garments. At last we have found our inner freedom, real inner joy. We drink water in clay jugs as if it were wine, and the sun likes a refectory better than a restaurant. Apples, bread, the potato — from now on they will appease not merely physical but spiritual hunger as well. The Christian — and every cultivated man is a Christian now — knows not a merely physical hunger or a merely spiritual nourishment. For him, the word is also flesh, and simple bread is happiness and mystery.

*

Social distinctions and class antagonisms pale before the division of people into friends and enemies of the word. Literally, sheep and goats. I sense, almost physically, the unclean goat smell issuing from the enemies of the word. Here, the argument that arrives last in the course of any serious disagreement is fully appropriate: my opponent smells bad.

The separation of culture from the state is the most significant event of our revolution. The process of the secularization of our political life has not stopped with the separation of church and state as the French Revolution understood it. Our social upheaval has brought a deeper secularization. The state now displays to culture that curious attitude we might best call tolerance. But at the same time, there is a new kind of organic connection binding the state to culture as the appanage princes used to be linked to the monasteries. The princes would support the monasteries for the sake of their *counsel*. That says all. The state's exclusion from cultural values places it in full dependence on culture. Cultural values ornament political life, endow it with color, form, and, if you will, even with sex. Inscriptions on government buildings, tombs, gates, safeguard the state from the ravages of time.

Poetry is the plow that turns up time so that the deep layers of time, the black soil, appear on top. There are epochs, however, when mankind, not content with the present, longing for time's deeper layers, like the plowman, thirsts for the virgin soil of time. Revolution in art inevitably tends to Classicism. Not because David [3] reaped Robespierre's harvest, but because that is how the earth would have it.

One often hears: that might be good, but it belongs to yesterday. But I say: yesterday hasn't been born yet. It has not yet really come to pass. I want Ovid, Pushkin, Catullus afresh, and I will not be satisfied with the historical Ovid, Pushkin, Catullus.

In fact, it's amazing how everybody keeps fussing over the poets and can't seem to have done with them. You might think, once they'd been read, that was that. Superseded, as they say now. Nothing of the sort. The silver horn of Catullus—*"Ad claras Asiae volemus urbes"* [4]—frets and excites more powerfully than any futuristic mystification. It doesn't exist in Russian, and yet it must. I picked a Latin line so that the Russian reader would see that it obviously belongs to the category of Duty; the imperative rings more resonantly in it. Yet this is characteristic of any poetry that is Classical. Classical poetry is perceived as that which must be, not as that which has already been.

Not a single poet has yet appeared. We are free of the weight of memories. For all that, how many rare presentiments: Pushkin, Ovid, Homer. When in the silence a lover gets tangled up in tender names and suddenly remembers that all this has happened before, the words and the hair, and the rooster that crowed outside the window had been crowing in Ovid's *Tristia*,[5] a deep joy of repetition seizes him, a head-spinning joy—

> Like dark water I drink the dimmed air,
> Time upturned by the plow; that rose was once the earth.

So that poet, too, has no fear of repetition and gets easily drunk on Classical wine.

What is true of a single poet is true of all. There's no point forming schools of any kind. There's no point inventing one's own poetics.

*

The analytic method, applied to style, movement, form, is altogether a legitimate and ingenious approach. Lately, demolition has become a purely formal artistic premise. Disintegration, decay, rot—all this is still *décadence.* But the Decadents were *Christian* artists; in their own way, the last Christian martyrs. For them, the music of decay was the music of resurrection. Baudelaire's "Charogne" is a sublime example of Christian despair. Deliberate demolition of form is quite another matter. Painless suprematism. A denial of the shape of appearances. Calculated suicide, for the sake of mere curiosity. You can take it apart, or you can put it together: it might seem as though form were being tested, but in fact it's the spirit rotting and disintegrating. (Incidentally, having mentioned Baudelaire, I would like to recall his significance, as an ascetic hero, in the most authentic Christian sense of the word, a *martyr.*)

A heroic era has begun in the life of the word. The word is flesh and bread. It shares the fate of bread and flesh: suffering. People are hungry. Still hungrier is the state. But there is something even hungrier: time. Time wants to devour the state. Like a trumpet-voice sounds the threat scratched by Derzhavin on his slate board.[6] Whoever will raise high the word and show it to time, as the priest does the Eucharist, will be a second Joshua, son of Nun. There is nothing hungrier than the contemporary state, and a hungry state is more terrible than a hungry man. To show compassion for the state which denies the word is the contemporary poet's civic "way," the heroic feat that awaits him.

> Let us praise the fateful burden
> Which the people's leader tearfully bears.
> Let us praise the twilight burden of power,
> Its intolerable weight.
> Whoever has a heart, he must hear, O time,
> How your boat goes to the bottom . . .[7]

One shouldn't demand of poetry any special quiddity, concreteness, materiality. It's that very same revolutionary hunger. The doubt of Thomas. Why should one have to touch it with the fingers? But the main point is, why should the word be identified with the thing, with the grass, with the object that it signifies?

Is the thing master of the word? The word is a Psyche. The living word does not signify an object, but freely chooses, as though for a dwelling place, this or that objective significance, materiality, some beloved body. And around the thing the word hovers freely, like a soul around a body that has been abandoned but not forgotten.

What's been said of materiality sounds somewhat different applied to imagery: *"Prends l'éloquence et tords-lui son cou!"* [8]

Write imageless poems if you can, if you know how. A blind man will recognize a beloved face by just barely having touched it with his seeing fingers; and tears of joy, the authentic joy of recognition, will spurt from his eyes after a long separation. The poem is alive through an inner image, that resounding mold of form, which anticipates the written poem. Not a single word has appeared, but the poem already resounds. What resounds is the inner image; what touches it is the poet's aural sense.

"And the flash of recognition alone is sweet to us!" [9]

These days, something like glossolalia manifests itself. In sacred frenzy, poets speak in the language of all times, all cultures. Nothing is impossible. Just as a room where a man is dying is opened to all, so the door of the old world is flung wide before the crowd. Suddenly everything has become common property. Come in and help yourself. Everything's available: all the labyrinths, all the hiding places, all the forbidden paths. The word has become, not a seven-stop, but a thousand-stop reed, instantly animated by the breathing of all the ages. In glossolalia the most striking thing is that the speaker does not know the language in which he speaks. He speaks in a totally obscure tongue. And to everyone, and to him, too, it seems he's talking Greek or Babylonian. It is something quite the reverse of erudition. Contemporary poetry, for all its complexity and its inner violence, is naïve: *"Ecoutez la chanson grise . . ."* [10]

A synthetic poet of modern life would seem to me to be not a Verhaeren, but a kind of Verlaine of culture. For him, the whole complexity of the old world would be like that same old Pushkinian reed. In him, ideas, scientific systems, political theories would sing, just as nightingales and roses used to sing in his predecessors. They say the cause of revolution is hunger in the interplanetary spaces. One has to sow wheat in the ether.

Classical poetry is the poetry of revolution.

(1921)
Translated by Sidney Monas

Notes

1. Pushkin, *The Gypsies*. In this passage the old Gypsy tells Aleko an old legend about Ovid in Moldavia, without recalling the poet's name or age. He tells it as if it happened yesterday.

2. Ovid, *Tristia*, I.3, lines 1–4.

    When the gloomy memory steals upon me
    of the night that was my last time in the city,
    when I bring to mind that night on which I left so many things
       dear to me,
    even now, the teardrops fall from my eyes.

3. Jacques Louis David (1748–1825). French painter. Before the Revolution, leading exponent of the Classical trend in painting; court painter to Louis XVI. Became an ardent republican, was elected to the Convention, and voted for the king's death. Later, under Napoleon, became first painter to the emperor. Under the Restoration spent his last years in Brussels.

4. Catullus, Number 46. "Away let us fly, to the famous cities of Asia."

5. Reference is to Ovid's *Amores*, I 4,65, not to the *Tristia*.

6. See Mandelstam's essay "The Nineteenth Century," which quotes in full the poem referred to here. See also "About the Nature of the Word," note 2, concerning Derzhavin, in *Selected Essays* (1977).

7. Mandelstam, Number 103.

8. Verlaine, "Art poétique," stanza 6. "Take eloquence and wring its neck!"

9. Mandelstam, Number 104.

10. "Listen to the tipsy song." This appears to be a misquoting of "Art poétique," stanza 2:

> Rien de plus cher que la chanson grise
> Où l'Indécis au Précis se joint.

(Nothing more precious than the tipsy song [or "gray song"] In which the Vague is joined to the Precise.)

Notes by Sidney Monas

Boris Pasternak

Some Statements

1

WHEN I TALK about mysticism or painting or the theater, I talk in that peaceable and unconstrained way in which any freely thinking reader considers things. When the talk turns to literature, I remember the book itself and become unable to consider things rationally. I have to be shaken awake and brought by force from a physical condition of dreaming about the book, as if from a swoon, and only then, and only with great reluctance, overcoming a slight revulsion, will I join in a conversation on any other literary subject, where the issue is not a book but something else, no matter what: public readings, say, or poets or schools or new developments in the arts, and so forth. But not for anything would I ever move of my own free will, uncompelled, out of the world of what deeply interests me, into this world of amateurs taking an interest.

2

Contemporary trends of thought imagine that art is like a fountain, whereas it is a sponge. They have decided that art should gush forth, whereas it should absorb and become saturated. They think it can be broken down into methods of depiction, whereas it is composed of organs of perception. The proper task of art is to be always an observer, to gaze more purely than others do, more receptively and faithfully; but in our time it has become acquainted with powder and the make-up room, and displays itself from a stage, as if there were two kinds of art in the world, and one of them, having the other in reserve, can permit itself the luxury of self-distortion, a luxury equivalent to suicide. It shows itself off, while it ought to be sunk in obscurity, in the back rows, hardly aware that its hat is aflame on its head, or that, though it has hidden away in a corner, it is stricken with a phosphorescence and a light-transparency, as with some kind of illness.

3

A book is a cubic piece of burning, smoking conscience — and nothing else.

Mating calls are the care nature takes to preserve the feathered species, her vernal ringing in the ears. A book is like a wood grouse calling in the spring. Deafened with its own sound, listening spellbound to itself, it hears nothing and nobody. Without it, the spiritual race would have had no continuation. It would have become extinct. Monkeys had no books.

A book is written. It grows, it gathers experience, it knocks about the world, and now it's grown-up and — this is what it is. It is not to blame for the fact that we can see right through it. That's how the spiritual universe is arranged. Yet not very long ago the scenes in a book were thought to be dramatizations. This is wrong — what should it want them for? People forgot that the only thing which lies in our power is to know how not to distort the voice of life that sounds within us.

Inability to find and tell the truth is a deficiency that cannot be covered up by any amount of ability to tell untruths. A book is a living being. It is quite conscious and in its right mind: its pictures and scenes are what it has brought out of the past and committed to memory, and is not prepared to forget.

4

Life hasn't just begun. Art never had a beginning. Always, until the moment of its stopping, it was constantly there.

It is infinite. It is here, at this moment, behind me and inside me, and, as if the doors of an Assembly Hall were suddenly flung open, I am immersed in its fresh, headlong omnilocality and omnitemporality, as if an oath of allegiance were to be sworn without delay.

No genuine book has a first page. Like the rustling of a forest, it is begotten God knows where, and it grows and it rolls, arousing the dense wilds of the forest until suddenly, in the very darkest, most stunned and panicked moment, it rolls to its end and begins to speak with all the treetops at once.

5

What is a miracle? It is that once upon a time there lived on earth a seventeen-year-old girl called Mary Stuart, and one October day, at her little window, with the Puritans jeering outside, she wrote a poem in French which ended with these words:

> *Car mon pis et mon mieux*
> *Sont les plus déserts lieux.*

Second, it is that once upon a time, in his youth, at a window with October carousing and raving outside, the English poet Charles Algernon Swinburne finished his *Chastelard*, in which the quiet plaint of Mary's five stanzas was thought up into the uncanny booming of five tragic acts.

Third, finally, it is that once, about five years ago, when a translator glanced through the window, he did not know which thing to find more amazing—the way the Yelabuga blizzard knew Scottish and, just as on that day, was distressed about the seventeen-year-old girl; or the way that girl and the English poet, her sorrower, had been able to tell him so well, so intimately, in Russian, what was still troubling them both as before and still pursuing them.

What does this mean?—the translator asked himself. What is going on over there? Why is it so quiet there today (and yet so stormy!)? It would seem that, because we're sending there, someone ought to be bleeding to death. And yet they are smiling there.

This is what a miracle is. It is the unity and identity of these three lives and of a whole host of others (bystanders and witnesses of three epochs—people, biographies, readers) in the authentic October of who knows what years, booming, and blinded, and growing hoarse, out there beyond the window, beneath the mountain—in art.

This is what it is.

6

Misunderstandings exist. They have to be avoided. Here there is room for boredom. A writer, people say, a poet . . .

Aesthetics does not exist. It seems to me that aesthetics doesn't exist as a punishment for the way it lies, pardons, panders, condescends. For the way, while knowing nothing about man, it spins its gossip about specialist subjects. Portraitists, landscapists, genre painter, still-life painter? Symbolist, acmeist, futurist? What murderous jargon!

Clearly, this is a science that classifies air balloons according to where and how the holes are placed in them, which interfere with their flying.

Inseparable from each other, poetry and prose are two opposite poles.

By its inborn faculty of hearing, poetry seeks out the melody of nature amid the tumult of the dictionary, and then, picking it up as one picks up a tune, abandons itself to improvisation upon that theme. By scent, and according to its level of inspiration, prose seeks and finds the human being in the category of speech, and if the age is deprived of him, it re-creates him from memory, secretly abandons him, and then, for the good of mankind, pretends it has found him in the midst of the contemporary world. These principles do not exist in isolation.

As it weaves its fantasies, poetry stumbles across nature. The live, real world is the only project of the imagination, which, having once succeeded, goes on forever, endlessly succeeding. Look at it continuing, moment after moment a success. It is still real, still deep, absorbing, fascinating. It is not something you'll be disappointed in next morning. For the poet it is an example, even more than a model or pattern.

7

It is madness to trust in common sense. It is madness to doubt it. It is madness to look ahead. It is madness to live without looking. But now and then to roll your eyes and, with your blood temperature rapidly rising, to hear how, stroke upon stroke, reminiscent of convulsions of lightnings on dusty ceilings and plaster casts, there begins to expand and resound, along your consciousness, the reflected mural of some sort of unearthly, rapidly passing, eternally springlike thunderstorm — this is *pure* madness, surely the very purest madness!

It is natural to strive for purity.

And so we go right up to the pure essence of poetry. It is disturbing, like the ominous turning of a dozen windmills at the edge of a bare field in a black year of famine.

(1922)
Translated by Angela Livingstone

Notes

Originally, Pasternak planned to call this piece "Quintessence."

Swinburne ... Chastelard: Swinburne wrote a trilogy of plays about Mary Stuart; the first play of the trilogy was *Chastelard* (1865), which Pasternak translated. According to Pasternak's "Autobiographical Sketch" he lost the translation in 1914 along with other books and manuscripts during anti-German riots in Moscow. (Pasternak happened to be tutor in a German household which was destroyed.)

Châtelard was a somewhat unbalanced young poet whose unseemly assaults on Mary's chambers led to his execution in 1563.

Mary herself did write poetry, in French, to Ronsard among others.

Yelabuga blizzard knew Scottish: that is, a Russian poet writing in a storm in the town of Yelabuga (where some thirty years later Tsvetaeva would hang herself) could translate Swinburne.

Notes by Carl Proffer

Federico García Lorca

The Duende: Theory and Divertissement[1]

WHOEVER INHABITS that bull's hide stretched between the Júcar, the Guadalete, the Sil, or the Pisuerga[2] — no need to mention the streams joining those lion-colored waves churned up by the Plata — has heard it said with a certain frequency, "Now that has real *duende!*" It was in this spirit that Manuel Torres, that great artist of the Andalusian people, once remarked to a singer, "You have a voice, you know all the styles, but you will never bring it off because you have no *duende.*"

In all Andalusia, from the rock of Jaen to the shell of Cádiz, people constantly speak of the *duende* and find it in everything that springs out of energetic instinct. That marvelous singer "El Lebrijano," originator of the *Debla*, observed, "Whenever I am singing with *duende*, no one can come up to me"; and one day the old Gypsy dancer "La Malena" exclaimed, while listening to Brailowsky play a fragment of Bach, "Olé! That has *duende!*" — and remained bored by Gluck and Brahms and Darius Milhaud. And Manuel Torres, to my mind a man of exemplary blood culture, once uttered this splendid phrase while listening to Falla himself play his "Nocturno del Generalife": "Whatever has black sounds, has *duende.*" There is no greater truth.

These "black sounds" are the mystery, the roots that probe through the mire that we all know of and do not understand, but which furnishes us with whatever is sustaining in art. Black sounds: so said the celebrated Spaniard, thereby concurring with Goethe, who, in effect, defined the *duende* when he said, speaking of Paganini, "A mysterious power that all may feel and no philosophy can explain."

The *duende*, then, is a power and not a construct, is a struggle and not a concept. I have heard an old guitarist, a true virtuoso, remark, "The *duende* is not in the throat; the *duende* comes up from inside, up from the very soles of the feet." That is to say, it is not a question of aptitude, but of a true and viable style — of blood, in other words; of what is oldest in culture: of creation made act.

This "mysterious power that all may feel and no philosophy can explain" is, in sum, the earth-force, the same *duende* that fired the heart of Nietzsche, who sought it in its external forms on the Rialto Bridge, or in the music of Bizet, without ever finding it, or understanding that the *duende* he pursued had rebounded from the mystery-minded Greeks to the dancers of Cádiz or the gored, Dionysian cry of Silverio's *siguiriya*.[3]

So much for the *duende*; but I would not have you confuse the *duende* with the theological demon of doubt at whom Luther, on a Bacchic impulse, hurled an inkwell in Nuremberg,[4] or with the Catholic devil, destructive, but short on intelligence, who disguised himself as a bitch in order to enter the convents, or with the talking monkey that Cervantes' mountebank carried in the comedy about jealousy and the forests of Andalusia.[5]

No. The *duende* I speak of, shadowy, palpitating, is a descendant of that benignest *daimon* of Socrates, he of marble and salt, who scratched the master angrily the day he drank the hemlock; and of that melancholy imp of Descartes, little as an unripe almond, who, glutted with circles and lines, went out on the canals to hear the drunken sailors singing.

Any man — any artist, as Nietzsche would say — climbs the stairway in the tower of his perfection at the cost of a struggle with a *duende* — not with an angel, as some have maintained, or with his muse. This fundamental distinction must be kept in mind if the root of a work of art is to be grasped.

The Angel guides and endows, like Saint Raphael; or prohibits and avoids, like Saint Michael; or foretells, like Saint Gabriel.

The Angel dazzles, but he flies over men's heads and remains in midair, shedding his grace; and the man, without any effort whatever, realizes his work, or his fellow feeling, or his dance. The angel on the road to Damascus, and he who entered the crevice of the little balcony of Assisi, or that other angel who followed in the footsteps of Heinrich Suso,[6] *commanded*—and there was no resisting his radiance, for he waved wings of steel in an atmosphere of predestination.

The Muse dictates and, in certain cases, prompts. There is relatively little she can do, for she keeps aloof and is so full of lassitude (I have seen her twice) that I myself have had to put half a heart of marble in her. The Poets of the Muse hear voices and do not know where they come from; but surely they are from the Muse, who encourages and at times devours them entirely. Such, for example, was the case of Apollinaire, that great poet ravaged by the horrible Muse with whom the divinely angelic Rousseau painted him. The Muse arouses the intellect, bearing landscapes of columns and the false taste of laurel; but intellect is oftentimes the foe of poetry because it imitates too much: it elevates the poet to a throne of acute angles and makes him forget that in time the ants can devour him, too, or that a great, arsenical locust can fall on his head, against which the Muses who live inside monocles or the lukewarm lacquer roses of insignificant salons are helpless.

Angel and Muse approach from without; the Angel sheds light and the Muse gives form (Hesiod learned of them). Gold leaf or chiton-folds: the poet finds his models in his laurel coppice. But the *Duende*, on the other hand, must come to life in the nether most recesses of the blood.

And repel the Angel, too—kick out the Muse and conquer any awe of the fragrance of the violets that breathe from the poetry of the eighteenth century, or of the great telescope in whose lenses the Muse dozes off, sick of limits.

The true struggle is with the *Duende.*

The paths leading to God are well known, from the barbaric way of the hermit to the subtler modes of the mystic. With a tower, then, like Saint Theresa, or with three roads, like Saint John of the Cross. And even if we must cry out in Isaiah's voice, "Truly, thou art the hidden God!" at the end, and at last, God sends to each seeker his first fiery thorns.

To seek out the *Duende*, however, neither map nor discipline is required. Enough to know that he kindles the blood like an irritant; that he exhausts; that he repulses all the bland, geometrical assurances; that he smashes the styles; that he makes of a Goya, master of the grays, the silvers, the roses of the great English painters, a man painting with his knees and his fists in bituminous blacks; that he bares a Mosen Cinto Verdaguer[7] to the cold of the Pyrenees, or induces a Jorge Manrique[8] to sweat out his death on the crags of Ocaña, or invests the delicate body of Rimbaud in the green domino of the *saltimbanque*, or fixes dead fish eyes on the Comte de Lautréamont in the early hours of the boulevard.

The great artists of southern Spain, both Gypsies and flamenco, whether singing or dancing or playing on instruments, know that no emotion is possible without the mediation of the *Duende*. They may hoodwink the people, they may give the illusion of *duende* without really having it, just as writers and painters and literary fashion-mongers without *duende* cheat you daily; but it needs only a little care, and the will to resist one's own indifference, to discover the imposture and put it and its crude artifice to flight.

Once the Andalusian singer Pastora Pavón, "The Girl with the Combs," a somber Hispanic genius whose capacity for fantasy equals Goya's or Raphael el Gallo's, was singing in a little tavern in Cádiz. She sparred with her voice — now shadowy, now like molten tin, now covered over with moss; she tangled her voice in her long hair or drenched it in sherry or lost it in the darkest and furthermost bramble bushes. But nothing happened — useless, all of it! The hearers remained silent.

There stood Ignacio Espeleta, handsome as a Roman turtle, who was asked once why he never worked, and replied, with a smile worthy of Argantonio, "How am I to work if I come from Cádiz?"

There, too, stood Héloise, the fiery aristocrat, whore of Seville, direct descendant of Soledad Vargas, who in the thirties refused to marry a Rothschild because he was not of equal blood. There were the Floridas, whom some people call butchers, but who are really millennial priests sacrificing bulls constantly to Geryon; and in a corner stood that imposing breeder of bulls, Don Pablo Murabe, with the air of a Cretan mask. Pastora Pavón finished singing in the midst of total silence. There was only a little man, one of those dancing mannikins who leap suddenly out of brandy bottles, who observed sarcastically in a very low voice, *"Viva Paris!"* As if to say: We are not interested in aptitude or techniques or virtuosity here. We are interested in something else.

Then the Girl with the Combs got up like a woman possessed, her face blasted like a medieval weeper, tossed off a great glass of Cazalla at a single draft, like a potion of fire, and settled down to singing—without a voice, without breath, without nuance, throat aflame—but with *duende!* She had contrived to annihilate all that was nonessential in song and make way for an angry and incandescent *Duende*, friend of the sand-laden winds, so that everyone listening tore at his clothing almost in the same rhythm with which the West Indian Negroes in their rites rend away their clothes, huddled in heaps before the image of Saint Barbara.

The Girl with the Combs had to *mangle* her voice because she knew there were discriminating folk about who asked not for form, but for the marrow of form—pure music spare enough to keep itself in air. She had to deny her faculties and her security; that is to say, to turn out her Muse and keep vulnerable, so that her *Duende* might come and vouchsafe the hand-to-hand struggle. And then how she sang! Her voice feinted no longer; it jetted up like blood, ennobled by sorrow and sincerity, it opened up like ten fingers of a hand around the nailed feet of a Christ by Juan de Juni[9]—tempestuous!

The arrival of the *Duende* always presupposes a radical change in all the forms as they existed on the old plane. It gives a sense of refreshment unknown until then, together with that quality of the just-opening rose, of the miraculous, which comes and instills an almost religious transport.

In all Arabian music, in the dances, songs, elegies of Arabia, the coming of the *Duende* is greeted by fervent outcries of *Allah! Allah!, God! God!,* so close to the *Ole! Ole!* of our bull rings that who is to say they are not actually the same; and in all the songs of southern Spain the appearance of the *Duende* is followed by heartfelt exclamations of *God alive!*—profound, human, tender, the cry of communion with God through the medium of the five senses and the grace of the *Duende* that stirs the voice and the body of the dancer—a flight from this world, both real and poetic, pure as Pedro Soto de Roja's over the seven gardens (that most curious poet of the seventeenth century), or Juan Calimacho's on the tremulous ladder of tears.

Naturally, when flight is achieved, all feel its effects: the initiate coming to see at last how style triumphs over inferior matter, and the unenlightened, through the I-don't-know-what of an authentic emotion. Some years ago, in a dancing contest at Jeréz de la Frontera, an old lady of eighty, competing against beautiful women and young girls with waists supple as water, carried off the prize merely by the act of raising her arms, throwing back her head, and stamping the little platform with a blow of her feet; but in the conclave of muses and angels foregathered there—beauties of form and beauties of smile—the dying *Duende* triumphed as it had to, trailing the rusted knife blades of its wings along the ground.

All the arts are capable of *duende*, but it naturally achieves its widest play in the fields of music, dance, and the spoken poem, since these require a living presence to interpret them because they are forms which grow and decline perpetually and raise their contours on the precise present.

Often the *Duende* of the musician passes over into the *Duende* of the interpreter, and at other times, when musician and poet are not matched, the *Duende* of the interpreter—this is interesting—creates a new marvel that retains the appearance—and the appearance only—of the originating form. Such was the case with the *duende*-ridden Duse, who deliberately sought out failures in order to turn them into triumphs, thanks to her capacity for invention; or with Paganini, who, as Goethe explained, could make one hear profoundest melody in out-and-out vulgarity; or with a delectable young lady from the port of Santa María whom I saw singing and dancing the horrendous Italian ditty "O Marie!" with such rhythms, such pauses, and such conviction that she transformed an Italian gewgaw into a hard serpent of raised gold. What happened, in effect, was that each in his own way found something new, something never before encountered, which put life blood and art into bodies void of expression.

In every country, death comes as a finality. It comes, and the curtain comes down. But not in Spain! In Spain the curtain goes up. Many people live out their lives between walls till the day they die and are brought out into the sun. In Spain, the dead are more alive than the dead of any other country of the world: their profile wounds like the edge of a barber's razor. The quip about death and the silent contemplation of it are familiar to the Spanish. From the "Dream of the Skulls" of Quevedo,[10] to the "Putrescent Bishop" of

Valdés Leal;[11] from La Marbella of the seventeenth century, who, dying in childbirth on the highway, says:

> The blood of my entrails
> Covers the horse.
> And the horses' hooves
> Strike fire from the pitch . . .

to a recent young man from Salamanca, killed by a bull, who exclaimed:

> My friends, I am dying.
> My friends, it goes badly.
> I've three handkerchiefs inside me,
> And this I apply now makes four . . .

there is a balustrade of flowering niter where hordes peer out, contemplating death, with verses from Jeremiah for the grimmer side or sweet-smelling cypress for the more lyrical — but in any case, a country where all that is most important has its final metallic valuation in death.

The knife and the cart wheel and the razor and the stinging beard points of the shepherds, the shorn moon and the fly, the damp lockers, the ruins and the lace-covered saints, the quicklime and the cutting line of eaves and balconies: in Spain, all bear little grass blades of death, allusions and voices perceptible to the spiritually alert, that call to our memory with the corpse-cold air of our own passing. It is no accident that all Spanish art is bound to our soil, so full of thistles and definitive stone; the lamentations of Pleberio or the dances of the master Josef María de Valdivielso are not isolated instances, nor is it by chance that from all the balladry of Europe the Spanish inamorata disengages herself in this fashion:

> "If you are my fine friend,
> Tell me — why won't you look at me?"
>   "The eyes with which I look at you
>   I gave up to the shadow."
> "If you are my fine friend
> Tell me — why don't you kiss me?"
>   "The lips with which I kissed you

I gave up to the clay."
"If you are my fine friend
Tell me — why won't you embrace me?"
    "The arms that embrace you
    I have covered up with worms."

Nor is it strange to find that in the dawn of our lyricism, the following note is sounded:

Inside the garden
I shall surely die.
Inside the rosebush,
They will kill me.
Mother, Mother, I went out
Gathering roses,
But surely death will find me
In the garden.
Mother, Mother, I went out
Cutting roses,
But surely death will find me
In the rosebush.
Inside the garden
I shall surely die.
In the rosebush
They will kill me.

Those heads frozen by the moon that Zurbarán[12] painted, the butter yellows and the lightning yellows of El Greco, the narrative of Father Sigüenza, all the work of Goya, the presbytery of the Church of the Escorial, all polychrome sculpture, the crypt of the ducal house of Osuna, the death with the guitar in the chapel of the Benavente in Medina de Río Seco — all equal, on the plane of cultivated art, the pilgrimages of San Andrés de Teixido where the dead have their place in the procession; they are one with the songs for the dead that the women of Asturias intone with flame-filled lamps in the November night, one with the song and dance of the Sibyl in the cathedrals of Mallorca and Toledo, with the obscure "In Recort" of Tortosa, and the innumerable rites of Good Friday that, with the arcane Fiesta of the Bulls, epitomize the popular triumph of Spanish death. In all the world, Mexico alone can go hand in hand with my country.

The Duende: Theory and Divertissement   35

When the Muse sees death on the way, she closes the door or raises a plinth or promenades an urn and inscribes an epitaph with a waxen hand, but in time she tears down her laurels again in a silence that wavers between two breezes. Under the truncated arch of the Ode, she joins with funereal meaning the exact flowers that the Italians of the fifteenth century depicted, with the identical cock of Lucretius, to frighten off an unforeseen darkness.

When the Angel sees death on the way, he flies in slow circles and weaves with tears of narcissus and ice the elegy we see trembling in the hands of Keats and Villasandino[13] and Herrera[14] and Bécquer[15] and Juan Ramón Jiménez.[16] But imagine the terror of the Angel, should it feel a spider—even the very tiniest—on its tender and roseate flesh!

The *Duende*, on the other hand, will not approach at all if he does not see the possibility of death, if he is not convinced he will circle death's house, if there·is not every assurance he can rustle the branches, borne aloft by us all, that neither have, nor may ever have, the power to console.

With idea, with sound, or with gesture, the *Duende* chooses the brim of the well for his open struggle with the creator. Angel and Muse escape in the violin or in musical measure, but the *Duende* draws blood, and in the healing of the wound that never quite closes, all that is unprecedented and invented in a man's work has its origin.

The magical virtue of poetry lies in the fact that it is always empowered with *duende* to baptize in dark water all those who behold it, because with *duende*, loving and understanding are simpler, there is always the *certainty* of being loved and being understood; and this struggle for expression and for the communication of expression acquires at times, in poetry, finite characters.

Recall the case of that paragon of the flamenco and demonic way, Saint Theresa—flamenca not for her prowess in stopping an angry bull with three magnificent passes—though she did so—nor for her presumption in esteeming herself beautiful in the presence of Fray Juan de la Miseria, nor for slapping the face of a papal nuncio—but rather for the simple circumstance that she was one of the rare ones whose *Duende* (not her Angel—the angels never attack) pierced her with an arrow, hoping thereby to destroy her for having deprived him of his ultimate secret: the subtle bridge that links the five senses with the very center, the living flesh, living cloud, living sea, of Love emancipated from Time.

Most redoubtable conqueress of the *Duende* — and how utterly unlike the case of Philip of Austria, who, longing to discover the Muse and the Angel in theology, found himself imprisoned by the *Duende* of cold ardors in that masterwork of the Escorial, where geometry abuts with a dream and the *Duende* wears the mask of the Muse for the eternal chastisement of the great king.

We have said that the *Duende* loves ledges and wounds, that he enters only those areas where form dissolves in a passion transcending any of its visible expressions.

In Spain (as in all Oriental countries where dance is a form of religious expression) the *Duende* has unlimited play in the bodies of the dancers of Cádiz, eulogized by Martial; in the breasts of the singers, eulogized by Juvenal; and in all the liturgy of the bulls — that authentic religious drama where, in the manner of the Mass, adoration and sacrifice are rendered a God.

It would seem that all the *duende* of the Classical world is crowded into this matchless festival, epitomizing the culture and the noble sensibility of a people who discover in man his greatest rages, his greatest melancholies, his greatest lamentations. No one, I think, is amused by the dances or the bulls of Spain; the *Duende* has taken it on himself to make them suffer through the medium of the drama, in living forms, and prepares the ladders for a flight from encompassing reality.

The *Duende* works on the body of the dancer as wind works on sand. With magical force, it converts a young girl into a lunar paralytic; or fills with adolescent blushes a ragged old man begging handouts in the wineshops; or suddenly discovers the smell of nocturnal ports in a head of hair and, moment for moment, works on the arms with an expressiveness which is the mother of the dance of all ages.

But it is impossible for him ever to repeat himself — this is interesting and must be underscored. The *Duende* never repeats himself, any more than the forms of the sea repeat themselves in a storm.

In the bullfight, the *Duende* achieves his most impressive advantage, for he must fight then with death, who can destroy him, on one hand, and with geometry, with measure, the fundamental basis of the bullfight, on the other.

The bull has his orbit, and the bullfighter has his, and between orbit and orbit is the point of risk where falls the vertex of the terrible byplay.

It is possible to hold a Muse with a *muleta*[17] and an Angel with *banderillas*,[18] and pass for a good bullfighter; but for the *faena de capa*,[19] with the bull still unscarred by a wound, the help of the *Duende* is necessary at the moment of the kill, to drive home the blow of artistic truth.

The bullfighter who moves the public to terror in the plaza by his audacity does not *fight* the bull—that would be ludicrous in such a case—but, within the reach of each man, puts his life at stake; on the contrary, the fighter bitten by the *Duende* gives a lesson in Pythagorean music and induces all to forget how he constantly hurls his heart against the horns.

Lagartijo with his Roman *duende*, Joselito with his Jewish *duende*, Belmonte with his Baroque *duende*, and Cagancho with his Gypsy *duende*, from the twilight of the ring, teach poets, painters, and musicians four great ways of the Spanish tradition.

Spain is the only country where death is the national spectacle, where death blows long fanfares at the coming of each spring, and its art is always governed by a shrewd *duende* that has given it its distinctive character and its quality of invention.

The *Duende* that, for the first time in sculpture, fills the cheeks of the saints of the master Mateo de Compostela with blood, is the same spirit that evokes the lamentations of Saint John of the Cross or burns naked nymphs on the religious sonnets of Lope.

The *Duende* who raises the tower of Sahagún or tesselates hot brick in Calatayud or Teruel, is the same spirit that breaks open the clouds of El Greco and sends the constables of Quevedo and the chimeras of Goya sprawling with a kick.

When it rains, he secretly brings out a *duende*-minded Velásquez, behind his monarchical grays; when it snows, he sends Herrera out naked to prove that cold need not kill; when it burns, he casts Berruguete[20] into the flames and lets him invent a new space for sculpture.

The Muse of Góngora and the Angel of Garcilaso[21] must yield up the laurel wreath when the *Duende* of Saint John of the Cross passes by, when

> the wounded stag
> peers over the hill.

The Muse of Gonzalo de Berceo[22] and the Angel of the Archpriest of Hita[23] must give way to the approaching Jorge Manrique when he comes, wounded to death, to the gates of the Castle of Belmonte. The Muse of Gregorio Hernández[24] and the Angel of José de Mora[25] must retire so that the *Duende* weeping blood-tears of Mena,[26] and the *Duende* of Martínez Montañés[27] with a head like an Assyrian bull's, may pass over, just as the melancholy Muse of Cataluña and the humid Angel of Galicia must watch, with loving terror, the *Duende* of Castile, far from the hot bread and the cow grazing mildly among forms of swept sky and parched earth.

The *Duende* of Quevedo and the *Duende* of Cervantes, one bearing phosphorescent green anemones and the other the plaster flowers of Ruidera, crown the altarpiece of the *Duende* of Spain.

Each art has, by nature, its distinctive *Duende* of style and form, but all roots join at the point where the black sounds of Manuel Torres issue forth — the ultimate stuff and the common basis, uncontrollable and tremulous, of wood and sound and canvas and word.

Black sounds — behind which there abide, in tenderest intimacy, the volcanoes, the ants, the zephyrs, and the enormous night, straining its waist against the Milky Way.

Ladies and gentlemen, I have raised three arches, and with clumsy hand I have placed in them the Muse, the Angel, and the *Duende*.

The Muse keeps silent; she may wear the tunic of little folds, or great cow-eyes gazing toward Pompeii, or the monstrous, four-featured nose with which her great painter, Picasso, has painted her. The Angel may be stirring the hair of Antonello da Messina,[28] the tunic of Lippi,[29] and the violin of Masolino[30] or Rousseau.[31]

But the *Duende* — where is the *Duende?* Through the empty arch enters a mental air blowing insistently over the heads of the dead, seeking new landscapes and unfamiliar accents; an air bearing the odor of child's spittle, crushed grass, and the veil of a Medusa announcing the unending baptism of all newly created things.

(1930)
Translated by Ben Belitt

Notes

1. The *"duende"*: Arturo Barea explains *(Lorca: The Poet and His People)*: "Characteristically, Lorca took his Spanish term for daemonic inspiration from the Andalusian idiom. While to the rest of Spain the *duende* is nothing but a hobgoblin, to Andalusia it is an obscure power which can speak through every form of human art, including the art of personality."

2. Júcar: river of east central Spain; Guadalete: river in southern Spain; Sil: river of northwestern Spain; Pisuerga: river of northern Spain. Plata: river of South America, used by Lorca in the present context to suggest the whole of the Hispanic world outside the borders of his native Spain.

3. Silverio's *siguiriya*: Silverio Franconetti, an Italian *cantaor* who came to Seville and cultivated the "deep song" *(cante jondo)* of the Andalusian Gypsy. According to Lorca, the *siguiriya* is a development of the *cante jondo* which combines elements of the primitive musical systems of India with the indigenous folk tradition of Andalusia. The flamenco style, which derives from the *cante jondo*, does not take form until the eighteenth century.

4. Nuremberg: Lorca is apparently in error here; it was at the electoral castle of Wartburg in Eisenach that the celebrated encounter occurred.

5. Here again Lorca is either in error or is indulging a playful hoax of his own.

6. Heinrich Suso (1300–1366): German mystic and theologian.

7. Mosen Cinto Verdaguer: Jacinto Verdaguer (1845–1902), Catalan poet, author of *La Atlantida.*

8. Jorge Manrique (1440–1479): Spanish poet and soldier, best known for the elegiac *Coplas* on his father's death.

9. Juan de Juni (1507–1577): Spanish painter, pupil of Berruguete.

10. Francisco Gómez de Quevedo y Villegas (1580–1654): Poet and satirist born in Madrid.

11. Juan de Valdés Leal (1630–1691): Córdovan painter.

12. Francisco de Zurbarán (1598–1669): Painter born in Estremadura.

13. Alfonso Alvarez de Villasandino (1350?–1424?): Writer of lyric and satirical verse, born in the province of Burgos.

14. Fernando de Herrera (1534–1597): Leader of the Andalusian school and innovator in the line of Góngora.

15. Gustavo Adolfo Bécquer (1836–1870): Romantic lyric poet born in Madrid, best known for his *Rimas.*

16. Juan Ramón Jiménez (1881–1958): Contemporary lyric poet born at Moguer.

17. Muleta: Cloth of scarlet serge or flannel, folded and doubled over tapered wooden stick, used by matadors for defense, the positional manipulation of the bull, "passes" to demonstrate the dexterity and daring of the fighter, and as an aid in the final kill.

18. Banderilla: A small dart with a bannerol for baiting bulls, thrust in a series of three pairs into the withers of the bull in the second phase of the bullfight.

19. *Faena de capa:* "Cape-task"; the sum of work done by matador in third phase of the fight.

20. Alonso Berruguete (1490?–1581?): Baroque sculptor and architect, pupil of Michelangelo.

21. Garcilaso de la Vega (1501?–1536?): Poet, statesman, and soldier, author of eclogues, elegies, and sonnets in the Italianate style.

22. Gonzalo de Berceo (c. 1180–c. 1246): Early Spanish poet and Benedictine priest.

23. Archpriest of Hita (Juan Ruiz) (died before 1351): Poet and priest, author of the *Libro de buen amor.*

24. Gregorio Hernández (1576–1636): Spanish sculptor born in Galicia.

25. José de Mora (1638–1725): Sculptor born in Granada.

26. Pedro de Mena (d. 1693): Sculptor born in Granada.

27. Juan Martínez Montañés (1580–1649): Sculptor born in Granada.

28. Antonello da Messina (1430–1479): Italian painter born at Messina.

29. Fra Filippo Lippi (1406–1469): Italian painter and Carmelite friar born in Florence.

30. Masolino da Panicole (1383–1447): Italian painter born near Florence.

31. Henry Rousseau (1844–1910): The French primitive painter, whose portrait of the poet Apollinaire *(La Muse Inspirant Le Poète)* is referred to earlier in the essay.

Notes by Ben Belitt

Luis Cernuda

Words Before a Reading

I CAN SAY that for the first time in my life I am risking a direct contact with the public. For me, the sensation is strange, since generally a poet cannot suppose that there is a public, listening to him. The poet is alone when he speaks or is with someone who scarcely exists in the outer reality. It's true that today the public is so reduced (and has even been called a "minority"[1]) that a poet may well address himself to it without thereby giving up that essential solitude in which he believes he hears divine voices.

I have always rejected any temptation to comment on my poems or explain what I meant to do in them. Why do I do so now? Perhaps because I believe that my own deficiency was unable to express in them what I wanted, or that the deficiency of others may not see in them everything I have put there. Although I accept the first possibility, since I know how few poets have been able to express entirely what they wished to express, it consoles me somewhat to recall that it may be enough to express a few of the fragmentary experiences which allow us to surmise the entirety of a poet's thought.

*

And I will be asked, "What is the poet's goal?" Permit me to relate poetry to my personal experience—an act that assumes no small amount of presumption, although a poet, if I may be permitted to call myself that, must inevitably relate to himself the poetic experiences which with his limited means he perceives. And when all is said and done, perhaps the poet's experiences, however unusual they may seem, are not so much so that they may not find an echo, along general lines, in other existences.

The poetic instinct was awakened in me thanks to a more acute perception of reality — experiencing with a deeper echo the beauty and attraction of the surrounding world. Its effect, as in some way occurs with that desire which provokes love, was the necessity — painful because of its intensity — of getting outside myself, negating myself in the vast body of creation. And what made that desire even more agonizing was the tacit recognition that it was impossible to satisfy it.

From that time, I began to distinguish a simultaneous, contradictory pair of currents within myself: toward reality and against reality, both attraction and hostility toward the real. Desire carried me toward the reality offered up to my eyes, as if only by possessing it could I attain some certainty of my own life. But since I have never achieved that possession except in a precarious way, the opposing current arises, of a hostility before the ironic attractiveness of reality. Since, as it seems, this or something similar has also been the experience of some philosophers and poets whom I admire, I join them in concluding that exterior reality is a mirage and that the only certain thing is my own desire to possess it. Thus, the essence of the poetic problem, as I understand it, lies in the conflict between reality and desire, between appearance and truth, which permits us to attain a glimpse of that complete world that we know nothing of, the "divine idea of the world that lies at the foot of appearances," according to the phrase of Fichte.

Given this preliminary experience, which surrounds what I regard as the motive of the poetic activity — at least of my own — we may now ask. This conflict between appearance and truth that the poet tries to resolve in his work — what phases, what possibilities does it go through in the course of the poet's life?

Perhaps poetry, at least in certain aspects, requires a youthful state of spirit, and it is not uncommon for poetry to prolong the power of youth in a poet, beyond the time allotted for it. Youth presupposes a capacity to love and to call forth love from others, and although a poet like any other mortal loses with time the ability to inspire love, it would be unlikely for him also to lose the capacity for falling in love. This aesthetic basis is what permits a poet, even in the worst of times, when everything seems to conspire against him, to retain, at the least, the dramatic intoxication of defeat. A confused acceptance of good and evil, of failure and of defeat, must seem to some a dangerous thing. I will be told that it presupposes a fatalistic attitude, and that fatalism is a pretty convenient attitude at that.

But this fatalism has deep causes. What can the poet do by himself? Nothing, since society has now reduced life to such narrow confines. And certainly the poet is almost always a revolutionary; I, for one, believe so. A revolutionary who like other men lacks liberty, but with the difference that he cannot accept this privation, and dashes against the walls of his prison. Today most people produce the impression of being amputated bodies, trunks cruelly pruned back.

Since two interpretations can be given to almost anything, someone will now recall that it is necessary to limit oneself, and this implies some maturity. I have not been among the last to recognize the value of limitation or of resignation, to call this virtue by its true Christian name. But this is no obstacle to my feeling, when I contemplate life, that I am attending some disagreeable mystery drama; and if other societies esteemed the artist or the philosopher, today's adores the detective. So I recognize that for me the immediate material possibilities of poetic activity seem negative.

*

But a poet not only struggles against his social surroundings; he also attends to another struggle, equally dramatic, perhaps even more dramatic, although the forces against which he struggles are in this case invisible. The poet tries to fix the transitory spectacle that he perceives. Each day, every minute, the urge to arrest the course of life falls upon him, a course so full at times that it would seem to merit an eternal continuation. It is precisely from this struggle that the poet's work arises, and although the impulse from which it springs seems clear to us, there is still much in it that is mysterious. The simplest, the clearest thing in this world has unknown roots.

Modern society, unlike societies that preceded it, has decided to do without the mysterious element that is inseparable from life. Unable to fathom it, modern society prefers to appear not to believe in its existence. But the poet cannot proceed in this way, and must depend in life on that zone of shadow and fog that floats around human bodies. This zone is the refuge of an undefined vast power that manipulates our destinies. At times I have perceived the influence of a demoniac power in life, or rather, a *daimonic* power, that acts on men.

What does this power consist of? I will confess a foreboding about definitions, because time ensures that our thought will exceed the definitions that we establish. In addition, the daimonic power to which I refer is closely tied to my poetic beliefs, and neither the daimonic nor the poetic can be defined. But I am going to be somewhat more precise on this point, regarding what affects my poetic beliefs.

Reading a study by a certain Arabist on the life and doctrines of a Moslem theologian, I found this reply offered by the latter to one of his disciples. While strolling down a street, one of them asked, when he heard the sound of a flute, "Master, what is that?" The master answered, "That is the voice of Satan, who weeps over the world." According to this theologian, Satan has been condemned to be smitten with a love for those things that pass away, and therefore he weeps; he weeps, like the poet, for the loss and destruction of beauty.

Here a definition is unavoidable and comes to us almost by fate: poetry fixes ephemeral beauty. Through poetry the supernatural and the human are united in spiritual nuptials, engendering celestial beings, and as in those Greek myths about a god loving a mortal, semidivine beings are born. So the poet tries to fix the transitory beauty of the world that he perceives, relating it to the invisible world that he senses, and when he grows weak and fails in this unequal struggle, his voice, like that of Satan in the Moslem theologian's reply, weeps, still enamored, for the loss of what he loves.

But this lamentation does not prevent the possibility that from the contemplation of beauty, however ephemeral, a terrible happiness will be born in the poet, because in our lives feelings rarely fail to come to us without being mixed with their opposites; only in the union of the extremes can we intuit a harmony in the powers of human understanding. How do we know what our life may be in the thoughts of the gods? We need and require everything, because in everything there vibrates an echo of poetry, and it is nothing but the expression of that dark daimonic force that governs the world.

Goethe alludes to this daimonic power in his conversations with Eckermann,[2] and perhaps it is the very same power that consumed the life of Hölderlin, like the fire in the burning bush that Moses saw. Mingled with the lyrical gift that has inhabited certain poets, it seems as if their physical powers could not resist it, as they saw themselves dragged toward destruction, finally reaching, beyond death, an enigmatic liberty.

Ask me no more about this power, because I would not know what to say. I sense it, but I do not understand it. Furthermore, how can one express in words those things that are inexpressible? Words are alive, and therefore betray; what they express today as true and pure, tomorrow is false and dead. One has to use them, knowing their limitations, and try not to let them overly falsify, when they translate it, that intuited truth that we try to express through them. At least, they may receive a part of that truth, perhaps, and remain impregnated with the meaning that it is given only to the poet to suggest: the mystery of creation, the hidden beauty of the world.

*

It was not my intention, as I said, to give a definition of what I think poetry is, for to do so is a vain and pretentious task, but only to relate, to a small audience of good will, several points in my own experience with regard to poetry. This task seemed to me a useful preliminary to a reading of a few of my poems, encouraging as far as possible that honest, deep sympathy that I would wish a few people to have. But if I were asked what answer a poet can expect in this world, I would reply that there is none, or if there is one, that it is so weak that it helps no one.

And here I say: enough. Perhaps these words have been nothing but a rough outline in the darkness.

(1935)
Translated by Reginald Gibbons

Notes

1. "The immense minority" was what Juan Ramón Jiménez called the constituency of literature. (Translator's note.)

2. "The Daemonic [Goethe said] is that which cannot be explained by Reason or Understanding . . . It manifests itself in the most varied manner throughout all nature — in the invisible as in the visible. Many creatures are of a purely Daemonic kind." [Wednesday, March 2, 1831.] "In poetry, especially in that which is unconscious, before which reason and understanding fall short, and which, therefore, produces effects so far surpassing all conception, there is always something of the Demoniacal." [Tuesday, March 8, 1831.] "The book [*Metamorphosis of Plants*] gives me more trouble than I expected; indeed, I was drawn into the undertaking, almost against my will, by some Demoniacal influence which I could not resist." [Friday, March 18, 1831.] (Cernuda's note.)

Wallace Stevens

The Irrational Element in Poetry

I

TO BEGIN WITH, the expression, the irrational element in poetry, is much too general to be serviceable. After one has thought about it a bit, it spreads out. Then too we are at the moment so beset by the din made by the surrealists and surrationalists, and so preoccupied in reading about them that we may become confused by these romantic scholars and think of them as the sole exemplars of the irrational today. Certainly, they exemplify one aspect of it. Primarily, however, what I have in mind when I speak of the irrational element in poetry is the transaction between reality and the sensibility of the poet from which poetry springs

II

I am not competent to discuss reality as a philosopher. All of us understand what is meant by the transposition of an objective reality to a subjective reality. The transaction between reality and the sensibility of the poet is precisely that. A day or two before Thanksgiving we had a light fall of snow in Hartford. It melted a little by day and then froze again at night, forming a thin, bright crust over the grass. At the same time, the moon was almost full. I awoke once several hours before daylight and as I lay in bed I heard the steps of a cat running over the snow under my window almost inaudibly. The faintness and strangeness of the sound made on me one of those impressions which one so often seizes as pretexts for poetry. I suppose that in such a case one is merely expressing one's sensibility, and that the reason why this expression takes the form of poetry is that it takes whatever form one is able to give it. The poet is able to give it the form of poetry because poetry is the medium of his personal sensibility. This is not the same thing as saying that a poet writes poetry because he writes poetry, although it sounds much like it. A poet writes poetry because he is a poet; and he is not a poet because he is a poet but because of his personal sensibility. What gives a man his personal sensibility I don't know and it does not matter because no one knows. Poets continue to be born not made and cannot, I am afraid, be predetermined. While, on the one hand, if they could be predetermined, they might long since have become extinct, they might, on the other hand, have changed life from what it is today into one of those transformations in which they delight, and they might have seen to it that they greatly multiplied themselves there.

III

There is, of course, a history of the irrational element in poetry, which is, after all, merely a chapter of the history of the irrational in the arts generally. With the irrational in a pathological sense we are not concerned. Fuseli used to eat raw beef at night before going to bed in order that his dreams might attain a beefy violence otherwise lacking. Nor are we concerned with that sort of thing; nor with any irrationality provoked by prayer, whiskey, fasting, opium, or the hope of publicity. The Gothic novels of eighteenth-century England are no longer irrational. They are merely boring. What interests us is a particular process in the rational mind which we recognize as irrational in the sense that it takes place unaccountably. Or, rather, I should say that what interests us is not so much the Hegelian process as what comes of it. We should probably be much more intelligently interested if from the history of the irrational there had developed a tradition. It is easy to brush aside the irrational with the statement that we are rational beings, Aristotelians and not brutes. But it is becoming easier every day to say that we are irrational beings; that all irrationality is not of a piece and that the only reason why it does not yet have a tradition is that its tradition is in progress. When I was here at Harvard, a long time ago, it was a commonplace to say that all the poetry had been written and all the paintings painted. It may be something of that sort that first interested us in the irrational. One of the great figures in the world since then has been Freud. While he is responsible for very little in poetry, as compared, for example, with his effect elsewhere, he has given the irrational a legitimacy that it never had before. More portentous influences have been Mallarmé and Rimbaud.

IV

It may be that my subject expressed with greater nicety is irrational manifestations of the irrational element in poetry; for if the irrational element is merely poetic energy, it is to be found wherever poetry is to be found. One such manifestation is the disclosure of the individuality of the poet. It is unlikely that this disclosure is ever visible as plainly to anyone as to the poet himself. In the first of the poems that I shall read to you in a moment or two the subject that I had in mind was the effect of the Depression on the interest in art. I wanted a confronting of the world as it had been imagined in art and as it was then in fact. If I dropped into a gallery I found that I had no interest in what I saw. The air was charged with anxieties and tensions. To look at pictures there was the same thing as to play the piano in Madrid this afternoon. I was as capable of making observations and of jotting them down as anyone else; and if that is what I had wished to do, I could have done it. I wanted to deal with exactly such a subject and I chose that as a bit of reality, actuality, the contemporaneous. But I wanted the result to be poetry so far as I was able to write poetry. To be specific, I wanted to apply my own sensibility to something perfectly matter-of-fact. The result would be a disclosure of my own sensibility or individuality, as I called it a moment ago, certainly to myself. The poem is called "The Old Woman and the Statue." The old woman is a symbol of those who suffered during the depression and the statue is a symbol of art, although in several poems of which *Owl's Clover*, the book from which I shall read, consists, the statue is a variable symbol. While there is nothing automatic about the poem, nevertheless it has an automatic aspect in the sense that it is what I wanted it to be without knowing before it was written what I wanted it to be, even though I knew before it was written what I wanted to do. If each of us is a biological mechanism, each poet is a poetic mechanism. To the extent that what he produces is mechanical: that is to say, beyond his power to change, it is irrational. Perhaps I do not mean wholly beyond his power to change, for he might, by an effort of the will, change it. With that in mind, I mean beyond likelihood of change so long as he is being himself. This happens in the case of every poet.

V

I think, too, that the choice of subject-matter is a completely irrational thing, provided a poet leaves himself any freedom of choice. If you are an imagist, you make a choice of subjects that is obviously limited. The same thing is true if you are anything else in particular and profess rigidly. But if you elect to remain free and to go about in the world experiencing whatever you happen to experience, as most people do, even when they insist that they do not, either your choice of subjects is fortuitous or the identity of the circumstances under which the choice is made is imperceptible. Lyric poets are bothered by spring and romantic poets by autumn. As a man becomes familiar with his own poetry, it becomes as obsolete for himself as for anyone else. From this it follows that one of the motives in writing is renewal. This undoubtedly affects the choice of subjects as definitely as it affects changes in rhythm, diction, and manner. It is elementary that we vary rhythms instinctively. We say that we perfect diction. We simply grow tired. Manner is something that has not yet been disengaged adequately. It does not mean style; it means the attitude of the writer, his bearing rather than his point of view. His bearing toward what? Not toward anything in particular; simply his pose. He hears the cat on the snow. The running feet set the rhythm. There is no subject beyond the cat running on the snow in the moonlight. He grows completely tired of the thing; wants a subject, thought, feeling; his whole manner changes. All these things enter into the choice of subject. The man who has been brought up in an artificial school becomes intemperately real. The Mallarmiste becomes the proletarian novelist. All this is irrational. If the choice of subject was predictable it would be rational. Now, just as the choice of subject is unpredictable at the outset, so its development, after it has been chosen, is unpredictable. One is always writing about two things at the same time in poetry and it is this that produces the tension characteristic of poetry. One is the true subject and the other is the poetry of the subject. The difficulty of sticking to the true subject, when it is the poetry of the subject that is paramount in one's mind, need only be mentioned to be understood. In a poet who makes the true subject paramount and who merely embellishes it, the subject is constant and the development orderly. If the poetry of the subject is paramount, the true subject is not constant nor its development orderly. This is true in the case of Proust and Joyce, for example, in modern prose.

VI

Why does one write poetry? I have already stated a number of reasons, among them these: because one is impelled to do so by a personal sensibility and also because one grows tired of the monotony of one's imagination, say, and sets out to find variety. In his discourse before the Academy, ten years or more ago, M. Brémond elucidated a mystical motive and made it clear that, in his opinion, one writes poetry to find God. I should like to consider this in conjunction with what might better be considered separately, and that is the question of meaning in poetry. M. Brémond proposed the identity of poetry and prayer, and followed Bergson in relying, in the last analysis, on faith. M. Brémond eliminated reason as the essential element in poetry. Poetry in which the irrational element dominated was pure poetry. M. Brémond himself does not permit any looseness in the expression "pure poetry," which he confines to a very small body of poetry, as he should, if the lines in which he recognizes it are as precious to his spirit as they appear to be. In spite of M. Brémond, pure poetry is a term that has grown to be descriptive of poetry in which not the true subject but the poetry of the subject is paramount. All mystics approach God through the irrational. Pure poetry is both mystical and irrational. If we descend a little from this height and apply the looser and broader definition of pure poetry, it is possible to say that, while it can lie in the temperament of very few of us to write poetry in order to find God, it is probably the purpose of each of us to write poetry to find the good which, in the Platonic sense, is synonymous with God. One writes poetry, then, in order to approach the good in what is harmonious and orderly. Or, simply, one writes poetry out of a delight in the harmonious and orderly. If it is true that the most abstract painters paint herrings and apples, it is no less true that the poets who most urgently search the world for the sanctions of life, for that which makes life so prodigiously worth living, may find their solutions in a duck in a pond or in the wind on a winter night. It is conceivable that a poet may arise of such scope that he can set the abstraction on which so much depends to music. In the meantime we have to live by the literature we have or are able to produce. I say live by literature, because literature is the better part of life, provided it is based on life itself. From this point of view, the meaning of poetry involves us profoundly. It does not follow that poetry that is irrational in origin is not communicable poetry. The pure poetry of M. Brémond is irrational in origin. Yet it communicates so much that M. Brémond regards it as supreme. Because most of us are incapable of sharing the experiences of M. Brémond, we have to be content with less. When we find in poetry that which gives us a momentary existence on an exquisite plane, is it necessary to ask the meaning of the poem? If the poem had a meaning and if its explanation destroyed the illusion, should we have gained or lost? Take, for instance, the poem of Rimbaud, one of *Les Illuminations*, entitled "Beaten Tracks." I quote Miss Rootham's translation:

> On the right the summer dawn wakes the leaves, the mists and the sounds in this corner of the park. The slopes on the left clasp in their purple shade the myriad deep-cut tracks of the damp highway. A procession from fairyland passes by. There are chariots loaded with animals of gilded wood, with masts and canvas painted in many colors, drawn by twenty galloping piebald circusponies; and children and men on most astonishing beasts; there are twenty vehicles, embossed, and decked with flags and flowers like coaches of by-gone days, as coaches out of a fairytale; they are full of children dressed up for a suburban pastoral. There are even coffins under their night-dark canopies and sable plumes, drawn by trotting mares, blue and black.

I do not know what images the poem has created. M. Delahaye says that the poem was prompted by an American circus which visited Charleville, where Rimbaud lived as a boy, in 1868 or 1869. What is the effect of this explanation? I need not answer that. Miss Sitwell wrote the introduction to the collection of Miss Rootham's translations of the poems of Rimbaud. Something that she said in the course of that introduction illustrates the way the true subject supersedes the nominal subject. She said:

> How different was this life [of the slum] from that sheltered and even rather stuffy life of perpetual Sundays that he had led when he was a little boy in Charleville, and on these ever-recurring days of tight clothing and prayer, when Madame Rimbaud had escorted him, his brother and two sisters, to the eleven o'clock Mass, along the bright light dust-powdery roads, under trees whose great glossy brilliant leaves and huge pink flowers that seemed like heavenly transfigurations of society ladies, appeared to be shaking with laughter at the sober procession.

Miss Sitwell herself could not say whether the eleven o'clock Mass suggested the bright light flowers, or whether the society ladies came into her mind with the great glossy brilliant leaves and were merely trapped there by the huge pink flowers, or whether they came with the huge pink flowers. It might depend upon whether, in Miss Sitwell's mind, society ladies are, on the one hand, great glossy and brilliant, or, on the other hand, huge and pink. Here the true subject was the brilliance and color of an impression.

VII

The pressure of the contemporaneous from the time of the beginning of the World War to the present time has been constant and extreme. No one can have lived apart in a happy oblivion. For a long time before the war nothing was more common. In those days the sea was full of yachts and the yachts were full of millionaires. It was a time when only maniacs had disturbing things to say. The period was like a stage setting that since then has been taken down and trucked away. It had been taken down by the end of the war, even though it took ten years of struggle with the consequences of the peace to bring about a realization of that fact. People said that if the war continued it would end civilization, just as they say now that another such war will end civilization. It is one thing to talk about the end of civilization and another to feel that the thing is not merely possible but measurably probable. If you are not a communist, has not civilization ended in Russia? If you are not a Nazi, has it not ended in Germany? We no sooner say that it never can happen here than we recognize that we say it without any illusions. We are preoccupied with events, even when we do not observe them closely. We have a sense of upheaval. We feel threatened. We look from an uncertain present toward a more uncertain future. One feels the desire to collect oneself against all this in poetry as well as in politics. If politics is nearer to each of us because of the pressure of the contemporaneous, poetry, in its way, is no less so and for the same reason. Does anyone suppose that the vast mass of people in this country was moved at the last election by rational considerations? Giving reason as much credit as the radio, there still remains the certainty that so great a movement was emotional and, if emotional, irrational. The trouble is that the greater the pressure of the contemporaneous, the greater the resistance. Resistance is the opposite of escape. The poet who wishes to contemplate the good in the midst of confusion is like the mystic who wishes to contemplate God in the midst of evil. There can be no thought of escape. Both the poet and the mystic may establish themselves on herrings and apples. The painter may establish himself on a guitar, a copy of *Figaro*, and a dish of melons. These are fortifyings, although irrational ones. The only possible resistance to the pressure of the contemporaneous is a matter of herrings and apples or, to be less definite, the contemporaneous itself. In poetry, to that extent, the subject is not the contemporaneous, because that is only the nominal subject, but the poetry of the contemporaneous. Resistance to the pressure of ominous and destructive circumstance consists of its conversion, so far as possible, into a different, an explicable, an amenable circumstance.

VIII

M. Charles Mauron says that a man may be characterized by his obsessions. We are obsessed by the irrational. This is because we expect the irrational to liberate us from the rational. In a note on Picasso with the tell-tale title of "Social Fact and Cosmic Vision," Christian Zervos says:

> The explosion of his spirit has destroyed the barriers which art . . . impressed on the imagination. Poetry has come forward with all that it has of the acute, the enigmatical, the strange sense

which sees in life not only an image of reality but which conceives of life as a mystery that wraps us round everywhere.

To take Picasso as the modern one happens to think of, it may be said of him that his spirit is the spirit of any artist that seeks to be free. A superior obsession of all such spirits is the obsession of freedom. There is, however, no longer much excuse for explosions, for, as in painting, so in poetry, you can do as you please. You can compose poetry in whatever form you like. If it seems a seventeenth-century habit to begin lines with capital letters, you can go in for the liquid transitions of greater simplicity, and so on. It is not that nobody cares. It matters immensely. The slightest sound matters. The most momentary rhythm matters. You can do as you please, yet everything matters. You are free, but your freedom must be consonant with the freedom of others. To insist for a moment on the point of sound. We no longer like Poe's tintinnabulations. You are free to tintinnabulate if you like. But others are equally free to put their hands over their ears. Life may not be a cosmic mystery that wraps us round everywhere. You have somehow to know the sound that is the exact sound, and you do in fact know, without knowing how. Your knowledge is irrational. In that sense life is mysterious, and if it is mysterious at all, I suppose that it is cosmically mysterious. I hope that we agree that it is at least mysterious. What is true of sounds is true of everything: the feeling for words, without regard to their sound, for example. There is, in short, an unwritten rhetoric that is always changing and to which the poet must always be turning. That is the book in which he learns that the desire for literature is the desire for life. The incessant desire for freedom in literature or in any of the arts is a desire for freedom in life. The desire is irrational. The result is the irrational searching the irrational, a conspicuously happy state of affairs, if you are so inclined.

Those who are so inclined and without reserve say: The least fastidiousness in the pursuit of the irrational is to be repudiated as an abomination. Rational beings are canaille. Instead of seeing, we should make excavations in the eye; instead of hearing, we should juxtapose sounds in an emotional clitter-clatter.

This seems to be freedom for freedom's sake. If we say that we desire freedom when we are already free, it seems clear that we have in mind a freedom not previously experienced. Yet is not this an attitude toward life resembling the poet's attitude toward reality? In spite of the cynicisms that occur to us as we hear of such things, a freedom not previously experienced, a poetry not previously conceived of, may occur with the suddenness inherent in poetic metamorphosis. For poets, that possibility is the ultimate obsession. They purge themselves before reality, in the meantime, in what they intend to be saintly exercises.

You will remember the letter written by Rimbaud to M. Delahaye, in which he said:

> It is necessary to be a seer, to make oneself a seer. The poet makes himself a seer by a long, immense and reasoned unruliness of the senses . . . He attains the unknown.

IX

Let me say a final word about the irrational as part of the dynamics of poetry. The irrational bears the same relation to the rational that the unknown bears to the known. In an age as harsh as it is intelligent, phrases about the unknown are quickly dismissed. I do not for a moment mean to indulge in mystical rhetoric, since, for my part, I have no patience with that sort of thing. That the unknown as the source of knowledge, as the object of thought, is part of the dynamics of the known does not permit of denial. It is the unknown that excites the ardor of scholars, who, in the known alone, would shrivel up with boredom. We accept the unknown even when we are most skeptical. We may resent the consideration of it by any except the most lucid minds; but when so considered, it has seductions more powerful and more profound than those of the known.

Just so, there are those who, having never yet been convinced that the rational has quite made us divine, are willing to assume the efficacy of the irrational in that respect. The rational mind, dealing with the known, expects to find it glistening in a familiar ether. What it really finds is the unknown always behind and beyond the known, giving it the appearance, at best, of chiaroscuro. There are, naturally, charlatans of the irrational. That, however, does not require us to identify the irrational with the charlatans. I should not want to be misunderstood as having the poets of surrealism in mind. They concentrate their prowess in a technique which seems singularly limited but which, for all that, exhibits the dynamic influence of the irrational. They are extraordinarily alive, and that they make it possible for us to read poetry that seems filled with gaiety and youth, just when we were beginning to despair of gaiety and youth, is immensely to the good. One test of their dynamic quality and, therefore, of their dynamic effect, is that they make other forms seem obsolete. They, in time, will be absorbed, with the result that what is now so concentrated, so inconsequential in the restrictions of a technique, so provincial, will give and take and become part of the process of give and take of which the growth of poetry consists.

Those who seek for the freshness and strangeness of poetry in fresh and strange places do so because of an intense need. The need of the poet for poetry is a dynamic cause of the poetry that he writes. By the aid of the irrational he finds joy in the irrational. When we speak of fluctuations of taste, we are speaking of evidences of the operation of the irrational. Such changes are irrational. They reflect the effects of poetic energy, for where there are no fluctuations, poetic energy is absent. Clearly, I use the word "irrational" more or less indifferently, as between its several senses. It will be time enough to adopt a more systematic usage, when the critique of the irrational comes to be written, by whomever it may be that this potent subject ultimately engages. We must expect in the future incessant activity by the irrational and in the field of the irrational. The advances thus to be made would be all the greater if the character of the poet was not so casual and intermittent a character. The poet cannot profess the irrational as the priest professes the unknown. The poet's role is broader, because he must be possessed, along with everything else, by the earth and by men in their earthy implications. For the poet, the irrational is elemental, but neither poetry nor life is commonly at its dynamic utmost. We know Sweeney as he is and, for the most part, prefer him that way and without too much effulgence and, no doubt, always shall.

(1937?)

René Char

from The Formal Share

I

IMAGINATION consists in expelling from reality several incomplete persons, and then using the magic and subversive powers of desire to bring them back in the form of one entirely satisfying presence. The latter is the inextinguishable, increate real.

II

It is from lack of *inner* justice that the poet suffers most in his relations with the world. Caliban's sewer window behind which Ariel's powerful and sensitive eyes are angry.

III

The poet turns defeat into victory, victory into defeat, indifferently—a prenatal emperor interested in nothing but gathering the sky.

IV

At times the poet's reality would have no meaning for him if he did not secretly alter the record of exploits in the reality of others.

V

The poet, a magician of insecurity, can have only adopted satisfactions. A cinder never quite burned out.

VI

Behind the closed eye of one of those pre-established laws that are insoluble obstacles to our desire, there is sometimes hiding a belated sun as sensitive as fennel, which at our touch effuses violently, enveloping us in its perfume. The obscurity of his love, his pact with the unexpected, are nobility heavy enough for the poet.

VII

The poet must keep an equal balance between the physical world of waking and the dreadful ease of sleep; these are the lines of knowledge between which he lays the subtle body of the poem, moving indistinctly from one to the other of these different states of life.

X

It is right for poetry to be indistinguishable from what is foreseen but not yet formulated.

XV

In poetry today still too many novices, at the racetracks of luxurious summer and with the finest thoroughbreds to choose from, insist on entering an old horse from the bull ring whose entrails, recently sewn back into him, are still quivering with repugnant dust! Until the dialectical embolism that strikes every poem fraudulently made works its justice on the person of the author for his unpardonable impropriety.

XVI

A poem is always married to someone.

XVII

Heraclitus points to the exalting union of contraries. In the first place, he sees in them the perfect condition and the indispensable motive of harmony. In poetry it happened that the moment these contraries were fused, there arose, from no definite source, a shock whose solitary and disintegrating force started a slide in the abysses which, in a way so contrary to physics, bear the poem. It is for the poet to put a stop to this danger by bringing to bear either something traditional, tested by reason, or the fire of a demiurge so miraculous that it stops the passage from cause to effect. The poet may then see contraries (those punctual and tumultuous mirages) joined, and their indwelling descendants become *personified*—poetry and truth, as we know, being synonymous.

XX

From your glowing window, look down on the features of this subtle stake and recognize the poet—a tumbril of burning reeds escorted by the unexpectable.

XXI

In poetry, only when there is communication and a free ordering of the totality of things among themselves, through us, are we ourselves engaged and defined, ready to take on our original form and our proven qualities.

XXIV

By intense physical work we keep even with the outer cold, and doing so, put down the risk of being taken over by it; likewise when we return to what is real—that is, not sustained by our desire—and the time has come to give over to its destiny the vessel of the poem, we find ourselves in an analogous situation. The wheels (junk!) of our petrified mill start turning, scooping deep and difficult waters. Our exertion learns again its proportion of sweat. And we go on, wrestlers downed but never dying, surrounded by exasperating spectators and indifferent virtues.

XXVII

Earth being an exquisite horrible quicksand, earth and the incongruous human condition seize and modify each other, mutually. Poetry is drawn from the exalted sum of iridescence on their surface.

XXVIII

The poet is the man of unilateral stability.

XXIX

The poem emerges from a subjective constraint and an objective choice.

The poem is an assemblage in motion of original determinant values in contemporaneous relation with *someone whom this circumstance puts first.*

XXX

A poem is the realization of love — desire that remains desire.

XXXI

Some ask that poetry be relieved of her armor; their wound is sick of an eternity of tweezers. But walking naked on her feet of reeds, her feet of pebbles, she lets herself be nowhere confined. Woman! On her mouth we kiss the madness of time; or side by side with the zenith cricket, she sings through the winter night in the bakery of the poor, under the softness of a loaf of light.

XXXII

The poet is not angry at the hideous extinction of death, but, confident of his own particular touch, he transforms everything into long wools.

XXXIII

Working in the new ground of the Word's universality, the poet—

being honest, avid, sensitive, and bold—will not sympathize with those undertakings that alienate the miracle of freedom in poetry; that is, of intelligence in life.

XXXIV

The being we do not know is an infinite being; he may arrive, and turn our anguish and our burden to dawn in our arteries.

Between innocence and knowledge, love and the void, the poet every day throws the bridge of his health.

XXXV

The poet, by translating intention into an inspired act, by converting a cycle of illness into a cargo of resurrection, forces an oasis of cold through all the pores of the windowpane of dejection, thus creating the prism, a hydra of struggle, wonders, rigor, and deluge, with your lips for wisdom and my blood for an altarpiece.

XXXVI

The place of the poet's lodging is of the vaguest; a gulf of sorrowing fire underlies his rough-wood table.

The poet's vitality is not a vitality from the beyond but a diamond point *here and alive* with transcendent presences and pilgrimaging storms.

XLI

In the poet two kinds of evidence are held: the first yields its whole meaning at once in the variety of forms available in external reality, it rarely goes deep, it is only pertinent; the second is inserted into the poem, it speaks the commandment and exegesis of the powerful and capricious gods who inhabit the poet, it is indurate evidence that can neither fade nor die. Its hegemony is its attribute. Spoken, it covers a considerable expanse.

XLII

To be a poet is to have an appetite for a certain anxiety which,

when tasted among the swirling sum of things existent or forefelt,
causes, as the taste dies, joy.

XLIII

The poem gives and receives from its plenitude the entire act of
the poet exiling himself from his secret chamber. Behind his shut-
ter of blood burns the cry of a force that will destroy itself because
it abhors force—its subjective and sterile sister.

XLV

The poet is the origin of two beings, one that projects and one that
holds. From the lover he borrows emptiness, from the beloved,
light. This formed couple, this double sentinel, pathetically gives
him his voice.

XLVII

Recognize two kinds of the possible: the *daily* possible and the *for-
bidden* possible. Make the first, if you can, the equal of the sec-
ond; put them on the princely way to the fascinating impossible,
that highest degree of the comprehensible.

XLVIII

The poet advises: "Read me. Read me again." He does not always
come away unscathed from his page, but like the poor, he knows
how to make use of an olive's eternity.

(1941–1943)
Translated by Jackson Mathews

Eugenio Montale

from Intentions

(Imaginary Interview)

— . . .

—If I've understood your question correctly, Marforio, you'd like to know at what moment, and due to what accidental cause, in front of what picture, I was able to declare prophetically "I too am a painter." How I became committed to and recognized in my own art, which isn't painting. It's very difficult to explain. I never suffered from an infatuation with poetry, nor from any desire to "specialize" in that sense. In those years almost no one was interested in poetry. The last success I remember from those days was Gozzano, but the strong-minded disparaged him, and I too (wrongly) shared their opinion. The better *littérateurs* who were soon to gather around the "Ronda" thought that poetry from then on should be written in prose. I remember that after my first poems had been published, in Debenedetti's *Primo Tempo*, I was treated ironically by my few friends (who were already immersed in politics, mainly anti-fascist, by 1922–1923). And Gobetti, who printed my first book in 1925, wasn't too happy when I sent him a political article for his *Rivoluzione Liberale*. He too believed, as the various Scrutators and Babeufs of Roman monarchical journalism believe today, that a poet can't and shouldn't make judgments in politics. He was wrong; not that I was very sure of being a poet.

— . . .

—Am I sure of it today? I wouldn't know. Besides, poetry is only one of a great many possible positives in life. I don't believe a poet stands taller than another man who really exists, that he is a some-body. I too acquired a smattering of psychoanalysis in its day, but even without recourse to its lights I soon came to think, and still think, that art is the form of life of the man who truly doesn't live: a compensation or a surrogate. Which is not to justify a delib-erate ivory-tower attitude: a poet mustn't renounce life. It's life that is trying to flee from him.

— . . .

—I wrote my first poems as a boy. They were humorous poems, with bizarre, truncated rhymes. Later, when I'd discovered futur-ism, I also made some *fantaisiste*—or, if you will, grotesque-cre-puscular—poems. But I didn't publish, and wasn't sure of myself. I had more concrete and stranger ambitions. At the time I was pre-paring for my debut as Valentino, in Gounod's *Faust*; then I learned the entire part of Alfonso XII in *La Favorita* and Lord Astor in *Lucia*. My experience, more than intuition, of the funda-mental unity of the various arts must have come to me from that source. The indications were excellent, but after the death of my teacher Ernesto Sivori, one of the first and most famous Bocca-negras, I changed direction (also, I was suffering from unrelieved insomnia). The experience was useful to me: there's a problem of pitch outside singing, too, in every human activity. And I believe I am one of the few persons surviving today who understands our melodrama. To Verdi we owe the surprising reappearance in the midst of the nineteenth century of a few sparks of the fire of Dante and Shakespeare. It doesn't matter that it's usually mixed up with the fire of Victor Hugo.

[. . .]

— . . .

—No, I knew even then how to distinguish between description and poetry, but I realized that poetry can't grind on nothing and that there can be no concentration until there has been diffusion. I didn't say *waste*. A poet shouldn't spoil his voice with too much *solfeggio*; he shouldn't lose those qualities of timbre which later he'll never recover. There's no need to write a series of poems where one exhausts a specific psychological situation, an occasion. In this sense the lesson of Foscolo, a poet who never repeated him-self, is exemplary.

— . . .

—Don't misunderstand me. I don't deny that a poet can or should exert himself in his calling, inasmuch as it is such. But the best exercises are internal, acts of meditation or reading. Reading of all kinds, not poetry: it's not necessary for the poet to spend his time reading the work of others, though he shouldn't be ignorant of what has been achieved, from the technical point of view, in his art. The language of a poet is a historicized language, a relationship. It is valid to the degree that it opposes or differentiates itself from other languages. And naturally, the great seedbed of any poetic discovery lies in the field of prose. At one time everything was expressible in verses, and these resembled, and sometimes were, poetry. Today only certain things are said in verse.

— . . .

—It's not easy to say what things. For many years poetry has been becoming more a vehicle of consciousness than of representation. Often it's called to a different destiny, and some would like to see it *in piazza*. But those who are deluded and go down into the marketplace are soon given the gate.

— . . .

—No, I'm not thinking of a philosophical poetry; that diffuses ideas. Who thinks of that anymore? The task of the poet is the search for a timely truth, not a general truth. A truth of the poet-subject which doesn't deny that of the empirical man-subject. Which sings what unites man with other men but doesn't deny what separates him and makes him unique and unrepeatable.

— . . .

—Those are big words, my dear Marforio. Directly, I know few existentialist texts, but many years ago I read a few writers like Shestov, a Kierkegaardian very close to the positions of that philosophy. After the first war, in 1919, the absolute immanentism of Gentile gave me a great deal of satisfaction, however badly I deciphered the very involved theory of pure act. Later, I preferred the great idealistic positivism of Croce; but perhaps in the years in which I wrote *Ossi di seppia* (between 1920 and 1925), the French philosophers of contingency, especially Boutroux, whom I knew better than Bergson, had an influence on me. For me, the miracle was manifest like necessity. Immanence and transcendence are inseparable, and to make a state of mind out of the perennial mediation of the two terms, as modern historicism proposes, doesn't resolve the problem, or resolves it with excessive optimism. We need to live our contradiction without loopholes, but also without enjoying it too much, without making it into polite gossip.

— . . .

—No, writing my first book (a book which wrote itself) I didn't commit myself to ideas like these. The intentions I'm outlining today are all *a posteriori*. I obeyed a need for musical expression. I wanted my words to stick closer than those of the other poets I'd read. Closer to what? It seemed to me I was living under a bell jar, and yet I seemed to be hearing something essential. A subtle veil, almost a thread, separated me from the definitive *quid*. Absolute expression would have meant breaking that veil, that thread: an explosion, the end of the illusion of the world as representation. But this was an unreachable goal. And my desire to stay close remained musical, instinctive, unprogrammatic. I wanted to wring the neck of the elegance of our old aulic language, even at the risk of a countereloquence.

[. . .]

— . . .

—With a change of scenery and occupation, and after I'd made a number of trips abroad, I never dared reread myself seriously, and I felt the need to go deeper. Before I was thirty, I'd hardly known anyone. Now I was seeing too many people, but I wasn't any less alone than at the time of *Ossi di seppia*. I tried to live in Florence with the detachment of a foreigner, of a Browning, but I hadn't taken into account the henchmen of the feudal authority on which I depended. Besides, the bell jar remained around me, and now I knew it would never be shattered; and I feared that that dualism between lyric and commentary, between poetry and the preparation for or spur to poetry, in my old experiments (a contrast I had once, with youthful presumption, recognized also in Leopardi) was seriously persistent in me. I didn't think of pure lyric in the sense it had later among us, too—of a game of sound suggestions—but rather of a result which would contain its motives without revealing them, or, better, without broadcasting them. Admitted that there is a balance in art between the external and the internal, between the occasion and the work-object, it was necessary to express the object and omit the occasion-spur. A new means, not Parnassian, of immersing the reader *in medias res*, a total absorbing of one's intentions in objective results. Even here I was moved by instinct, not by a theory. (Eliot's theory of the "objective correlative" did not yet exist, I believe, in 1928, when my "Arsenio" was published in *The Criterion*.) In substance, I don't feel the new book [*Le occasioni*] contradicted the achievements of the first: it eliminated some of its impurities and tried to attack that barrier between external and internal which seemed nonexistent to me even from the gnoseological point of view. Everything is internal *and* external for contemporary man; not that the so-called world is necessarily our representation. We live with an altered sense of time and space. In *Ossi di seppia* everything was attracted and absorbed by the fermenting sea; later I saw that the sea was everywhere for me, and that even the Classic architecture of the Tuscan hills was also in itself movement and flight. And in the new book, too, I continued my struggle to unearth another dimension in our weighty polysyllabic language, which seemed to me to reject an experience such as mine. I repeat, the struggle was not programmatic. Perhaps the unwelcome translating I was forced to do was helpful to me. I've often cursed our language, but in it and through it I came to realize I am incurably Italian—and without regret.

The new book was no less romantic than the first, although the sense of a poetry which delineates itself, watching it physically form itself, gave *Ossi di seppia* a flavor some have regretted. If I'd stopped there and repeated myself I would have been wrong, but others would have been happier.

— ...

—*Le occasioni* was an orange or rather a lemon that was missing a slice: not really that of pure poetry in the sense I first indicated, but of the pedal, of profound music, contemplation. My work to date ends with the poems of *Finisterre*, which represent, let us say, my "Petrarchan" experience. I projected the Selvaggia or Mandetta or Delia (call her what you will) of the "Motets" against the background of a war both cosmic and earthly, without end and without reason, and I pledged myself to her, lady or shade, angel or petrel. The motive had already been contained and anticipated in "Nuove Stanze," written before the war; it didn't take much then to be a prophet. *Finisterre* contains a few poems, written in the incubus of 1940–1942, perhaps the freest I've ever written, and I thought their relationship to the central theme of *Le occasioni*

from *Intentions (Imaginary Interview)*   69

was evident. If I had orchestrated and diluted my theme, I would have been better understood. But I don't go looking for poetry; I wait to be visited. I write little, with few revisions, when it seems to me I can't abstain. If even then I fail to avoid rhetoric then it means (at least for me) it's inevitable.

[…]

— …

—The future is in the hands of providence, Marforio: I can go on and I can stop tomorrow. It doesn't depend on me. An artist is a driven man; he doesn't have freedom of choice. In this field, more than in others, there's an effective determinism. I've followed the path my time imposed on me; tomorrow others will go in other directions; I myself may change. I've always written like a poor fool, not a professional man of letters. I don't possess the intellectual self-sufficiency some would attribute to me, nor do I feel invested with an important mission. I've had a sense of today's culture, but not a shadow of the culture I'd have wished for, and with which I probably never would have written a line. When I sent my first poems to the printer I was ashamed of them for a while, now I can speak of them almost with indifference. Perhaps I would have done wrong not to write and publish them. I've lived my time with the minimum of cowardice consigned to my feeble forces, but there are those who have done more, much more, even if they haven't published books.

(1946)
Translated by Jonathan Galassi

George Seferis

from A Poet's Journal

Tuesday, June 4, 1946

Crazy about the land. Every day carried away more and more by this drunkenness. The sea, the mountains that dance motionless; I found them the same in these rippled chitons: water turned into marble around the chests and the sides of headless fragments. I know my whole life won't be long enough to express what I have been trying to say for so many days now: this union of nature with a simple human body, this worthless thing—superman they'd say today. As I'm writing now, I make desperate gestures in the void and express nothing.

And yet I'm crazy about these things, in this light.

"And you see the light of the sun"—

as the ancients used to say. I could analyze this phrase and advance toward the most secret love. But to say what you want to say, you must create another language and nourish it for years and years with what you have loved, with what you have lost, with what you will never find again.

Friday, October 18

Yesterday after lunch I cut wood. The body functions more easily;

the animal is more relaxed; no elation. That's it. The head is empty, emotions settled down. Not at all in a poetic mood. It doesn't matter; for the time being it's better so. Don't forget that you must leave and return. Shut-up rooms warp you with bad habits; the room where I lived in recent years was stifling. I think of nothing now.

In the morning to the village with Mina. We climbed the narrow paths up to the Clock. Friday is washday, clothes hanging out; you pass beneath them to continue and feel them damp on your face. We returned by boat. Rowing, cutting wood, swimming; clouds and sunshine. I don't want to be anything today; tomorrow, we'll see.

Monday, October 21

Marouli and company left today at dawn; Mina left too. About six, voices woke me up: "The sun! The sun!"

I opened my eyes. By my bed was the pitcher from Aegina which I brought to my room the other day (a big open poppy, surrounded by green branches, painted on yellow clay); on the wall the sun's rays, coming in parallel lines through the shutters, painted long, narrow, rose streaks. I opened the window toward the sea beyond the Training Camp. The huge disk of the sun, still bisected by the horizon, had a color I had never seen before: it was the color of blackberry juice, a bit lighter. The sea was breathless, without a ripple; the pine needles motionless as sea-urchin spines in clear depths. On the horizon a black ship crawled very slowly, just like on the Karaghiozis screen, underlined that amazing disk, and vanished. Then, heels tapping on the wooden steps, suitcases, words, fingers—they all left. (Writing this, I'm still drunk, with the unpleasant feeling of being a drunkard; only rarely and with difficulty can I stand being drunk.)

I went out onto the veranda facing the sea; the time was now 8:30, the sun high. It was impossible to separate the light from the silence, the silence and light from the calm. Sometimes the ear would catch a noise, a distant voice, a faint chirping. But these were in some way *enclosed elsewhere*, like your heartbeat, felt for a moment and then forgotten. The sea had no surface; only the hills opposite didn't end at the earth's rim, but advanced beyond, below, starting all over again with a fainter image of their shape which vanished softly into faraway emptiness. There was a sense that another side of life exists. (I write with difficulty, trying to avoid generalizations, trying to *describe* the indescribable.) You perceived the surface of the water by watching the oars in the distance, as they dipped with a dry glitter like a windowpane struck by the sun; or again, later, when a boat passed below the house, its raised sails flapping, *perfectly* mirrored in the water like a picture on a deck of cards. The feeling that if the slightest crack opened up in this enclosed vision, all things could spill out beyond the four points of the horizon, leaving you naked and alone, begging alms, muttering imprecise words, without this amazing preciseness you had seen.

I returned to my room, dizzy, as I said, almost a visionary, and closed the east shutters, letting in only the dim light of the north.

Wednesday, October 23

Yesterday and today, verse-making. Cavafy is waiting. The feeling that my fingers have hardened lamentably against writing verses; I've abandoned them for so many years. Military discharge, restoration: you thought it was the war, the difficult circumstances which would end with some sort of "peace." Suddenly you discover that you'll spend your entire life in disorder. It's all that you have; you must learn to live with it.

This light, this landscape, these days start to threaten me seriously. I close the shutters so that I can work. I must protect myself from beauty, as the English from the rain and the Bedouins from the *chamsin*. You feel your brain emptying and lightening; the long day absorbs it. Today I understood why Homer was blind; if he had had eyes he wouldn't have written anything. He saw once, for a limited period of time, then saw no more.

Friday, October 25

Why does one write poems? Why, although they are such secret things (for him who writes them), does he consider them more important than anything else in life? This vital need.

Saturday, October 26

Yesterday morning verse-making; exercise on a given theme; very instructive. Contra tempo, observation of a line starting out from an insignificant beginning. Such exercises are necessary. Why does a pianist pound on his piano so many hours a day?

Thursday, October 31

Evening. In the afternoon I cut wood until it grew dark. I returned home sweating, my hands coated with resin. A bath, and then I sat at my table. I finished the poem. Title: "Thrush." I don't know if it's good; I know that it's finished. Now it must *dry*.

Friday, November 1

Copying "Thrush" and making minor corrections. From 10:00 on, half-naked, I cut wood. It's November, yet I dipped in the sea three times. I think the ending of the poem isn't bad (Part III) because it's well sustained by the first two parts and at times it comes close to the preciseness I want. As for the last lines of that part, the allegro, I would call it, or the "lyric," others would (a tone that I haven't used for several years), this is strange: before I left yesterday afternoon for the garden, I left on my table very obscure verses (emotionally, I mean); the tone was constantly diminishing. Coming down from the mountain, I thought of Bashō's teaching to Kikakou:

> We shouldn't abuse God's creatures. You must reverse the haiku, not:
> A dragonfly;
> remove its wings —
> pepper tree.
> but:
> A pepper tree:
> add wings to it —
> dragonfly.

When I picked up the pen again, I did *reverse* the lines I had written; this was the right tone.

Saturday, November 2

One cannot easily tear oneself away from a poem which is finished; the fibers can't be cut easily. All day long I've still been *fumbling* with the "Thrush": finishing touches, corrections, additions of fine tones. I still feel bruised by the poem. It has drawn heavily on my experience of life in the past years and on ideas for verses jotted down at random since last January.

This morning: wood, swimming. A fisherman passed and offered fish; his boat is a *kourita*. Here people do not know these boats. Those I asked said "something like a gondola." I, too, asked him: "What do you call your caique?" "Kourita," he answered. I understood that he was from Asia Minor. I asked him other questions, knowing what he would answer, and was pleased that he said what I expected. "Does she go by sail?" "Yes, she soars; I came from Smyrna on her, from the Englezonesi . . ." "Without a keel, do you use leeboards?" "These don't need leeboards; with the sail, their side serves as a keel . . . From Smyrna to here? . . . This one went to Egypt in 1913 with four or five others; she's the only one that came back. They took them to the Nile and sold them. Look at her warped planks." I looked. I was pleased with the workmanship, the beautiful old wood. The carvings on the prow and stern recalled icons from my past. I observed this boat with much joy.

Sunday morning, November 3

I've been here almost a month. Essentially, by nature I must be a man like Rodakis (of the house on Aegina), caring or molding his house all his life. The poems would be extra — gifts of God.

There's been no electricity since the day before yesterday; the fuses are burned out. Today we tell Evangelia about the mishap. She replies: "In my sleep I saw you distressed; this must be it." It's natural that the language of dreams pertains even to trifles; messengers condescending even to humble errands. The intellectuals have made them speak only with the trumpet of Jericho or with bagpipes.

Tuesday, November 5

The cyclamen become deeper and deeper in color as winter approaches. With more character.

In essence, the poet has one theme: his live body.

Monday, January 20, 1947

For almost a month now I have been working poorly; for many reasons, including Athens. The fever of the sick city and at the same time the feeling of a beauty or a vivacity or an acceptance; a pillar of light before me refuses to let me articulate a word.

Wednesday, January 22

And yet in the background is this pillar of light, this untouched thing that remains wedged in the heart of change like a diamond in a brook. There is a dreadful affirmation of one's whole being in such moments, like a Bach chorale, you think, that continues, irrevocably; *you know* that even if they suddenly machine-gunned instruments and musicians and listeners it would not stop. I feel now that this exists *behind* the best of what I've written (whether or not apparent). Around this pivot, this thread, my functioning images and their shadows are crystallized. Hard to say this with precision; I should write a poem. It is similar to the expression — it's just occurred to me — perfectly applicable to a kind of sudden and indestructible humaneness. Prometheus' cry *"O sacred ether"* had a similar effect on me when I read it one chilly afternoon in Johannesburg and burst into an exile's sobs. The same with Makriyannis' words: "And you don't hear us, and you don't see us" — or his talk at Mega Spelio. The same with certain moments of the war, in the face of danger.

Adverse moments are not moments of discouragement; even when this feeling is not at its height, I know the untouchable thing exists. There may be moments of endurance, sometimes of agonizing search, sometimes of sarcastic defense of the organism in the face of disgust. This is not the dead end; the dead end, still worse, is the consciousness of a standstill.

April 6, Palm Sunday

In March I worked steadily and hard every day (the Ministry uses me now for subordinate jobs which I do at home). I can't complain; it's better.

I've finished the poems "of setting out for Ithaca." Now it's more difficult. The feeling you have after the effort of the pen finding the groove in the paper is gone. The situation around me is unhealthy — damned, I should say — in this morass of souls and bodies to which Greece has been reduced. You think indeed that at times everything is spinning incoherently. They insult, yell, are scurrilous with constantly accelerating frenzy, and yet there's no end to it. The distance from here to the point where you yourself won't be able to keep your sanity is minimal. A strange psychology is created within you, to hold on to whatever is alive — a body, a kitten, a tender shoot; anything, in short, that has a throb of truth. You feel an unrestrained desire to howl to God, or to something that must exist above this thick mire, "Don't you hear us? Don't you see us?" And then you wonder: Must I perhaps be punished because I insist on not becoming like the others; for this *hubris*?

Last night I stayed out late with friends. At Psaras' and then to a patisserie at Omonia until two in the morning. I think it must be the first time I have stayed out at night like this since last January. I listened to their discussions — art, politics, social events — trying to put together what they wanted to say. Impossible; words kept leaping into my ears — outbursts of profundity, anger, or cleverness, without coherence, that stopped unexpectedly with an exclamation or somebody's joke. Then silence, and the thing began all over again.

I could face all this, the hell with it, if I had the means (that is, only the daily bread for my wife and me) to devote myself to the work I want and know I can do — so that I wouldn't be working like a crippled man. The degradation of money. Yesterday I had the most humiliating idea I may ever have had in my life: to stop writing for a period of time — five or ten years, I don't know — to find a job that would allow me to save a little money, and then do what I want. A ridiculous thought; for living things there's no deferment.

Wednesday, March 1, 1950

The dreadful war nature wages to prevent the Poet from existing.

Wednesday, March 15

Among the books Z was kind enough to send from Paris, I received Stendhal's diary. It begins like this:

"Milan, le 28 Germinal an IX — J'entreprends d'écrire l'histoire de ma vie jour par jour. Je ne sais si j'aurais la force de remplir ce projet, déjà commencé à Paris. Voilà déjà une faute de français; il y en aura beaucoup par ce que je prends pour principe *de ne pas me gêner et de n'effacer jamais.*" (The emphasis is mine.)

I've been thinking about that passage this week. It's been a long time since I started putting in order my personal notes from 1925 on — sporadically, the year before last; intensively, after our return from Bursa until the end of '49, with the interruption of our autumn trip to Constantinople. I also wrote, much more irregularly, "sans me gêner et sans effacer." But I didn't plan "to write the story of my life, day by day." Day by day we live our life; we don't write it — writing, no matter what you do, is only a part of life.

Evening

I passed through periods of great doubt concerning the value my works would have. I proceeded in life, all alone, without help (but who has help?), except for two men not connected with letters, and my own perseverance. As I look back on the past, I would call it the perseverance of a Negro. Until 1936 the years were very difficult. Nor do I forget that, after *Strophe* there were friends who showed me both love and dedication. But I don't mean that; when I say help, I mean the man who helps at the critical moments of doubt and accepts, *while they're still fresh*, your daring attempts. This I lacked.

But now — these days when I am fifty — I know what I am. I know who may accept me and who reject me. I am interested in the former, and, among the latter, in those better than I. I add without hesitation that I pray better ones may appear, even if they efface me from the memory of men. It is not *my* work that interests me above all else; it is *work*, without a possessive pronoun, that must live, even if our personal contributions are consumed in it.

I am fully conscious that we do not live in a time when the poet can believe that fame awaits him, but in a time of oblivion. This doesn't make me less dedicated to my beliefs; I am more so. At the same time it causes me to endure with greater peace of mind the indescribable "intellectual" men of Attico-Boeotia.

Thus, just as I published *Strophe*, just as I published *Mythisto-rema*, although others considered my whims crazy, I sat down and undertook, during this *stopover* at Ankara, the clearing out of these papers — still another "bottle into the sea," personal this time. Who knows? This, too, may help other *seafarers* like me.

Another reason: to fulfill my release.

Wednesday, April 12

I once heard one younger poet saying to another, in a critical tone: "You of course write beautifully" (see "*Days M.E.*").* Not in the sense we say that so-and-so writes with many flourishes, without content, with many embellishments, but as we say to someone we envy for the material comfort fortune has endowed him with: "You of course clip coupons." The other in vain tried to explain that he had sweated to learn the Greek language he was writing. I was irked by the invidious tone of the first; now I think sympa-

* Days, Middle East, is a part of Seferis' unpublished diary.

thetically about that embittered man. For one who crosses the threshold, how many have remained below the ceiling? How many pitchers are broken for each that survives?

Among the many ways that there are to study poets, the simplest, it seems to me, is the best: to look at what their works show us. And it is not improbable that they show things which we were looking for; "which we would not have sought if we had not found them already," as someone else says; or, to remember the ancient sage, "knowledge is memory." Thus, poets complement us and we complement them. I do not intend to advise arbitrariness when we read poems. A poem is not reason enough for us to unleash our imagination in reckless wanderings. Rather, what I want to say is this: that poets, if their poetry is good, draw on a deep-rooted experience of life, which all of us, young and old, have within ourselves; how much we feel this, I don't know. These are the roots through which they communicate with us. What forms, what vestments this common experience, this common feeling of life, will take in a historical moment no one can tell. It depends, I think, not only upon the idiosyncrasy of the individual who expresses himself but also upon many intellectual, social, and political mores of the time. A poem written from a purely erotic impulse may become in another era the expression of the feeling of human humiliation, of deceit, of degradation, because the era in some way has brought such sentiments to the surface; it has made them, let's say, public. And the praise of a rose or a ray of sunlight may convey the impression of human grandeur at moments when human grandeur flashes like lightning, as Solomos would say. These variations, as time passes, indicate that poems are alive and are nourished; they have the power to complement us and they ask us to complement them. If poetry were not sustained by this kind of human solidarity, in this human community, it wouldn't have lived very long. Poetry does not express truths in the scientific meaning of the word, nor does it discover philosophies and life theories. It uses science *and* the philosophy of others, if it needs them. Poetry is not for personal confessions; if it makes them, it is not they that save it. It does not try to express the personality of the poets, but, as Eliot has written, tries rather to abolish it. But in doing this, it expresses another personality that belongs to everyone; whosoever loses his life will find it, the Gospel says. Thus, let us not ask from the poet, in order to understand him, the petty, everyday details of his life which we think he is expressing. These petty events, if they have become poetry, are events belonging to you and me, and to those who have gone before, and to those who will come after us. If it were not so, poetry would not exist. You can make the experiment yourselves. Read a rhapsody of Homer and see if whether, at the parts that move you, what you feel is merely an archaeological reference alone, or if perhaps it is a sentiment nurtured by all the human experience that has occurred from that ancient era down to your present moment.

Saturday, November 25

In the evening at dinner, as I was talking with two young supporting actresses, one of them said: "When I'm around fifty-five, I can hope to be a good tragic actress." I was impressed by this remark in a time when we have become accustomed to seeing the young always in a hurry. This young girl reckoned that she had twenty-five years of hard work before her. The work of the past day is added to the work of the day to follow: I like this tempo. Not for one man only but also for the generations after him. During my student years in Paris, I once visited with a friend the apartment of a bow maker (for violins). It was on the top floor of a house in the vicinity of the Gare du Nord. To the right, as I entered, an orderly pile of unplaned wood. "All this," I asked; "will you make it into bows?" "Not I," he replied. "It will be made into bows by my son; the wood has not dried yet." I was impressed by this consciousness of continuity. How many know to wait for the wood to dry.

Translated by Athan Anagnostopoulos

Delmore Schwartz

The Vocation of the Poet
in the Modern World

TO HAVE a vocation is to have a calling, to be called. One may be called by the powers of evil as well as the powers of good, but it is clear that one must respond with the whole of one's being. In this sense it is also clear that to have a vocation is very much like being in love. Being in love and being called to write poetry are often linked, and many people feel the need to write poetry when they are in love. As there are many errors in love, so there are many errors in the writing of poetry. And as there is puppy love, there is adolescent poetry.

Since there are errors and since a calling is a very important matter, since one is called during the formative and decisive years of existence, there is much doubt and hesitation about the fact of having a calling, and a period of trial is prescribed in some vocations, while one of the reasons for going to school, after a certain point, is to determine if one has a true vocation, if one has truly been called; and it is in some kind of school that we prepare ourselves to be adequate to our vocation.

In poetry, it is particularly true that many are called and few are chosen. And to be a poet in the modern world means a certain important renunciation which does not hold of all vocations: it means that there is little hope or none of being able to earn a living directly by the writing of poetry; and this has been true in the past, although in other ways, as well as in the modern life; for example, Dryden speaks of "not having the vocation of poverty to scribble." In the modern world, it is hard to think of any poet who has had from the start any real economic support for the writing of poetry. There are prizes, grants, patrons, and poetry is honored by much generosity and much prestige. Unfortunately, these are provided after the poet has established himself—and not always then—but during the first and perhaps most difficult years of being a poet, the best a poet can do is to get some other job to support his effort to be a poet. In recent years, the job of teaching English has provided a good many positions which help the poet during his first years, but it is not entirely clear that this is a good thing. For to have a vocation means that one must respond with the whole of one's being; but teaching should be a vocation too, and not a job, and when the poet takes teaching as a job, he may injure or weaken himself as a poet, or he may not be adequate to all that the task of teaching requires. All the temptations of the world, the flesh, and the devil combine to lure the poet to success as a teacher and to the rewards of successful academic ambition. At the same time that the poet resists these temptations, he must resign himself to the likelihood that a genuine poetic reputation can be achieved only among others who are poets—for it is mostly poets who read any poetry except what is to be found in anthologies—and the kind of fame (that last infirmity of noble mind, as Milton said) which he would like will come to him, if it comes at all, only in middle age.

What I have just said should distinguish roughly the difference between being a poet in the modern world from what it may have been in other historical periods. If we turn again to the wisdom, tried and inherited for so many years, to be found in the origins of words, we remember that to be a poet is to be a maker, to be the maker of something new, to make something new by putting things and words together. The distinguishing mark of the poet, that aptitude which more than any other skill of the mind makes him a poet, is metaphor, according to Aristotle. Now metaphor is literally a bearing-across, or a bringing-together of things by means of words. And composition, which is what the poet accomplishes by all the elements of his poem when they are brought together in a unity, structural, formal, intuitive, and musical—composition means putting things together, bringing them together into a unity which is original, interesting and fruitful. Thus the poet at any time may be said to be engaged in bringing things together, in making new things, in uniting the old and the new, all by the inexhaustible means which words provide for him. In this way, the poet as creator and metaphor-maker and presiding bringer of unity is a kind of priest. He unites things, meanings, attitudes, feelings, through the power, prowess, and benediction of words, and in this way he is a priest who performs a ceremony of marriage each time he composes a poem. Unfortunately, not all marriages are happy.

*

In the modern world, the poet who has been truly called cannot respond as poets did in idyllic and primitive periods, when merely the naming of things, as Adam named the animals, was enough to bring poems into existence. On the contrary, he must resist the innumerable ways in which words are spoiled, misused, commercialized, deformed, mispronounced, and in general degraded. We can see clearly how much this resistance is part of the vocation of the poet if we consider the recurrent references to language itself in the poems of that truly modern poet, T. S. Eliot. These references occur in his poems from the very start, continue in each volume he has published, and culminate in a passage in his most recent book of poems, *Four Quartets*:

> So here I am, in the middle way, having had twenty years—
> Twenty years largely wasted, the years of *l'entre deux guerres*—
> Trying to learn to use words, and every attempt
> Is a wholly new start, and a different kind of failure
> Because one has only learnt to get the better of words
> For the thing one no longer has to say, or the way in which
> One is no longer disposed to say it.

Elsewhere in his work there is a sensitivity to colloquial speech—and a kind of horror or anguish about it—which arises from the fact that for a modern poet, as for any poet, words are the keys to what he wants.

Eliot's play in verse *Sweeney Agonistes* is the best example of this aspect of his feeling about language, which is used to express a profound anguish about human beings and human existence. When language is degraded in speech, then the basis in community life for the art of poetry is diseased; and it is appropriate and perhaps inevitable that the great modern poet who should have felt this fact with as much acuteness as any other poet should at the same time be an author who acquired an English accent after arriving at the age of reason. Nevertheless, just as certain kinds of disease make for a greater sensitivity to experience or a more precise observation of reality (the blind know more about how things sound and how they feel to the touch than those who have normal vision), so, too, the disease which degrades language in the modern world may help to bring about the remarkable and often multilingual sensitivity of the modern poet to the language which is the matrix from which he draws his poems.

"Degradation" and "disease" are strong words of condemnation, and a great claim is also made when one says that the degradation and disease to which poetry is subjected in the modern world are also one of the fruitful and necessary conditions of genuine poetry and of a genuine vocation for the art of poetry. For the sake of justifying these claims, let us examine small and convenient examples. The word "intrigue" is a noun which has four legitimate meanings. It means something which is intricate; it means "a plot, or a plotting intended to affect some purpose by secret artifice"; thirdly, it is "the plot of a play or romance"; fourthly, it is "a secret and illicit love affair; an amour; a liaison" (this fourth meaning probably derives from the third). And the synonyms of intrigue are plot, scheme, machination, and conspiracy. Notice that there is no sense in which the word means something overwhelmingly attractive and fascinating, unless one thinks of secret and illicit love affairs as overpowering in their fascination. However, at present, the use of the word as a noun has fallen into decay. Although there are still references to schemers who engage in conspiracies and intrigues, the noun has become a verb in popular usage: anyone who is said to be "intriguing" is said to be very attractive, in fact, fascinating like a Hollywood star, or like the spy Mata Hari. An intrigue was something unpleasant, dishonorable, underhand, and immoral. But now to be intriguing is to be wonderfully desirable or interesting and has no unfavorable or dishonorable association. The sense of the same word has thus been turned upside down; it has changed, in popular usage, from signifying something unscrupulous to representing in a vague but unmistakable way something which is extremely interesting, desirable, or beautiful, and has no immediate connotations of moral disrepute.

What has happened to one word has happened to many words and can happen to many more. And the causes are not, as is sometimes supposed, limited to a poor teaching of English, or a disregard of the dictionary. In this instance, the shift is probably involved in the radical trial which conventional morality has undergone in the last twenty-five years, and certainly there is also involved the influence of newspapers, the stage, the films, and the *literary* zest with which most people read of the sins of others.

This example does not make clear how a degradation in the meaning of a word can be fruitful as well as foolish. There is a shift of meaning and a new richness of meaning, of course, but some of the exactness has already been lost and more is going to be lost. Let me point out two more examples in which the complicated and mixed benefits and losses of the change may appear more fully. For a number of years I taught English composition. I taught because I was unable to support myself by writing poetry. (For the most part, however, I like to teach very much.) When I began to teach, I was confounded by simple misuses of languages of which "intrigue" is a fairly representative example. One student wrote that "swimming is my chief *abstraction*," and another student said that "a certain part of my native city is *slightly ugly*." A third student who was attempting to describe the salutary effects of higher education upon all members of the fairer and weaker sex said that it was good for a girl to go to college because "it makes a girl *broader*." When I corrected the last word in accordance with my instructions as to the proper usage of English — and with a physical sense of one of the meanings of "broader" — the student protested that I had a peculiar mind; otherwise I would not object to the way in which she used "broader" instead of "broadens."

These errors — errors at least from the point of view of conventional and prescribed usage — made me reflect upon the character I played as a teacher of composition. The students thought I was pedantic when they did not think I was idiosyncratic. The difficulty was that so many of them made the same errors that, in a way, they were no longer errors. Moreover, the longer I thought about some of the errors, the more they seemed to be possible enlargements of meaning and association which might be creative. There was a real sense in which swimming, for an urban human being, was an abstraction as well as a distraction. So too, to say that something was slightly ugly was to suggest that a word or words denoting degrees of ugliness from homeliness and plainness to what was utterly ugly were lacking in English. And finally, it was true enough that education might make a girl broader as well as broaden a girl's outlook, although I doubt that this would have occurred to me if it had not been for this fruitful error.

The experience of teaching English literature and English poetry directly confronts the poet who teaches English with what can only be described as the most educated part of the population. Before the poet has taught English, he may well have been under the impression that no one except poets reads modern poetry (with a few and misleading exceptions). When he teaches poetry in the classroom, he finds out something which may be a great hope or a great delusion. It may be a delusion now and a hope for the future. At any rate, he does discover that he can persuade any student to understand any kind of poetry, no matter how difficult. They understand it as long as they are in the classroom, and they remain interested in it until they depart from school. Since so many poets have more and more undertaken the teaching of English and of poetry, it does seem possible that this may be the beginning of a new audience trained in reading and aware of how marvelous and exalted the rewards of poetry can be. But this is a matter which must be realized in the future. In the present, it is true that as soon as the student leaves school, all the seductions of mass culture and middle-brow culture, and in addition the whole way of life of our society, combine to make the reading of poetry a dangerous and quickly rejected luxury. The poet who teaches has immediate experiences in the classroom which give him some reason to hope for a real literary and poetic renaissance. As soon as he departs from the pleasant confines of the university, he discovers that it is more and more true that less and less people read serious poetry. And the last straw may be the recognition that even poets do not read very much poetry: Edwin Arlington Robinson confessed that during the latter half of his life, he read hardly any poems except his own, which he read again and again, and which may explain the paralysis of self-imitation which overcomes many good poets in midcareer. Here then is another trait which distinguishes the vocation of the modern poet from poets of the past: he not only knows how language is inexactly and exactly used; he also knows that for the most part only other poets will read his poems.

*

One reason that language is misused, whether fruitfully or not, is that in modern life experience has become international. In America itself the fact of many peoples and the fact that so large a part of the population has some immigrant background and cherishes the fragments of another language creates a multilingual situation in which words are misused and yet the language is also enriched by new words and new meanings. To make fun of errors in the use of language and to make the most comedy possible of foreign accents—or for that matter, an English accent—is an important and vital part of American humor, which is itself a very important part of American life. Moreover, the pilgrimage to Europe has for long been an important episode in the national experience. The American tourist in Europe, Baedeker in hand, has for generations spelled out the names of places and works of art and delicious foods. And, most crucial of all, the experience of two world wars has made Americans conscious of the extent to which the very quality of their lives depends upon the entire international situation. Whether the danger is from Germany or from Russia, whether a banking scandal occurs in Paris, or Spain becomes fascist, or the Vatican intervenes in American politics and American morality and American education, no one at this late date can fail to be aware of the extent to which the fate of the individual is inseparable from what is happening in the whole world.

These facts are, of course, in one sense platitudes; and yet it may not be clear how they affect the modern poet in his vocation as such. I want to resort to examples again before trying to define the way in which the international scene and an involvement with it affect the poet as a poet and have to do with his calling.

To quote once more from that truly modern poet, T. S. Eliot, here is a passage from one of his best poems, "Gerontion." Christ, the protagonist says, is:

> To be eaten, to be divided, to be drunk
> Among whispers; by Mr. Silvero

With caressing hands, at Limoges
Who walked all night in the next room;

By Hakagawa, bowing among the Titians;
By Madame de Tornquist, in the dark room
Shifting the candles; Fräulein von Kulp
Who turned in the hall, one hand on the door.

Let us think a little merely of the names of the people he remembers, Mr. Silvero, Hakagawa, Madame de Tornquist, Fräulein von Kulp. Is it not evident that the experience which provides the subject matter of the poet or inspires him to write his poem is not only European, but international, since Hakagawa is presumably Japanese; and involves all history, all culture, since the reference here to Titian is matched elsewhere by allusions to ancient Egypt, Buddhist sermons, and the religion of classical Greece? Another aspect of the same involvement and of how it has a direct impact on the writing of the poetry is illustrated in *Sweeney Agonistes*, where "two American gentlemen here on business" arrive in London and rehearse the clichés of colloquial American speech. London, one of them explains with great politeness to his English friends, is "a slick place, London's a swell place,/London's a fine place to come on a visit—," and the other adds, with equal politeness, "Specially when you got a real live Britisher/A guy like Sam to show you around./Sam of course is at *home* in London,/And he's promised to show us around." In the same work, at a moment of great anguish, another character reiterates the poet's extreme sensitivity to and concern for language when he says, "I gotta use words when I talk to you."

If Eliot as a transplanted American in Europe seems to be a special case (a great poet, however, is always a special case, if one chooses to regard him in that light), the example of James Joyce should help to reinforce the somewhat complicated (because ubiquitous) thesis I am trying to elucidate. Joyce was an impoverished Irishman. As Eliot had to toil for some time in a bank while he tried to write poems, Joyce supported himself during the composition of *Ulysses* by teaching in a Berlitz school in Trieste during the First World War. The publication of *Ulysses*—an event which was described by a French critic as marking Ireland's spectacular re-entry into European literature—was sufficiently a success to make a rich Englishman provide Joyce with financial security almost until the end of his life. Two years before, Joyce had completed his last and probably his best work, the stupendous *Finnegans Wake*, a book which would in itself provide sufficient evidence and illustration of the vocation of the modern poet* in modern life. All that has been observed in Eliot's work is all the more true of *Finnegans Wake* — the attention to colloquial speech, the awareness of the variety of ways in which languages can be degraded and how that degradation can be the base for a new originality and exactitude, the sense of an involvement with the international scene and with all history. But more than that, the radio and even television play a part in this wonderful book, as indeed they played a part in the writing of it. Joyce had a shortwave radio with which he was able to hear London, Moscow, Dublin — and New York! In *Finnegans Wake*, I was perplexed for a time by echoes of American radio comedy and Yiddish humor until I learned about Joyce's radio and about his daily reading of the Paris edition of the New York *Herald-Tribune*. The most important point of all, however, is that *Finnegans Wake* exhibits in the smallest detail and in the entire scope of the work the internationality of the modern poet, his involvement in all history, and his consciousness of the impingement of any foreign language from Hebrew to Esperanto upon the poet's use of the English language.

*

It is foolish to speculate about the future of anything as precarious as the vocation of poetry — an eminent critic said some years ago that the technique of verse was a dying one, but Joyce may have persuaded him to change his mind — but to think of the future is as inevitable as it is dubious. Joyce's last book suggests certain tentative formulations about the future of the writing of poetry. It suggests that there can be no turning back, unless civilization itself declines as it did when the Roman Empire fell. Yet it is also clear that poets cannot go forward in a straight line from the point at

---

* Joyce's two best works, *Ulysses* and his last book, are not poems in the ordinary sense of the word; and he wrote several volumes of poetry, most of which consist of verses far inferior to anything in his major books. But any view of poetry which excludes *Finnegans Wake* as a poem and Joyce as a poet merely suggests the likelihood that Joyce transformed and extended the limits of poetry by the writing of his last book. If we freeze our categories and our definitions (and this is especially true in literature), the result is that we disable and blind our minds.

which *Finnegans Wake* concluded. What they can do is not evident in the least, apart from the fact that a literal imitation or extension of Joyce would be as mechanical as it is undesirable: too much in the very nature of his work depends upon personal and idiosyncratic traits of the author, his training as a Jesuit, his love of operatic music, the personal pride which was involved in his departure from Ireland, and the infatuation with everything Irish, which obsessed him in this as in his other books. There are other important elements in Joyce's work and in his life which do lead, I think, to some tentative generalization about the future of poetry and the vocation of the poet. One of them was pointed out to me by Meyer Schapiro (who has influenced me in much of what I have said throughout): the question has been raised as to why Joyce, both in *Ulysses* and in *Finnegans Wake,* identified himself with Jews, with Leopold Bloom, an Irish Jew, and with the character of Shem in his last book. (Shem is, among other of his very many kinships, a son of Noah, and he is compared with Jesus Christ, to the ironic denigration of both beings.) The answer to the question of Joyce's identification with Jews, Schapiro said, is that the Jew is at once alienated and indestructible, he is an exile from his own country and an exile even from himself, yet he survives the annihilating fury of history. In the unpredictable and fearful future that awaits civilization, the poet must be prepared to be alienated and indestructible. He must dedicate himself to poetry, although no one else seems likely to read what he writes; and he must be indestructible as a poet until he is destroyed as a human being. In the modern world, poetry is alienated; it will remain indestructible as long as the faith and love of each poet in his vocation survives.

(1951)

Karl Shapiro

What Is Not Poetry?

THIS CHAPTER is divided into two parts; the first part is autobiographical and the second is theoretical. The first part tells the story of how I became a critic and the second part is an outline of my poetics, such as they are. These are two views of the same subject and I hope each section will throw light on the other.

The present essays are intended to be the last criticism I shall ever write. In this book I am getting together those few essays which I think worth keeping and which I hope will be of some help to young poets and would-be critics. It is the small mass of my own discarded criticism which I want to mention here before going on to my ideas of the theory and practice of poetry.

Whenever I meet a young poet I ask him among other things how much he knows about criticism. If he says he knows nothing I breathe a sigh of relief for both of us; if he begins to talk about criticism instead of poetry I know the conversation will soon grind to an embarrassing halt. On the other hand, whenever I meet a young critic I quickly confide to him that I am what he calls an "impressionistic" critic — an expression that has some of the overtones of "up from the city streets" — and we can then chat politely and patronizingly with each other. With full-grown and famous critics my experiences have been briefer and sometimes bristling, but I have not cultivated many friendships of this kind.

As long as I can remember, I have had an instinctive dislike for criticism of almost every description, whether it is Freud's on Dostoyevsky, Jones's on *Hamlet*, Richards' on theory, or for that matter Aristotle's, and nearly all the moderns. I once enjoyed the *Biographia Literaria*, at least the parts that deal with Wordsworth or *Venus and Adonis* (the sections about the imagination always struck me as being either unintelligible or unconvincing). One of the things I like best about the book is that it is a scrapbook, not a full-scale esthetic. Critics like Sainte-Beuve have held my attention for a while but I have never really learned anything from them. Among modern critics I like to read Edmund Wilson — especially when he is not talking about literature — George Orwell, Van Wyck Brooks and other "impressionistic" writers. I have never been able to make sense out of a history of criticism, primarily because I do not believe that criticism has a history. My favorite essay is Longinus' "On the Sublime," but philosophical essays in general are beyond me. I cannot retain a philosophical concept in my head for more than five minutes and I suspect any poet who can. If poetry has an opposite, it is philosophy. Poetry is a materialization of experience; philosophy the abstraction of it.

In spite of the few names I have mentioned, I have tried consistently to avoid reading criticism all my life. But life has pushed criticism under my nose. I discovered to my horror when I began to teach modern poetry that it was not really poetry I was teaching for the most part, but criticism. It was only about ten years ago that it began to dawn on me that the poetry called Modern is little more than a façade for various philosophies of criticism, literary maneuvers, and cultural propaganda for one or another persuasion. As my acquaintance with this vast literature grew, I began to understand the poetry anthology of our time, the university textbook of modern poetry, the purpose of the literary quarterly, the existence of great international prize committees, the strange political pronouncements of certain poet-critics, the public anger at modern poetry, and the innocence of my own bits and pieces of criticism. And, like most poets of our time, the deeper I became involved in criticism, the less desire I had to write poetry or even read it. The chill fell on my soul. Finally, I began to understand the criticism of my poems which people had spoken about from time to time and which I could never make sense of. One thing that had puzzled me greatly was the disaffection of certain critics who originally praised my poems far out of proportion to their merit and who later condemned the same poems. It was because they now understood my "critical position" that they disliked poems which had previously appeared to them of a high order of work!

For five years I edited *Poetry* magazine and was forced to read a great deal of book-review criticism for publication. My only aim as editor of this famous magazine was to keep its reputation what it was reputed to be. Because of the intensity of modern critical activity I had no difficulty getting well-known writers to give us reviews. The one famous piece of criticism I solicited was W. C. Williams' review of Sandburg's *Collected Poems*. Sandburg never forgave this essay by Williams and my part in it; but it is the best essay on Sandburg ever written. Unfortunately for everybody concerned, it was quite negative.

The poetry, by and large, I printed in this magazine was mostly "critical" poetry or academic poetry. It was the kind of poetry that came; it was the official poetry, the poetry à la mode, and I printed it. Had I been editing a magazine of my own making, I would probably have published an entirely different sort of verse. Editing *Poetry* was a job for me, not a vocation, certainly, and I let the magazine coast as it had for forty years. I was afraid to tamper with its respectability. The critics invariably complimented me on my editing; I was not aware of what they meant until I knew their criticism. They meant that I was holding the line for them.

It is still a mystery to me that I was chosen to edit this magazine. My first poems of any worth had been printed in *Poetry* ten years before I became editor. Immediately upon acceptance of the poems, the editor asked if I would undertake to write a review. Thinking it some kind of obligation or perhaps *honor* I accepted and wrote my first review; the books were by Edmund Blunden and Siegfried Sassoon, I think, and I struggled with the piece. At about the same time, the *Partisan Review* asked me to write them a letter for publication about the army camp I had become a member of. These were my initiation into criticism. From then on I took it for granted that I was expected to write essays or reviews when asked, and I almost never refused. By the time I was discharged from the army several years later, my poetry had become sufficiently well known for me to be invited to lecture before literary audiences. Thus I took the final plunge and became a bona-fide critic. My lectures evidently sat well with the listeners, for I was shortly offered a job as associate professor at an excellent university. This was a great honor for me because I had left that university as a sophomore and was still a sophomore. It is not uncommon for poets to leave the university before they get a degree, and I sometimes advise young poets to do the same. The scholarly profession is the one I respect above all others (I do not consider literature a profession), but the poet who can also be a good scholar is a very rare beast. And literary scholarship has been so contaminated by modern criticism in our time that it is dangerous for the poet to attempt to become a scholar, unless he can keep his wits about him.

I am not going to render an account of all the essays and reviews I have published. I don't know what I have written myself; I have no records, no clippings, no bibliography. Now and then someone will ask me about a certain article or poem I wrote and I do not even remember writing it, much less where it appeared. Much of my criticism has been written for publication in a foreign language and I have no original of the thing I penned. The only reason for this slovenliness is my lack of ambition as an essayist or critic or *littérateur*. Several of my lectures, however, have been published in *Poetry*, the only place I ever attempted to print them. On one occasion three lectures of mine were printed as a small book called *Beyond Criticism*; a few copies were sold and the rest remaindered. Generally, these essays tried to state the same opinions I offer here, but in a more general fashion.

My chief venture into criticism, however, was with the verse *Essay on Rime*, which I wrote in New Guinea to amuse myself. Reviewed on the front page of the *New York Times Book Review*, it sold about ten thousand copies and brought down upon me the wrath of all the gods of criticism. For saying what I thought of Modern poetry and naming names, I was henceforth on the intellectual blacklist. Even William Carlos Williams felt called upon to rap my knuckles.

Lest this recital become completely pointless, I want to mention the drift of my previous lectures. Nearly all of them have in one way or another dealt with the need for the poet to dissociate himself from criticism. Only on one occasion did I depart from this principle: that was after the Bollingen Prize controversy when, like other writers, I was shocked at the accusations of the *Saturday Review of Literature* against all of us who were members of that literary jury, and I went to the defense of the jurors. I voted against giving Pound that prize, but I believed all the same that the jurors acted in good faith. Since then I have boned up on their criticism, and I no longer believe that they acted in good faith. The methods used by the *Saturday Review* were unspeakable (calling the prize a Fascist plot), but it now seems to me that the jurors, led by Eliot himself, acted in a distinctly underhanded manner. The journalistic outburst in the *Saturday Review* against our Bollingen committee drove me to write a defense of—the New Criticism, of all things! My first act on becoming editor of *Poetry* was to publish that silly essay. A New York publicist who was trying to raise money for *Poetry* said to me, "I see you have joined the T. S. Eliot covered wagon." He knew more about criticism than I did.

That was my chief lapse of critical sense. On one other occasion—to conclude this *mea culpa*—I jumped on Robert Graves for lumping together all modern poets and throwing them into limbo. It was particularly his criticism of Dylan Thomas that upset me, but I also said the usual mealy-mouthed words about Eliot, Pound, and Auden. This was before I had read *The White Goddess*, which immediately became one of my favorite books, one which can stand in place of all the New Criticism ever written. Graves has a world view, which is part of a tradition older and deeper than any tradition employed by the Modernists. Of his part in this great stream of criticism, I was unaware.

Every poet of my generation grew up in the shadow of the criticism of T. S. Eliot. Whether he read this criticism or not, he was influenced by it. Every vestige of opposition to Eliot had been erased by the mid-thirties, when I began to write verse in earnest. How could a young writer not admire Eliot when even a radical high-brow publication, not to mention all the high-brow right-wing magazines, fell to their knees before this strange puritanical American? Those who didn't, like Williams or Hart Crane, were considered rustics. My tastes and affections had always been with Hart Crane and Williams, but the intellectuals told me otherwise. It took me years of teaching and editing and poring over modern criticism to see the light. It was not poetry the big pontifical magazines wanted: it was Culture. Poetry was only a handy tool of culture. I firmly believe that whatever good poetry I have written was written because of my ignorance of criticism; I just as firmly believe that every poet of our age who has been too close to criticism has either given up poetry completely or has ruined his work because of it. There is no question that Hart Crane was driven to distraction by the niggardliness of his critics, and that poets with the great gifts of Ransom and Tate and Warren have cut their poetry to fit the cloth of the critic. The greatest freedom poets can hope for in the twentieth century is freedom from critical theorizing and a return to the *laissez faire* amateur criticism of the audience. The remarks that follow, although they are not consecutive or logical, will attempt to point the way back to a poetry which is not restrained or informed by Modern Criticism or the poetry that has been written out of this criticism.

*

It has always seemed to me that everyone except the critic knows what poetry is—I am not trying to be facetious—and that poets and other artists must from time to time remind the audience that the criticism stands between them and poetry. There is one extraordinary fallacy which lies at the bottom of most literary criticism and which is such an obvious fallacy to the ordinary reader and the poet that it seems a profundity when anyone mentions it. The fallacy is that of meaning, the treatment of poetry as language. One might, in the jargon of the age, call it "the understanding fallacy" or "the semantic fallacy." Poetry is not language; its raw material is language, but from this point on the poet goes in one direction while the critic goes in the opposite direction. The *word* in poetry is not a word in any already existing sense, and I call it a not-word.

*

The most obvious and salient fact about the natural separation of poetry from criticism is that in the greatest ages of poetry there has been little or no criticism. Criticism comes, if at all, after the art.

*

Criticism is a department of philosophy, not of literature. The function of criticism is not to "correct taste," as Eliot would have it, but to understand the nature of art. This kind of inquiry is of no interest whatever to the audience or to the artist. Once the artist begins to puzzle about the nature of poetry, he moves into the realm of philosophy, his language takes on the gray cast of abstraction, and he ceases to experience that unity with the world which is the poet's characteristic quality. All "philosophical" poetry, whether in Dante, Blake, Lucretius, Milton, Shelley, Bridges, or Eliot, is weak to the extent that it philosophizes. This is pointed out by critics themselves at times when criticism is honest and regards itself as a branch of philosophy.

*

There is an accidental similarity between philosophy and poetry: neither takes language seriously. Philosophy is suspicious of language; poetry sees language as one of the manifestations of nature (the one closest to the poet). To the poet, as to the philosopher, language is in a constant state of flux. The philosopher tries to arrest this flux; the poet only tries to keep up with it.

*

When critics remark upon poetry as a kind of game, they are naming the wrong object. Poetry is never play to the poet; language is. In trying to follow the play of language, the poet is trying to follow the play of nature. The painter follows nature through color, the composer through harmony, the poet through the squawks of the human voice box.

*

The relationship between poetry, Nature, and mysticism is something like this: the poet substitutes Language for Nature. Everything he knows he knows through the medium of language. The poet has a natural affinity with Nature, whether trees and daffodils or armadillos and scarabs or human beings. (In intellectual, self-conscious times the poet tries to see the "nature" of societies and civilizations, as Yeats, Auden, and Pound and Eliot do. This is the ragged edge of poetry that soon breaks out into politics and theology.) The poet's natural affinity with nature makes him contiguous to all forms of mysticism, good and bad. The weak poet is magnetized toward some popular mystique or even religion. The strong poet is always the heretic and the saint. Even in weak poets like Eliot and Pound there are traces of "religious heresy."

*

All the great scriptures were probably penned by poet-mystics. Mysticism is not an aim of art (nor is it an aim of mystics!): mysticism is a pejorative used by critics in a rational age to denote a departure from the established meanings of words. Every good poet is a "mystic"; that is, he departs from the dictionary, as the painter departs from the straight line and the perfect circle.

*

The departure from the dictionary is not intentional but natural. In the great ages of poetry and the other arts there are no dictionaries or encyclopedias. Shakespeare didn't know how to spell. We know how to spell and have no Shakespeare. Classicism is the attempt to write the dictionary of forms. In our time the Classicism of Eliot, Pound, and Yeats has attempted to arrest the forms of poetry via the amazing stratagem of arresting the forms of society.

*

The meaning of poetry, as far as language is concerned, is the meaning of *hey-nonny-nonny.* To the poet, *hey-nonny-nonny* means what the other words in the poem failed to say.

> It was a lover and his lass
>   With a hey and a ho and a hey-nonny-no
> That o'er the green corn-field did pass
> In the spring time, the only pretty ring time
> When birds do sing, hey ding a ding a ding,
>   hey ding a ding a ding, hey ding a ding a ding
> Sweet lovers love the spring.

The critic will pipe up and chirp: Onomatopoeia!

*

Living in an age of literacy, we have lost contact with the sources of poetry and see everything through books. The modern poet has turned his back on modern life and views it with undisguised hostility. This psychological provincialism gives modern poetry its tone, whether in Eliot or in Robinson Jeffers. In fact, *The Waste Land* and the *Cantos* have all the characteristics of a hillbilly poetry: broken dialect, broken tradition, a desperate desire to hold on to a half-forgotten past, and a provincial viciousness involving a fundamentalist interpretation of scripture, and tar and feathers.

*

The rational person is least able to understand poetry. Or rather, it is his understanding of it that prevents him from seeing it as anything but a series of words in meters, with various rhetorical devices and "levels" of meaning. He does not perceive, as all other people perceive, including children and savages, that poetry is a way of seeing things, not a way of saying things. Poetry is "different," not because of meters and figures of speech and symbols (these things exist in advertisements), but because it is a way of seeing a thing differently. The reaction of an audience to good poetry is laughter—the laughter of delight and discovery, not of derision. In fact, the basic emotion aroused by any work of art, however somber or tragic, is joy, even hilarity.

*

The poet really does see the world differently, and everything in it. He does not deliberately go into training to sharpen his senses; he is a poet because his senses are naturally open and vitally sensitive. But what the poet sees with his always new vision is not what is "imaginary"; he sees what others have forgotten how to see. The poet is always inadvertently stripping away the veils and showing us his reality. Many poets, as we know, go mad because they cannot bear the worlds of illusion and falsehood in which most human beings spend their lives.

*

The mystic condemns what is called loosely the Imagination. The imagination is the fool in the house, says Saint Theresa. The poet thinks in terms of reality, not in terms of the imagination. Reality in his mind is not very far from what the mystics and ecstatics mean by reality. Most uses of imagination in poetry indicate a forcing of one's way toward reality. And in times when the poet theorizes about the imagination, poetry moves dangerously close to rationalism. Notice the mechanistic, highly rational Poe forcing the imagination to create "effects."

*

The poet never says this to himself, but in effect this is what he means when he begins a poem: he is asking "what is the poetry of..." whatever he happens to be dealing with. By poetry, he means the reality of, the totality of. What is the poetry of love at first sight? What is the poetry of desperate ambition? What is the poetry of myself, my consciousness? And the poet with his peculiar way of seeing breaks down each particle of the experience into "the poetry of." "Landscape plotted and pieced." The turtle is "large and matronly and rather dirty." But this is silly: one could go on to quote every poem ever written; and it would be a poem because it created the reality of whatever it happened to be about. Whenever the poet is not "oned" with the experience we can always detect the forcing, the insincerity.

*

When we hear critics talk about paradox, ambiguity, conceit, and so forth, we should be on guard. They are talking about forced poetry, poems in which the author has tried by violence to break through the habitual delusions into reality. The violence of much modern poetry stems from this cold-blooded forcing of reality.

*

Critics are inclined to misinterpret the poet or artist's use of the ugly; they think either he is making a social statement or a paradox. In good poetry and painting that use the ugly, the poet and painter are, on the contrary, writing about the beauty of ugliness.

*

There is no borderline between poetry and prose. Even verse (meter) is no distinction. There is only greater or lesser heat. The novel is simply the narrative poem in extension. The novel deals with the poetry of character, the poetry of situation, the poetry of history. It is possible to speak of more or less poetry in a writer, meaning more or less vision-of-reality. Everyone is part poet; it is the poet in each of us that responds to the whole poet. The poet may be a biological sport or a freak. The prose man is the man of average sensibilities, the man who limits his experience of life. The most common universal experience of reality is love. The prose man falls in love once or twice, or according to some psychologists, thrice. If he keeps it up, he is in danger of becoming a poet.

*

Critics frequently speak of rhymes, stanzas, meters, and so on as a kind of ritual in which the poet "objectifies" experience. This is nonsense. The forms are not rituals at all but realities. The Greek meters, for instance, were dance steps; the rhythms so produced expressed a mode of thought. On the other hand, when meters are used arbitrarily we get faked poetry. "Iambic pentameter" represented the poetry of English rhythm for a thousand years. This was not "ritual"; it was "the poetry of" the rhythm of our language. The situation in America demanded a new rhythm which we are still trying to find the poetry of.

*

Keats noted that the poet is generally without "character"; he is a fluid, open, and vulnerable character, much like a child. Everyone has observed this about poets. In general, the chief characteristics of any poet are his honesty, his self-acceptance, and his vulnerability.

*

Poetry is no more language than the landscape is paint. Poetry is a version of language, a reading of it. But poetry, as a version of language, is also a version of nature and of human nature. Most human transactions are carried out without language, without speech or writing, language being employed as an aid to more direct forms of communication. As everyone knows, more can be conveyed by the language of glances than poetry can tell; Proust speaks of the language of clothes, and so forth. Buying a ticket at a station window, one reveals more by tones of voice, pace, dress, facial expression, and so on, than any passage by a great novelist can convey. The poet recognizes the limitations of human language and is always slightly outside language. He sees that language is in a state of becoming and cannot be arrested; poetry is rhythmic because the poet takes language at flood and goes with it. He senses the wave of language.

*

There is usually no criticism during ages of great poetry because at such times it is understood that poetry is not language pure and simple. In our time, when rationalism is worldwide and the intellectuals are the chief spokesmen for everything, the tendency is to think of poetry as language, or language treated in a particular way. Actually, poetry is the "poetry of" language, just as painting is the "poetry of" line, color, and mass, sculpture is the poetry of solids, and so on. Poetic, picturesque, sculpturesque are all derogatories denoting the failure to penetrate the realities of the material.

*

The association between poetry and religion is always tenuous; both are emotionally centered modes of behavior and as such they sometimes meet. Poetry seems to have a natural aversion for religion, however, as it does for all form of organization. There is some reason to believe that most Scriptural poetry (poetry admitted to Bibles) is not "religious" to begin with but is the work of some particular poet or of some folk. This poetry may have a basis in secular experience or it may be "the poetry of" revelation of one kind or another. The best example of the first is the Song of Songs, very likely a collection of Semitic marriage poems, later given theological or allegorical interpretations by the Hebrews, the Catholics, and the Protestants. The Psalms, on the other hand, are God-poetry, the poetry of worship, thanks, supplication, etc.

*

It is idle to claim that poetry is either a secular art or an art of the supernatural. These are critical dualisms, secular and supernatural, which solve nothing. The poet does not distinguish between them. The natural poet, the primitive poet, the "lyrical" poet, cannot make any such distinctions because they do not exist for him. The poet is always "one" with his experience; to that extent he does inhabit the realm of the supernatural. All artists search for a unification of the elements of a particular experience, the photographer cropping a negative no less than the painter choosing his landscape or model, or the poet looking for the poetry of the thing that engages him at the moment. The artist is different from other people in that he is in a constant state of "oneness" with his experience. When he is not, he is out of Paradise; he has fallen into the world of rationality where all dualisms run riot. It is a fact, I think, that to most poets the ordinary world seems insane; and quite naturally the poet seems mad to the pedestrian or rational mind. Pure science bears most of the characteristics of art; chiefly what is different about the work of abstract science is the absence of the emotional center of motivation; but scientists are, in the popular rational mind, also considered mad.

*

Modern criticism has waged war against science in the same way that it has waged war against poetry. Modern criticism is really a branch of what is called Social Science — a better name would be Moral Science — the hybrid science which includes such dubious sciences as economics, political science, psychology, sociology, and even history. History, which used to be a true literary art, like poetry, has been debased in our time to a pseudoscience. Criticism tries to debase science and subvert poetry. The removal of this criticism and its pseudosciences should be a primary aim of educators. Sociology is a poetry substitute, not a science. Most sociologists are poets who are working in the wrong medium. I mean this literally.

*

The great men of science in our time are not honored by the poets. Why is this? Because Modern Criticism in a war against positivistic thinking lumps all science under materialism. This jealousy of Science, whether abstract or practical, comes from the puritanical critics, such as Eliot and Pound, who know or care nothing about the aims or achievements of science, and is only one of many criticisms of contemporary life. In poetry it has been a fad, since Eliot, to condemn every aspect of contemporary life, with science as the enemy. The other arts are free of these shallow hates and envies. Whitman's love of science is one of the reasons for his condemnation by modern criticism. It is notable that the culture poets and other ideocrats make free use of the pseudosciences but ignore true science. Sociology is the poetry of the twentieth century. It writes about such things as Car Culture, et cetera.

*

All true poetry is absolutely amoral. What is the moral of *Hamlet*? What is the moral of Mozart's Twentieth Piano Concerto? These are nonsense questions. Even when a work of art becomes "literary," like much Renaissance painting, using biblical subject matter, it lies beyond the reach of religion. Poetry is eternally out of favor with all forms of authority, not because it is antagonistic to authority (only inferior poetry battles against society) but because it does not recognize the reality of authority as it is practiced in society. All art is polarized toward some humanistic point of view, on the one hand, and toward some nonauthoritarian *mystique* on the other. Thus it is always close to "the people" and always slightly beyond the reach of the authorities. Poetry dedicated to the "elites," the authorities, is degenerate, moralistic, authoritarian poetry.

*

It is true that poetry represents not only the periphery of language but the periphery of a certain kind of consciousness. The poet or artist explores this consciousness constantly until it becomes habitual with him. Robert Graves puts it this way: "The function of poetry is religious invocation of the Muse—its use is the experience of mixed exaltation and horror that her presence excites."

*

As everyone is aware, poetry exists among the most ancient and primitive peoples as well as among the most civilized. It is one of the first forms of communication among children; that is, one of the primary manifestations of the sense of joy. There is probably no other form of art which is universal in the way poetry is. The uses of poetry are always self-limiting, however, and bear no relationship to history or to society. Modern poetry's attempt to interpret poetry as a refined or pure form of language or as an implement of civilization violates all the known facts about poetry. Poetry exists in a dimension outside civilization, as Plato said or seemed to say.

*

Everything shows progress except poetry. The reason is that the poet exists in past, present, and future together. History to the poet is a fairy tale. Nor does the poet recognize Literature; he sees this poem and that poem, but not in time, in sequence. The poet understands also that the events of one's own time rarely touch the poet or artist. His knowledge of the present is not a knowledge of wars, what's in the newspaper, and the latest high-brow opinion, but of how his contemporaries talk.

*

All good poetry has an immediate impact upon its audience. This is proved simply by the existence of the greatest poetry in the form of drama or narrative. Nearly all Modern poetry fails in impact, immediate or otherwise. Even Dante, a poet enmeshed in theology, sought out the common language, the language of the street, for his epic poem. By modern standards, he should have chosen Latin for his poem. If there is only one law of art, it is that the work must be capable of apprehension as a whole and at once. This is the nature of art, that it is wholly and immediately apprehended, like a tree or a woman.

*

The question of the low taste of the audience is always the chief argument for criticism. Actually there is no way to determine the taste of audiences except on the spot. What we know of "taste" is always interpreted by critics and is thus merely a written record of learned opinion. The famous gaffes in literary taste are made by critics, not by audiences.

*

What modern criticism does not take into account, respecting the audience, is that there is not one audience but innumerable audiences. It seems painfully obvious to point out — but there is a difference between the Punch and Judy audience and the opera audience. There is a different audience for ballad poetry than for epic and tragic poetry. All appreciation, however, rises from the bottom and does not descend from the top. The sickness of modern poetry is the sickness of isolation from any living audience. There is no healthy literature that does not grow out of naïve, folk, and "primitive" art. It is notable that every art in the twentieth century except poetry has drawn richly from jazz, the movies, advertising, the comic strip, commercial design, and even radio and TV. Poetry is somehow deprived of its contact with contemporary art on the popular and even commercial levels. It is only poetry in its rebellious aspects that has tried to regain contact with popular art, without which there can be no sophisticated art. We should write off Modern Poetry, the poetry of the American expatriates of 1915, as a failure to seize power, or as a temporary counterrevolution. If someone would draw up a tentative list of the true poets of our time, those who have abstained from culture bolshevism and who have maintained their touch with popular art, we would find that nearly all those poets lie outside the English language; that is, outside the influence of the poetry-criticism of our time.

*

Probably the most profound idea in the writings of T. S. Eliot is that of the split between the rational functions of the mind and the creative functions. (He does not use these terms and his dating of the "split" is a very late one.) The extraordinary thing about Eliot's recognition of this process was the use he made of it; instead of aiming at some process for reunifying sensibility, as he called it, he deliberately chose the nostalgic prescientific path of religion. Thus, there is no place in Eliot's system for modern science, out of which the split had grown. This contempt for objective science has crippled modern poetry and made it incapable of dealing with our world. The schizophrenic spiderweb of the *Cantos* shows where the antiscience prejudice leads. Pound's rejection of the modern world of science has a purely esthetic motive — art over all. Yeats's rejection of science also destroys any possibility of a reunified sensibility in his work.

But the poet should not be the creator of Unified Sensibility in the first place, but only one of the expressions of it. Poetry cannot change or influence history; or, if it can, it is only by example. A good poem or any true work of art is a projection of a whole, organic, "biopsychic" personality. Most of our so-called great modern poems are sick poems, poems split either against Reason or against the Supernatural or against Society. Whereas a poem such as "Song of Myself" is a demonstration of man's unity with Nature and with man's condition.

A "solution through poetry" is therefore a misnomer, and all modern poetics fall apart at this point. The problem of a true twentieth-century criticism must be to separate out all rationalistic poetry (the poetry of social criticism, culture propaganda, all poetry that is sectarian or based upon idea systems) from truly unified poetry. Such poetry lies in a different dimension from politics, religion, or philosophy. It accepts all these things, without being dominated by them.

Art with consequences is by definition bad art. Poetry can do no more than affirm the unification of human with nonhuman nature. If God enters the poet's work, religion cannot. Morality cannot. "Sin" cannot. The Baudelairean travesty upon man's wholeness is seen in his hatred of society and his involvements with historical ideas. All such poetry — which is the model for Modern poetry — ends up as Idealism, the rejection of the whole for the part. Poe's idealization of Beauty ends up as the worship of the beautiful female dead body and the invention of the Whodunit.

*

The poet is not, in the vulgar saying, either a dreamer or an idealist, but a realist in the highest sense of the word. Modern poetry has given us schemes and blueprints, nightmares, analyses, programs, politics, and metaphysics. Where true poetry is benign and liberating to the human psyche, Modern poetry is a dangerous psychological evil, reinforcing every form of split between man and his world.

*

All forms of this split in man's consciousness begin with the cynical impudent question: What is Art? The moment this question is posed, the split appears and critics begin to talk about form and content, prose and poetry, image and idea, body and soul, innocence and guilt, anxiety and felicity, and good and evil. To the poet none of these dualisms represent reality. Poetry says of all such dualisms — they do not exist.

*

Poetry has not been taken seriously since the Renaissance (Eliot's date) because it has been considered an art. We consider it ornamentation, recreation, a higher amusement for leisure time and for the educated. Yet modern painting has found its way to every level of our world; music also; architecture especially. Primitive painting is encouraged all over the world, but we cannot name a single primitive poet or child poet of our time. Painters and sculptors have rediscovered the great works of the Etruscans, Minoans, of Mohenjo-Daro, of the African. Literature has rediscovered nothing. Poetry is literally buried alive today; where it exists, it is virtually unheard of. It is, as I have reiterated *ad nauseam*, the fault of no one but the poets themselves and their arty self-consciousness that we have evolved an Alexandrian, Byzantine, Neoclassical art, and not poetry. But the world will have poetry at any cost. *The real poetry of the modern world is advertising*, probably the most debased form of poetry in history but the only authentic poetry we have. Advertising is pure poetic activity—debased to the nth degree, dishonest in intention, vulgar past all imagination, but poetry, the true poetry of modern commerce. Advertising is the poetry of the American masses; sociology is the poetry of the educated middle class; and academic poetry the poetry of cultural officialdom. The aim of advertising is not to sell things (nobody believes the claims of advertisers), but to convince the defenseless victim that he is happy. It is not necessary to own the latest gadget or patent medicine but only to know that the manufacturer loves us. Russia has successfully stamped out poetry because propaganda is a good substitute for it; propaganda is national advertising and it is rapidly becoming the poetry of our masses, too. I think people accept sociology in the same way that they accept advertising and propaganda—as a poetic version of our life. But where is the authentic American poetry of our century? Probably in hiding, if anywhere. Or under our noses, if we really want to find it.

(1960)

A. D. Hope

The Three Faces of Love

NO ONE, so far as I know, has thought much about the education of poets in our society. This is hardly surprising in a society which makes no provision for poets even to live. But it is proper for poets to think about it, for they have to contrive to survive in spite of their society; and there seem to be reasons for thinking that their education should differ from that of other kinds of artists and from that of other kinds of men.

As far as other artists are concerned, there is no apparent reason why there should not be schools of poetry in which young writers are taught their craft just as painters are trained to paint, sculptors to cast and hew and model, musicians to compose and perform, actors to act, and dancers to dance. Yet when one ponders the question, there seem to be good reasons why poets should always have differed from other artists, in the fact that they conduct their own education in the craft. One reason is that the other arts all involve a physical dexterity which nature does not provide. In each case this physical dexterity, to be of any use, has to be pushed to the point of exquisite control that is required, for example, by champion billiard players or by jugglers, though these professions are not fine arts. In consequence, any painter or musician or dancer has to spend years of concentrated effort under a teacher before he can give even a rudimentary performance of his art. To become an accepted artist, of course, requires further years of independent and intelligent practice. Now little of this preliminary training is needed to become a writer. The physical skill required is negligible and one that all literate people possess. Only in countries like China is calligraphy actually a part of the literary skill, and sometimes the most important part of it.

But there is perhaps a more important reason why writers, unlike other artists, are usually self-taught, and that is the fact that all the other arts manipulate their material, whether it is paint or stone or the muscles of the body, or a musical instrument making audible sounds. Quite apart from the dexterity this manipulation asks for is the fact that it is something the learner can see before him, or hear, or which his teachers can see and hear. A clumsy stroke, an awkward gesture, a false note or badly delivered phrase is immediately obvious. The whole process takes place outside the operator, and the gap between what he meant to do and what he actually succeeds in doing is therefore open to external criticism. But a poet composing a poem is doing it very much more inside himself, in a private world that nobody else can share until he has done it and translated it into words. Writing from the beginning is a solitary process; the material shaped by the mind is the material of the mental life itself.

The last and I think the most important difference of all is that a sort of serious play enters into the business of learning to write very much more than it does in the practice of the other arts—though it does have a place in all of them. Children and young animals train themselves for grown-up life by play which is an end in itself: the essence of much of this play is make-believe. Children playing at hospitals or mothers and fathers are imitating and imagining at the same time. They know that they are not actually being what they play at. So the rules of the game are variable and full of fantasy. Young writers are much the same while they are learning. The game is simply played in the mind instead of on the nursery floor. Bestride a stick and you have a horse and nobody worries that the stick does not look in the least like one. Make up a story about a horse and what you tell yourself is the horse in much the same way that the stick becomes a horse. It is only little by little that you learn to tell a horse story that will be truly and convincingly "horsey." But the young painter is only starting to control his pictorial imagination and therefore to be free to let his imagination "play" at the point when he can make a horse look like a real horse. One might say that in painting, skill releases the imagination; in writing, a released imagination leads to discovery of the skill.

But if poets, in common with other writers, need a different kind of education in their craft from that needed by other sorts of artist, it is also, I think, true that in common with other artists they need a different sort of education from that which society generally provides. They need in fact an education based on a recognition of the fact that theirs is a mode of life different from that of other men. Before this can happen, society must recover a sense of different modes of human life. I am not concerned with the ways in which the occupations of men can be classified into trades and professions or callings. Nor am I primarily concerned with the psychological divisions of men into well-marked types, nor with special gifts and abilities, though these have some bearing on my subject. The social and the psychological aspects of man occupy so much of the attention of modern science that what I call the properly philosophical aspect of man tends to be overlooked or neglected even among philosophers. Yet it was once a matter of prime concern to consider human life as a subject for metaphysical inquiry and not simply as material for empirical research and generalization in the fields of social and psychological science.

What I mean by the modes and kinds of human life is the kind of thing that Saint Thomas Aquinas is discussing in the 179th question of the Secunda Secundae Partis of the *Summa Theologica*. The question is divided into two parts in which Saint Thomas first asks whether life is fittingly to be divided into active and contemplative, and second, whether this division is adequate or not. To both he answers: Yes. My object is to ask and answer the same double question, though I shall not conduct the argument in scholastic or Aristotelian terms and I shall, with great regret, have to dispense with the charming type of argument, to which Saint Thomas gives some, though not the chief, weight: the argument that since Leah and Rachel in the Old Testament, and Mary and Martha in the New, symbolize the active and the contemplative life respectively, this is the proper division — otherwise one must suppose that God would have given Jacob three or more wives and Lazarus three or more sisters.

In my own mind, the idea itself did not actually start from what Saint Thomas has to say about the active and the contemplative life. It began from a consideration of what Dante has to say about the nature of love in the eighteenth canto of the *Purgatorio*. In the previous canto, Virgil has been explaining to Dante the nature of Purgatory, the nature of sin, and the nature of love. Love is what moves anything in the direction of another, not only man to his kind and man to God, but the stone toward the ground when it falls, or the fire toward the sky as it burns. Dante asks for further information and definition of the nature of this universal force. Virgil explains that the mind is created with a special aptitude or tendency to love. When it is stimulated by an object pleasing to it, it creates within itself an impression or image of the object, and if the mind inclines toward the object, that inclination or movement of the mind is what Virgil defines as love.

> Then even as fire moves upward by reason of its form, whose nature it is to ascend . . . so the mind once captivated enters into desire, which is a spiritual movement, and never rests until the object of its love makes it rejoice.

Later in the same discussion he explains that man does not know the sources of the natural appetites in himself which make love possible: "They are in you," he says, "just like the instinct in bees to make honey." It was from these two hints that I began thinking about the modes of love in scholastic terms in which they can still, to some extent, be validly distinguished.

In the first place, as we are concerned with man, we can accept the controversial notion of a final cause. Because men, unlike stones or moths, are conscious of themselves and the world about them, because they have memory and intelligence, they can propose to themselves ends of action which then become causes of their behavior, though these ends may be far in the future and may even be illusory or imaginary.

The ends that men propose to themselves arise from their impulses and desires, and these in turn are determined by the natures of the men who have them. Because he is conscious, man is able to know his own nature and his own desires and to choose between them. Unlike the stone or the moth, his actions and pursuits can be free insofar as he submits them to the intellect; that is to say, insofar as he knows all the conditions of choice implied by the conditions of his own nature and that of the world he lives in. Unlike the lower animals, his impulses are not specific, nor, as instinctive urges are, tied to specific predetermined ends. He is free therefore to propose to himself any end within the range of his knowledge.

Nor is his knowledge limited, as that of animals probably is, by the range of objects which his practical ends dictate. Knowledge, no doubt, arises in the first place as a device of the organism for the better pursuit of its practical ends. But it develops beyond this precisely because the human organism lacks specific instinctive mechanisms such as those of nest-building. Because the objects of human knowledge are not tied to such specific mechanisms, nothing in the range of possible knowledge is irrelevant to the successful attainment of man's practical ends, and this is the means of freeing knowledge from practical ends altogether.

Thus we see in man what so often occurs in nature, the extension or transference of functions for which certain organs and organization have been developed to other purposes which the same organs serve. The most remarkable case of this is perhaps the organs of the tongue, mouth, larynx, lungs, and nose. Originally developed for the intake of food, drink, and air, they have developed a secondary function as the organs of speech. Similarly with the organ of knowledge and consciousness, the brain; originally evolved to improve the creature's ability to pursue its practical ends of survival, there has developed in man, perhaps from an original animal curiosity such as we see in monkeys, an independent faculty of knowing for its own sake the contemplative intellect. The intellect is now not simply a faculty which draws its prime urge from the need to acquire food or love or power. It has its own specific impulse, to know, and its own specific desire, as specific as hunger or sexual desire or the desire to dominate, and its own specific pleasure or gratification, which is the pleasure or joy of contemplation of the objects of knowledge. And just as the power of speech opens a whole new range of powers to the formerly speechless animal, so the emergence of the free or contemplative intellect opens a new range of powers and possibilities to the human creature. It is, in fact, what differentiates him most from other animals. It is his distinguishing human characteristic.

The activities of men, therefore, can be satisfied in two principal ways: by the possession of the objects of desire or by the contemplation of these and of all the other possible objects of knowledge. This is the valid basis of the distinction between the active way of life and the contemplative way of life. The two ways of life are naturally not mutually exclusive. Contemplation is itself an activity and may involve continual active striving to attain its ends as it does in science and scholarship. Nor is it a stasis, for the fruition of knowledge always raises the possibility of further knowledge, and the pleasure of contemplation always contains in itself the urge to know further. Active life continually demands the results of contemplative knowledge to achieve its practical ends. Because man is a complex creature endowed with both sorts of urge, he cannot in any case avoid being both active and contemplative. The philosopher who neglects to provide a means of eating will soon cease to be able to pursue philosophy. It is the sort of fruition that each aims at which differentiates the active from the contemplative man.

It is because, in the first place, any man has only limited time to spend in the world that he is forced to choose among his possible activities. In the second place, while all men may feel both sorts of urge, some have a special gift or ability, similar to the special gifts of creative genius, which disposes them to concentrate their energies either on active ends or on contemplative ends. Below the ranks of the chosen, of those with a special genius for one or the other which we see in the great sages or the great men of action, there is a second class of men who are aware that to do a thing supremely well, or to achieve one end to the fullest extent, they need to sacrifice everything else to that end. The first class are the chosen, the second class those who choose to follow one way of life as much as possible to the exclusion of the other. There is therefore a sound basis for Saint Thomas' division of the types of human life into two sorts distinguished by the nature of the ends they pursue, though we may agree that for the majority of men there is a third way of life which combines the two in varying degrees. We cannot all be specialists, and it would be a serious thing for society if we were.

Just as there are the two sorts of life, with their two sorts of end and fruition in view, so there are, in Saint Thomas' sense, two corresponding sorts of love, each with an initial and a final stage. One may love a beautiful woman and desire to possess her. Her beauty awakens the desire to possess her, and the process of attracting her attention, then her interest, and finally the response of love often takes a long time and is a complex practical activity. During this time the man is said to be *in love*. In spite of the miseries of lovers on which the poets have so much to say, being in love is an exciting and a pleasurable state. But the gratification and fruition of love is the end proposed, and when it comes it is an altogether different and a better sort of happiness. This is an instance of the active life. But there is another sort of love of which the beauty itself is the object, and the fruition and gratification consist in its contemplation. This is closely allied to the contemplative pleasure we take in music or painting or in the observation of nature. In contemplative activity there are also two stages of gratification which are more clearly seen in the pursuit of knowledge than in the contemplation of beauty. The process of getting to know is itself pleasurable, a form of love, but the fruition of the process is to hold and reflect on what one knows in its completeness, and this, like the fruitions of the active life, is a higher and intenser gratification. We could give the first the name of Science or Knowledge, and the second the name of Wisdom. In this age we are so used to thinking of knowledge or the pursuit of science as a means to an end, that the notion of wisdom as an end in itself, the proper end of the contemplative life, has almost been lost from view. The contemplative life itself is associated in most people's minds with yogis and hermits, mystics and recluses — characters whose occupations suggest withdrawal from life rather than the pursuit of wisdom which is nothing less than the crown of life in all completeness.

My main purpose, however, is to suggest that there are not two but three main *ways of life* which together comprise all the modes of man's existence. The third way of life I should call the *creative way*. It is distinguished from the others in the same manner: by a distinct relation of man to the ends he proposes and desires and by a distinctive emotion which attends the pursuit and the fruition of those ends. As the mark of the active way of life is to possess the objects of desire, and the mark of the contemplative way of life is to enjoy the knowledge of the objects of desire, so the mark of the creative way of life is to bring new objects of desire into being. Those who have this gift or urge have it, as Dante says, as bees have the instinct to make honey. The composers of music, painting, poems, and dances do not compose these things in order to possess them or to contemplate them, but rather in order that others may be able to possess them and contemplate them. Once created, of course, the works of art and imagination may become objects of active or contemplative desire like any other existing objects, even for their creators, but these are not the desires that bring them into being. Creation is a separate mode of human activity, and, with those who have the gift, it constitutes a third and distinct way of life. And like the other ways of life it has its own separate and distinct sorts of pleasure, that which attends the process and that which consists of joy in fruition—its own mode of love. Jacob really should have had three wives and Lazarus three sisters.

If we ask why Saint Thomas did not recognize this third mode, the answer should probably take two forms, though they are related answers. In the first place, Saint Thomas, though he was a poet, did not pay much attention to art, and took little trouble to find a place for it in his metaphysical system. Creation is for him an attribute of God and not of man—creation, that is, in the sense of the power to create something new that never existed in the world before. In the second place, he apparently follows Aristotle and the Aristotelian tradition in regarding art as a species of imitation and as being concerned therefore with the representation of things already existing in the world. God is the only creator *ab initio*. The creation of works of art would therefore come under the head of the active life, as the enjoyment of works of art would come under that of the contemplative life. But the essential difference, as I have already pointed out, is this—that the writer of a poem or the composer of a symphony has, as his end, neither possession nor contemplation, but the bringing of a new sort of thing into the world. The poet or the painter may indeed give us recognizable likenesses of the forms of common experience; to this extent they use imitation as a means to their further ends. But the poem or the painting in itself is a thing in itself and not an imitation of anything any more than the symphony is an imitation of anything already in the world. It is *sui generis*, a new creation, and belongs to a different order of being from anything it imitates. W. B. Yeats speaks of the poets as people whose work exists not primarily to help or to inform us. When we read them, he says, we "have added to our being, not to our knowledge." It is the impulse to "add to being" which is the distinctive mark of the creative way of life.

This excursus into a neglected field of human philosophy may seem no more than a mental exercise undertaken for its own sake.

But it has a direct bearing on the modern world because of the sort of education we impose on all our citizens. In the first place, it is a uniform sort of education for everybody. In the second place, it is specifically designed for the way of life which is bound to be led by nearly everybody—what I described earlier as the mixed way of life, which inevitably has a bias toward the active life. It is largely dominated by practical ends. In the third place, it is subtly permeated by the view that because Jack is as good as his master, there is a taint of privilege and exclusiveness in providing a different sort of education for people with special gifts and powers. Education in the past was not very specific in preparation for the work of the world and because it was limited to a few, it was aristocratic in its temper. But modern education is democratic in temper and becomes yearly more specific in its adjustment of educational needs to social ends. In the past, the people destined to devote themselves as fully as possible to one way of life were able to struggle through to their achievement more or less successfully. Today, the more excellent and effective their education, the more they tend to be diverted from their true bent, particularly in the cases of the contemplative life and the creative life. In the past, a universal church provided an open door for anyone who felt in himself a gift for the contemplative life, and it was able to provide a discipline and a training to help him attain it. But now the church opens this door only to its own members, and more and more citizens are left with none. The very idea of the contemplative life hardly enters into secular education at all. In the universities nobody talks about wisdom anymore and the ideal is often a narrow research in which the end in view is nearly always the practical applications of the knowledge acquired.

In the field of creative energies things are perhaps a little better. The purely imitative view of art, which dominated Europe to the end of the eighteenth century, has gone, but the arts seem to have lost purpose, direction, and coherence with their traditions. The arts are fostered and discussed as never before and yet the works of genius comparable to those of the past somehow fail to appear. This is particularly true of the art of poetry.

If one asks what is wrong, I think that one important answer lies in the sort of education we provide. Our education, as I said, is specific. It aims at turning out well-molded definite characters which will fit without friction into the society that provides this education. Whether it succeeds in this is not important. The important thing is that this sort of thing might be quite the wrong sort of education for an artist, whose vocation for the creative life may need quite another approach. What most people need to cope with their world is perhaps the training of positive capability. Because the end is known, the means can be adapted to it. But what the artist needs, beyond training in the technical skills necessary for his craft, is not positive capability but what Keats called *negative* capability. This is how Keats describes it in one of his letters:

> I had . . . a disquisition with Dilke, on various subjects; several things dove-tailed in my mind, and at once it struck me what quality went to form a Man of Achievement especially in literature and which Shakespeare possessed so enormously — I mean *Negative Capability*, that is, when a man is capable of being in uncertainties, mysteries, doubts, without any irritable reaching after fact and reason.

In a later letter he continues the description:

> As to the Poetical Character itself . . . it is not itself — it has no character — it enjoys light and shade; it lives in gusto, be it foul or fair, high or low, rich or poor, mean or elevated — it has as much delight in conceiving an Iago as an Imogen . . . A Poet is the most unpoetical of anything in existence because he has no identity — he is continually in for — and filling some other Body — the sun, the moon, the sea and men and women who are creatures of impulse, are poetical and have about them an unchangeable attribute — the poet has none; no identity.

It is precisely because the end of the creative life is something not predictable, something unknown and truly creative, that artists need the sort of education that allows them to develop negative capability, as much as possible, and that our sort of education is unsuited to them.

The essential thing about education for the creative life as distinct from education for the active or the contemplative life is this: that what is truly autonomous must be self-initiating, or it stops being autonomous. For the active life the ends in view are practical ends which depend for their formulation on the known facts about man and society. The form that education for the active life should take can therefore be determined in advance. Similarly, for the contemplative life the world as it exists is its object and perhaps God insofar as he is knowable. The conditions of the contemplative life can therefore be set out in advance. But the ends of the creative life can only be surmised, and the great difference between its conditions and the other two modes of human existence is that what is truly creative must create itself. This is the axiom on which any view of education for the creative life must be based.

One of the tasks of a revived philosophy of man would be to reexamine and restore to public consciousness the basic notion of the ways of life as I have described them and particularly to restore the sense of the true nature of the contemplative life and the creative life. The active life is perhaps well enough provided for and can, by its very nature, take care of itself.

(1965)

Hugh MacDiarmid

Poetry and Science

ASKED IF HE DID NOT SENSE that the public resistance to the sort
of most basic ideas in science is changing at all, Jacques Monod,
the molecular biologist, who is Professor of the Faculty of Science
in the University of Paris and head of the Department of Meta-
bolic Chemistry in the Pasteur Institute — also 1965 joint winner
of the Nobel Prize for Medicine — replied in a recent interview:

> "I don't think so and I think it is a great danger and a tragedy. Sci-
> ence has molded our whole society, by technology, but even more
> by the creation of new ideas and new outlooks at the universe;
> and the fact that this is not fully understood and recognized by
> the general public and governments and the Church and the uni-
> versities and the philosophers is one of the causes of what we
> might call the neurosis of modern societies."

One effort to solve this problem, in a particular direction at
least, may be seen in the new methods of teaching mathematics.
Mathematics is the structure of human ideas and hypotheses con-
cerning abstract concepts based on the "real" world. Its processes
and concepts are particularly amenable to analysis, description,
and recording by concise symbols and patterns of symbols, and
this fact, coupled with the extreme practical importance of some
parts of the subject, accounts for the rapid expansion of math-
ematics over the centuries and its present unfortunate position —

the position or fact that it is quite possible to get good results in math examinations at any level up to and including honors degree by sheer facility and practice with techniques and procedures yet with almost negligible appreciation of the ideas and concepts involved. Math is not about symbols on a blackboard or piece of paper, which is the impression most people are hard put to avoid from the time they enter infant school onward. The object of the present attempted change in the teaching of mathematics is to try to get across to people the ideas and concepts first before bothering about how to write them down—just as children are taught to write a language only after they have become thoroughly familiar with its use.

There is a passage in Chekhov's story *The Wife* which runs:

> I listened to her doctor, and, according to my habit, applied my usual measures to him—materialist, idealist, and so forth, but not a single one of my measures would fit even approximately, and, curiously, while I only listened to him, and looked at him, he was a man perfectly clear to me, but the moment I began applying my measures to him, he became, despite all his sincerity and simplicity, an extraordinarily complex, confused, and inexplicable nature.

Is not this what the great majority of critics do to literature—applying their formulae of this kind or that, until the wood cannot be seen for the trees? Even with the best of them we feel as the Portuguese poet Eugenio de Castro describes himself as feeling on awaking to catch a glimpse of himself in the antique looking-glass of a Toledo hotel—he could not see himself, as he thought he really looked, but only as he might have been painted perhaps by an imitator of El Greco.

Susan Glaspell in her play *Bernice*[1] deals with the problem very well in the following dialogue between her two characters Margaret and Craig.

> MARGARET: We give ourselves in fighting for a thing that seems important, and in that fight we get out of the flow of life. We had meant it to deepen that flow—but we get caught. I know people like that. People who get at home in their fight and stay there and are left there when the fight's over. You write so well,

Craig—but what of it? What is it is the matter with you—with all you American writers—most all of you? A well-put-up light, but it doesn't penetrate anything. It never makes the fog part. Just shows itself off—a well-put-up light! *(Growing angry)* It would be better if we didn't have you at all. Can't you see that it would? Lights which only light themselves keep us from having light—from knowing what the darkness is. *(After thinking)* Craig, as you write these things, are there never times when you sit *dumb,* and know that you are glib and empty?

CRAIG: Did you ever try to write, Margaret?

MARGARET: No.

CRAIG: I suppose you think it's very simple to be real. I suppose you think we could do it—if we wanted to. Try it. *You* try.

MARGARET: So you do this just to cover the fact that you *can't* do anything? Your skill—a mask for your lack of power?

That's it. That's what we want—Chekhov's clearness before the application of "measures."

We are all, more or less consciously, troubled as we read, as Katherine Mansfield was when writing her stories. "I feel," she said, "that this kind of knowledge is too easy for me, it's even a kind of trickery. I know so much more. I know exactly where I fail, and yet when I have finished a story, and before I have begun another, I catch myself actually *preening* my feathers. It is disheartening. This interferes very much with work. I look at the mountains—and I think of something *clever.*"

Most writers—certainly all but a few poets—never look at the mountains at all, of course, and are to be condemned because, as J. Russell Lowell said, "Not failure but low aim is crime." As the Scottish poet John Davidson said,[2] "The want of poetical power is the impelling force in the case of most versifiers. They would fain be poets, and imagine that the best way is to try to write poetry and to publish what they write. They will never see their mistake. *Equus asinus* still believes that the possession of an organ of noise is sufficient, with a little practice, to enable him to sing like a nightingale."

It was said of Davidson—and so truly that it largely accounts for the way he has been neglected ever since neglect made him commit suicide in 1909—"He states fact in terms of poetry, and the statement sears one's consciousness. He is the first poet to digest the new wonders of science which have subtly changed the old cosmogony, and made the very foundations of existence crumble away." That is why I myself wrote, "The relation of John Davidson's thought to Nietzsche's is more important than all the drivel about 'Home, Sweet Home' four million cretins iterate. And if we can't throw off the world, let us hear of no 'Old Grey Mother' at all, but of Middle Torridonian Arkose with local breccias, or the pillow lavas at Loch Awe." Davidson knew what he was about, all right. "The insane past is the incubus," he said; "the world is really a virgin world awaking from a bad dream. These are some of the seeds of the new thing I bring, of the new poetry which the world will make. Poetry is the flower of what all men are maturing in thought and fancy; I reap a harvest unsown; I come a hundred years before the time — that time foreseen by Wordsworth 'when what is now called science, familiarized to men, shall be ready to put on a form of flesh and blood.' "

There has recently been a great debate between the critic F. R. Leavis and C. P. Snow, now Lord Snow, the novelist, about the two cultures — the gap of mutual unintelligibility and antipathy between science and the arts, a local application of that increasingly divisive force which springs from the fact that the sciences are becoming so greatly a matter of specialization that it is becoming virtually impossible for the specialist in one to communicate at all with the specialist in another, and general understanding — the ability to think or understand not in bits and pieces, but all round the circle — seems out of the question altogether.

To get these considerations into perspective, we should consider in conjunction with them what James Harvey Robinson says in his *The Mind In The Making*[3] on "the general show-up of man's thought throughout the ages." "The astonishing and perturbing fact that almost all that has passed for social science, political economy, politics, ethics in the past may be brushed aside by future generations as mainly 'rationalizing' — the opposite of thinking" — and, in particular, the paragraph in which he says,

> When we are offered a penny for our thoughts, we always find that we have recently had so many things in mind that we can easily make a selection which will not compromise us too nakedly. On inspection we shall find that even if we are not down-

right ashamed of a great part of our spontaneous thinking it is far too intimate, personal, ignoble or trivial to permit us to reveal more than a small part of it. We find it hard to believe that other people's thoughts are as silly as ours, but they probably are.

It has been truly said then that

the inventions and organizations that have produced the peculiar opportunities and dangers of the modern world have been the work so far of a few hundred thousand exceptionally clever and enterprising people — a very small percentage of mankind, which has been a constant throughout the whole of human history, and if that small percentage could be eliminated all the vast remaining mass of mankind could do nothing whatever to reconstitute the arts and sciences, or, in other words, èven such measure of civilization as we have so far achieved. The rest of mankind has just been carried along by that tiny minority, and has remained practically what it was a thousand years ago. Upon an understanding and competent minority, which may not exceed a million or so in all the world, depends the whole progress and stability of the collective human enterprise at the present time. They are in perpetual conflict with hampering tradition and the obduracy of nature ... For a number of generations at any rate a deadweight of the dull, silly, under-developed, weak and aimless will have to be carried by the guiding wills and intelligences of mankind. There seems to be no way of getting rid of them. The panics and preferences of these relatively uneducable minds, their flat and foolish tastes, their perversities and compensatory loyalties, their dull gregarious resistances to comprehensive efforts, their outbreaks of resentment at any too lucid revelation of their inferiority, will be a drag, and perhaps a very heavy drag, on the adaptation of institutions to modern needs and to the development of a common knowledge and a common conception of purpose throughout mankind ... The struggle of intelligent and energetic minds throughout the world to clear out their own lumber and get together for the conscious control of the affairs of the strangely mingled multitude of our kind to develop the still largely unrealized possibilities of science and to organize a directive collective will is the essential drama of human life.

What is the relation to all this of poets today — are poets still "the unacknowledged legislators of mankind," "the movers and shapers of the world for ever it seems"? I have said in one of my poems:[4]

> Once again we seek to heal the breach
> Between genius and scholarship, literature and learning,
> (These two which share the knowledge
> Of a broken unity of the human spirit,
> Which to genius appears
> Mainly a moral and personal disaster
> To be mended by intuition, by divination,
> But to the second, equally conscious
> Of the discontinuity of tradition,
> Of the accidents of time, language, place and race
> That hinder sympathy and understanding,
> Presents itself as an intellectual trouble
> To be solved by piecing together
> Minute particulars of evidence)
> Which, since consummate learning is far more rare
> Than genius, has led to the ridiculous condition
> That the world, which holds out both hands to genius,
> Is unhappy in the presence of scholarship,
> Often contemptuous, sometimes even resentful of it,
> Siding naturally with the spiritual valour
> Which dashes itself to pieces
> On the unbreachable walls which fence Truth
> But having little sympathy
> With the slow and cautious movement of learning,
> Yet we all know now the world might get on better
> If it ceased to produce great men of action;
> Speculative genius is a mixed boon too.

In the same very long poem I quote Paul Valéry's statement: "We have the privilege — or the great misfortune — to be present at a profound, rapid, irresistible and total transformation of all the conditions of human activity and of life itself." And I comment, "In this connection it is true of Joyce, as was said by and of another poet: 'I will not leave a corner of my consciousness covered up, but saturate myself with the strange and extraordinary new conditions of this life.'" This willingness and ability to let himself be "new born into the new situation, not subduing his experience to his established personality, is a large part if not the whole secret of the character of Joyce's best work. It was his exposure of his

whole personality that gave his work its quality of impersonality."
And I wrote that it is said in the twelfth chapter and second verse
of Luke, "For there is nothing covered that shall not be revealed,
neither hid that shall not be known."

The general predicament I have been describing leads me in the
same poem, which is an enormous In Memoriam poem to James
Joyce, to say:

> The ancestors of oysters and barnacles had heads,
> Snakes have lost their limbs,
> And ostriches and penguins their power of flight.
> Man may just as easily lose his intelligence.
> Most of our people already have.
> It is unlikely that man will develop into anything higher
> Unless he desires to and is prepared to pay the cost.
> Otherwise we shall go the way of the dodo and kiwi.
> Already the process seems far advanced,
> Genius is becoming rarer,
> Our bodies a little weaker, with each generation.
> Culture is slowly declining.
> Mankind is returning to barbarism
> And will finally become extinct.

What then is the use of the incredible stratagems of words in
which Joyce describes *Finnegans Wake* or Ezra Pound devises his
Cantos? I answer as follows:

> All but an infinitesimal percentage of mankind
> Have no use whatever for versatility and myriad-mindedness.
> Erudition means less than nothing to them
> (Larvae, hallucinated automata, bobbins,
> Savage robots, appropriate dummies,
> The fascinating imbecility of the creaking men-machines,
> Set in a pattern as circumscribed and complete
> As a theory of Euclid — essays in a new human mathematic)
> Yet, as Gaudapada says, even as a bed
> Which is an assembly of frame, mattress, bedding and pillows,
> Is for another's use, not for its own,
> And its several component parts render no mutual service,
> Thence it is concluded that there is a man who sleeps upon this
> bed
> And for whose sake it was made; so this world

Of words, thoughts, memories, scientific facts, literary arts,
Is for another's use. Ah, Joyce, enough said, enough said.
Mum's the word now! Mum's the word!
Responsibility for the present state of the world
And for its development for better or worse
Lies with every single individual;
Freedom is only really possible
In proportion as all are free.
Knowledge, and, indeed, adoption *(Aneignung)*
Of the rich Western tradition,
And all the wisdom of the East as well
Is the indispensable condition of any progress.
World-history and world-philosophy
Are only now beginning to dawn;
Whatever tribulation may yet be in store for men
Pessimism is false. Let us make ourselves at home
In das Umgreifende, the super-objective,
The final reality to which human life can attain.
Short of that every man is guilty,
Living only the immediate life,
Without memory, without plan, without mastery,
The very definition of vulgarity;
Guilty of a dereliction of duty,
The "distraction" of Pascal,
The "aesthetic stage" of Kierkegaard,
The "inauthentic life" of Heidegger,
The "alienation" of Marx,
The self-deception *(mauvaise foi)* of Sartre.

I believe it will be in every connection soon
As already in the field of colour
Where the imitative stage
Has long been passed
And coal-tar dyes are synthesized no more
To imitate the colours of nature,
Whether of Autumn or Spring.
The pattern cards of dye-stuff firms today
Display multitudes of syntheses
That transcend Nature to reach
Almost a philosophic satisfaction
Of the aesthetic sense of colour.
Apart from a handful of scientists and poets
Hardly anybody is aware of it yet

(A society of people without a voice for the consciousness
That is slowly growing within them.)
Nevertheless everywhere among the great masses of mankind
With every line it is growing and emerging
Like a mango tree under a cloth
Stirring the dull cloth,
Sending out tentacles,
—It's not something that can be stopped
By sticking it away in a zinc-lined box
Like a tube of radium
As most people have,
Calling all who approve of it mad,
The term they always apply
To anyone who tries to make them think.

For Schoenberg was right, the problem involved
In mental vocalization
Is not that the evolution of music
Must wait on the human ear,
But that the human ear must catch up
With the evolution of music.
As with Schoenberg's so, Joyce, with your work
And scant though the endeavour be
Of progress here we have ample proof
(While yet the vast majority of mankind
Are but inching to close the infinite gap
And may succeed in a few billion years perhaps)
That the complicated is Nature's climax of rightness,
And the simple at a discount. The Apocrypha is right.
Of our Muse, "She needs no simple man!"
We have learned the lesson of the Caddoan saying:
"When a woman grinds the corn with one hand
Don't let it into your belly!"
As in the clash between Red Indian and White Man
Sophistication was with simplicity everywhere
With only one possible conclusion. There can be no doubt
That the bed of which I have spoken will be filled,
All life's million conflicting interests and relationships,
Even as nerves before ever they function
Grow where they *will* be wanted; levers laid down in gristle
Become bone when wanted for the heavier pull
Of muscles which *will* clothe them; lungs, solid glands,
Yet arranged to hollow out at a few minutes' notice

When the necessary air shall enter; limb buds
Futile at their appearing, yet deliberately appearing
In order to become limbs in readiness
For an existence where they *will* be all-important;
A pseudo-aquatic parasite, voiceless as a fish,
Yet containing within itself an instrument of voice
Against the time when it *will* talk;
Organs of skin, ear, eye, nose, tongue
Superfluous all of them in the watery dark
Where formed — yet each unhaltingly preparing
To enter a daylit, airy, objectfull, manifold world
They *will* be wanted to report on. Everywhere we find
Prospective knowledge of the needs of life
Which are not yet, but are foreknown.
All is provided. As Aristotle says,
"To know the end of a thing is to know the why of it!"
So with your work, vastly outrunning present needs
With its immense complication, its erudition,
(The intricacy of the connections defies description.
Before it the mind halts, abased, *In tenuis labor*)
But providing for the developments to come.
Even so long before the foetus
Can have either sensation or motion,
When, in fact, its cellular elements
First begin to differentiate themselves,
The various nerves which are to govern
The perceptions and reactions essential in life
Develop, as they shape themselves, a faculty
For discovering and joining with their "opposite numbers,"
Sensory cell "calling" to motor cell
By a force we may call Cytoclesis.
Nor is this mysterious call
A phenomenon of the nervous system only.
Throughout the body cell calls to cell
That the elaborate and intricate development
Of tissues may proceed aright.
Thus in the case of the kidney tubules
The myriad secreting tubules are formed
In one portion of the primordial embryonic tissue
Budded out from the ureter.
Nevertheless although these two entities
Are involved in the completion of all the kidney tubules

> There is the marvel that results in each secreting tubule
> Meeting a collecting tubule
> Accurately end to end.
> Each complete duct is composed of two sections
> Preformed from different embryological elements
> But guided to meet each other by a "call,"
> A "call" so wonderful that each kidney tubule
> Meets each ureteric tubule end to end
> And so completes the canal.

The program for poetry I advocate is in Walt Whitman's words: to conform with and build on the concrete realities and theories of the universe furnished by science, and henceforth the only irrefragable basis for anything, verse included: and like Whitman I cry: "Think of the absence and ignorance hitherto of the multitudinousness, vitality, and the unprecedented stimulants of today. It almost seems as if a poetry with cosmic and dynamic features of magnitude and limitlessness suitable to the human soul were never possible before. It is certain that a poetry of absolute faith and equality for the use of the democratic masses never was."

More attention should have been — and should be — paid to Sir Compton Mackenzie's declaration that

> a new kind of man is beginning to reveal himself. Speed is the basic foundation of this new man. The mind has already begun to change its processes to take advantage of the speed with which every day the body is being more and more richly endowed. It seems, indeed, that unless some catastrophe of war or pestilence on a scale immensely greater than anything the world has yet known by exacerbating the struggle for existence intervenes to prolong the way of human thought since Genesis, the second millennium of the Christian era will see humanity launched upon a way of thought a thousand times more different from our present ways of thought than ours from the thought of neolithic man.

It is impossible to agree with Edwin Muir that when some postulation of a transcendental reality — the belief in eternity — fails, "imagination suffers an eclipse, and if that belief were to fail completely and for good it is possible that it would mean the final end of all imaginative literature and art."

I believe that all such beliefs will speedily fail and forever, and that that will be the beginning of imaginative literature and art for everybody—not, as hitherto, only for a favored few. The effective alternative to Mr. Muir's "belief in eternity which is natural to man" is Mr. Santayana's "primal and universal religion, the religion of will, the faith which life has in itself because it is life and in its aims, because it is pursuing them"—"the heart and mystery of matter lies in the seeds of things, *semina rerum*, and in the customary cycles of their transformation."

Discussing Professor Morris Cohen's *Reason and Nature*[5] an American critic observed:

> Professor Cohen states that his greatest debt is to Bertrand Russell's *Principles of Mathematics*, and a comparison of the chief traits of the two men may perhaps be fruitful. Russell and Cohen have in common two valuable characteristics. Both possess minds of immense logical acuteness and neither has confined himself to a single field of endeavor, but has ventured with great success into many domains of thought. Their range of interests is practically co-extensive, but each exhibits the same surprising limitations. In fields where the aesthetic content predominates over the intellectual, neither displays any special knowledge or aptitude. In *Reason and Nature* the literary allusions are almost non-existent. A few names of the first magnitude, such as Sophocles, Shelley, and Dante, are invoked to illustrate a point. There is an unfortunate reference to Sainte-Beuve—wrongly spelled and with the Sainte abbreviated into the contraction for a street and there is (for philosophical scientists) the inevitable quotation in the original German from *Faust*. It is perhaps a biological peculiarity that intellectual and aesthetic mastery unite so seldom in a single individual.

A still more significant case is that of Professor A. N. Whitehead in his *Science and the Modern World*.[6] He stresses the need to draw out habits of aesthetic apprehension—to foster the creative initiative toward the maintenance of objective values. He devotes a whole chapter to showing that the literature of the nineteenth century, especially English poetic literature, is a witness to the discord between the aesthetic intuitions of mankind and the mechanism of science. "The romantic reaction was" he contends, "a protest on behalf of value"—and an invaluable corrective to current scientific misconceptions and precursor of the better scientific understanding since attained. But in propounding his own new doctrines he does not take advantage of that important discovery and stop to ask what the relations between poetry and science today may disclose of a like sort. He deals with Wordsworth and Shelley, but subsequent poetry is apparently completely out of his ken, while the importance of his thesis in the chapter in question should surely have compelled him to widen his inquiries into the poetry of the period and not confine himself to two or three English poets and exclude the poets of other countries. And his conclusion that the passage in Shelley's *Prometheus Unbound* beginning, "I spin beneath my pyramid of night" could only have been written by someone with a definite geometrical design before his inward eye—a diagram it has often been my business to demonstrate to mathematical classes—is of course thoroughly unscientific. Shelley may have come at the conception in question quite independently: science itself abounds in instances of unrelated researchers arriving independently—and from different angles of approach—at identical discoveries. G. B. Dibblee's really epoch-making book *Instinct and Intuition*,[7] with all its abundant knowledge and extreme dialectical ability, illustrates to a lamentable extent how the growth of civilization can yet leave the spiritual stature of man not increased by one iota, and Mr. Dibblee's inept illustrations, jejune personal recollections, and lack of recourse to the very people who embody the "refined spiritual faculties" with which he is concerned, is just another sorry instance of the failure of most scientists and philosophers to avail themselves of the aid they could have derived from a really thorough and up-to-date knowledge of poetry. To give only one illustration, Paul Valéry for example made a present of his speculations in *L'Idée fixe* to the medical profession. What has the medical profession made of this important gift from a man of an intellectual stature to which few of its own members can ever aspire?

We have got a long way in this discussion from one of my own simple perceptions which at the outset of my career as a poet I expressed as follows:

> The rarity and value of scientific knowledge
> Is little understood—even as people
> Who are not botanists find it hard to believe

Special knowledge of the subject can add
Enormously to the aesthetic appreciation of flowers!
Partly because in order to identify a plant
You must study it very much more closely
Than you would otherwise have done, and in the process
Exquisite colours, proportions, and minute shapes spring to light
Too small to be ordinarily noted,
And more than this — it seems the botanist's knowledge
Of the complete structure of the plant
(Like a sculptor's of bone and muscle)
— Of the configuration of its roots stretching under the earth,
The branching of stems,
Enfolding of buds by bracts,
Spreading of veins on a leaf
Encircles and snakes three dimensional
His awareness of its complex beauty.

So I conclude that it is supremely desirable that every writer
should be able to lay his hand on his heart and say, with Anton
Chekhov,

> Familiarity with the natural sciences and with scientific methods
> has always kept me on my guard, and I have always tried, where it
> was possible, to be consistent with the facts of science . . . I may
> observe in passing that the conditions of artistic creation do not
> always admit of complete harmony with the facts of science. It is
> impossible to represent on the stage a death from poisoning
> exactly as it takes place in reality. But harmony with the facts of
> science must be felt even under these conditions — that is, it
> must be clear to the reader or spectator that this is only due to the
> conditions of art and that he has to do with a writer who under-
> stands. I do not belong to the class of literary men who take up a
> sceptical attitude toward science: and to the class of those who
> rush into anything with only their own imagination to go upon, I
> should not like to belong.

(1967)

Notes

1. London: Ernest Benn, 1924.

2. *Sentences and Paragraphs* (London: Lawrence and Bullen, 1893)

3. London: C. A. Watts, 1949.

4. *In Memoriam James Joyce* (Glasgow: Maclellan, 1955).

5. New York and London: Collier-Macmillan, 1953.

6. Cambridge: Cambridge University Press, 1936.

7. London: Faber and Faber, 1929.

Günter Kunert

Why Write

THE REASON is perfectly simple: to live. Not in the sense of keeping oneself physically alive, but in a different sense, which I shall attempt to explain in what follows.

In recent years the number of possible modes of existence that one might give oneself over to has seemed to be unlimited; so many possibilities present themselves that in the face of the ostensible fullness of life the intellect or at least the will stands still in any attempt to decide quickly in favor of one of those possibilities. You try this and that, get married (usually) a number of times, increase the population lawfully or unlawfully, change jobs, cities, dwellings, ideals, only to reach no satisfactory final outcome. You feel you've wasted your abilities, forfeited your options, while others were smart enough to decide in time. But even the others, who apparently have undergone a continuous development for decades, turn out to be dissatisfied: they in turn consider the experimental, open-ended life a marvelously full one and regard failure as a kind of success. That comes from a deep distrust of the course their own lives have taken, because almost every one of them sees and judges his own from an unreal perspective, often one drawn from popular culture. Hardly anyone tries to grasp his existence as something peculiar to him; most people pattern themselves on models, but this never leads to full contentment. Each one of these models is not an archetype but presumably a stylized functional object, more or less moderately removed from reality and thus not practicable in reality. The attempt is still made, however, again and again, and this finally leads to frustration.

This only apparently digressive introduction, which records a general pattern of behavior, is here to provide the contrast necessary for making oneself visible. For me, then, neither the alleged diversity nor the supposed constants were valid. Without an occupation in which I could have advanced or which I might have left, I came early to writing, at the age of seventeen, and succumbed immediately to this strange trade. I could do nothing else and — what was more decisive for the future — I never wished that I could do anything else. Only once, more pushed than attracted, did I attempt to ally myself to a relatively "normal" occupation; namely, that of editor, but it was a thoroughgoing failure. My aversion and my dismay in the face of the mechanism that suddenly was consuming me, and at being shrunk to a mere function, magnified even more my lack of practical talent: the uneasy suspicion that I was being filled increasingly with something forced and mechanical, utterly paralyzed me and actually made me ill. This experiment so long ago did teach me, however, that I am no good for any useful purpose. Even if the others had shown me the good will that I was unable to muster, I was of no reasonable use — if one is inclined to consider empty utilitarianism, which ravages the world, to be a manifestation of human reason. All I could do was to dangle from a fine thread of my own spinning over each day's abysses. And only after a while did I notice that this was not a supplement, not an accidental property adhering to the intrinsic, but the intrinsic itself. The more I tried, as I wrote, to dissolve into what I was writing, the more severely the number of themes and subjects was reduced (as if that were the price) — however inexhaustible I had formerly believed them, as others believed in the diversity of life. With increasing identity of text and author, the author's role as clown or teacher ends; every moral impetus loses its imperative aspect and becomes viewpoint and style, the frequency of the literal essence into which the author withdraws. The lack of freedom in every literary effort increases proportionally, and variability decreases, because all that succeeds is what promotes transformation; everything else comes about halfheartedly or not at all. Many considerations become secondary. And yet it seemed so simple at the beginning: one knew the alphabet and a bit of grammar, so why not write about the beauty of wood lice, the joys of idiocy, love for mankind, and other phantasmagories? After all, the function of language is to be of use to everyone and for everything. Why am I incapable of all this? Why not carry out every task like an honest workman who yields to the wishes of his customers, even if he considers them foolish?

It doesn't work for the simple reason that one would have to turn into something one is not, something that actually does not exist, and that therefore seems terrible: a consciously practiced example of self-alienation. One would be destroyed if one had to convert one's own real personality into a mere semblance, devoid of reality. That would be suicide by means of linguistic transformation into nothingness. Afterward, if you're there at all, it's as a living corpse, available for viewing. If a person is forced to transform his individual self—if he has one—violently into a fixed idea, he ceases to be as a person: that's murder on a high plane.

To write: because the process of transformation in which I become a text is a dialectical process of regeneration: I lose and win at the same time. This produces increased tension, like all seeking and finding; what is sought and found, however, is the unforeseen. One goes out into the world; that is, the world of oneself, to discover the impersonal, the general, that one has inside one's very self. To write: so that something happens that everyone secretly wishes—that the moment, for a moment, might be lasting and might be reawakened again and again. To write: a wavelike spreading out in all directions that knows no boundaries and encompasses and illuminates ever more, and ever more the unknown.

To write: because writing constitutes nothing final but only provides impulses; because it is an endless beginning, a constantly new first time, like intercourse or pain. As long as one writes, ruin is averted, it doesn't all slip away; and that's why I write: to bear the world as it steadily crumbles into nothingness.

(1972)
Translated by James Hulbert

Wendell Berry

The Specialization of Poetry

FOR SOME TIME I have been gathering and reading a number of examples of the newest of literary genres, the interview-with-a-poet. I have at hand interviews with Philip Levine, James Dickey, Galway Kinnell, William Matthews, Adrienne Rich, Anne Sexton, Louis Simpson, and Mark Strand. At first my interest rose mainly from curiosity as to the reasons for the growth of this genre. What does it mean that the work habits, personal circumstances, and casual opinions of poets have come lately to be held in such regard by the editors of magazines, by at least some readers, and evidently by the poets themselves? But various ones of the interviewed poets were expressing ideas that have been common in writings and discussions of poetry for a good many years, and as I read and made notes and reread, I realized how several of these ideas work together to define a specialization of poetry that parallels the specialization of other disciplines.*

My understanding of this specialization of poetry is, of course, indebted to the work of many other writers. The subject has been

---

* In writing this essay, I would have preferred to avoid controversy by setting out my own opinions without reference to the contrary opinions of other people. But my essay developed so particularly in response to the interviews I have quoted that it would have been difficult and even dishonest to leave them out. Because I have no appetite for the enmity that often goes with literary controversy, I would like to say that I intend no disrespect toward these poets themselves, even when I obviously dislike some of their opinions.

dealt with most ably, among writings known to me, in John Crowe Ransom's essay "Poets Without Laurels" and in Edwin Muir's lucid book *The Estate of Poetry*. Mr. Ransom spoke of the purification or the puritanization of poetry, which he saw as a part of the general dissociation of "the elements of experience" and of the "faculties" of the modern mind; and Muir of the diminishment of poetry's "estate," which he defined as its "effective range and influence." The Ransom essay was published in *The World's Body* in 1938, when the catastrophe of dissociation was still in its adolescence. *The Estate of Poetry* comprises the Charles Eliot Norton Lectures delivered by Muir in 1955–1956. By then the dissociation of which Mr. Ransom wrote had produced a working model of doomsday, and though Muir's book is not apocalyptic, it is informed by the historical urgency that burdens his later poems. Applied science (not necessarily "applied" by scientists) had had its *tour de force* in World War II, and Muir had understood the ferocious logic that was upon us.

Because of the proliferation of so-called protest poetry, and the widespread involvement of poets in public issues, after about 1964, it became possible to suppose that the concerns of Ransom and Muir had become somewhat dated. For a while during the sixties I hoped, and even believed, that the effort of many poets to speak out against public outrages might recover some of the lost estate of poetry; and I think that I was by no means the only one who hoped and believed this. But the political "involvement" of poets appears now to have subsided, leaving the "effective range and influence" of poetry no larger than before.

Having had several years in which to write my own protests, and several more in which to consider them and their effect, I conclude that I was wrong. I do not mean that I feel the protests to have been wrong, or that I would not—or that I do not now— protest against the outrages that I know to be taking place. I was wrong in assuming that protest, in itself, might alter the status of poetry. Poetry remains a specialized art, its range and influence so constricted that poets have very nearly become their own audience.

The primary aspect of specialization is practical; the specialist withdraws from responsibility for everything not comprehended by his specialty. Each specialization, Mr. Ransom says, "has had to resist the insidious charms of aesthetic experience before its own perfection could arise." But this is a perfection of a kind never before contemplated in human history — a perfection that depends upon the abandonment of all the old ideals of harmony, symmetry, balance, order, in favor of the singular totalitarian ideal of control, which is typically achieved by leaving out or discounting or destroying whatever is not subject to control. Our achievement of this sort of control over certain particles of the creation has given rise to the supposition that such control is possible on a much grander scale, which would permit us to bring nature and history into line with our intentions. There is no need, I think, to dwell upon the moral degeneracy, the spiritual misery, the abuses and wastes of power that are the result of this ambition. And of course we are every day surrounded by more evidence of its futility. Human control on any grand scale is impossible, and the technological and political controls that *are* possible are frequently the opposite of order; any viable human order must come to terms with the impossibility of an absolute control.

The so-called practical disciplines, then, shrugged off the claims of esthetics — among other things. Their withdrawal from the concern for esthetics defined that as the proper "field" for artists. And the artists specialized their various disciplines, Mr. Ransom says, by breaking down "the union of beauty with goodness and truth," which until then was "common enough to be regarded as natural." In reaction to the utilitarianism of other disciplines, the arts became defiantly nonutilitarian.

It is immediately necessary to amend Mr. Ransom's version of the modern role of the poet. First, it must be made to accommodate his own obvious concern with the larger responsibilities of poets — likewise that of Allen Tate, one of whose poems Mr. Ransom cites as an example of the "obscure" or unmoral poem. One must mention such self-consciously "national" poets as Yeats, Williams, and MacDiarmid, and a poet so determinedly a teacher as Pound. It must be said that some poets have resisted the claims of beauty, that others have attempted to be moralist or mages or priests or politicians. So much said, it remains true that the poet is isolated and specialized, and that the old union of beauty, goodness, and truth is broken. It remains true that, in Muir's words, "the public has become one of the subjects of poetry, but is no longer its audience."

I believe that the sudden rise and growth of the genre of the interview is itself a symptom of the specialization of poetry, and that it reveals some of the dangers. It suggests, as a sort of implied premise, that poets are of a different kind from other people; hence the interest in what they *say* as opposed to what they write. (The popularity of poetry readings, which about parallels the vogue of the interview, probably owes something to the same feeling, though I believe that the readings have a more legitimate function.) There has come to be a class of what might be called poet-watchers, who seem to be convinced that, whereas their own lives are routine and dull, the life of poets is constantly "different" and exciting. Judging from their tone and their lack of controversy, I conclude that most interviews with poets are conducted by poet-watchers. The purpose cannot be a dialogue between two beings of the same general kind; that, surely, would lead to hard questions or, better, to argument. Nor can the purpose be to learn what the poet has to say about his art, for that could be better done in an essay; if it is to be done at all, it *ought* to be done in an essay. The idea, obviously, is to *examine* the poet, to study as unobtrusively as possible whatever privacies may be disclosed by the inadvertences of conversation. The interviewer operates in a blind of obsequiousness, hoping the poet will reveal himself as the strange creature *he really is.* The interviewer and his intended readers are so convinced of the poet's otherness that they need to stand in his presence and say, "Well, well, so that's a poet." At a poetry reading once I sat behind a group of such spectators who passed back and forth during the entire evening a pair of huge binoculars.

But poet-watchers have a limitation in common with bird-watchers. Some essential things will not be revealed to them, because their interest is too direct, too imbued with the excitement of a special occasion. They are too much agog. They cannot relate to a poet on the basis of the casual happenstance that they are fellow creatures and contemporaries. If to an attentiveness appropriately critical and calm, the words of a poet reveal something extraordinary, then an extraordinary response is certainly in order. But it is better to be agape afterward than agog beforehand.

The poet-watcher is a kind of absurdity. But insofar as they have helped to create him, and to the degree that they indulge or exploit or need his excitement, there is also an absurdity in poets. There is apparently now some widespread feeling among poets themselves that they are of a different kind, hence have some special explaining to do. And this explaining often involves an advocacy of the very ideas and conditions that made the explanation necessary in the first place.

One of the oldest doctrines of the specialist-poet is that of the primacy of language and the primacy of poetry. He has made virtually a religion of his art, a religion based not on what he has in common with other people, but on what he *does* that sets him apart from them. For a poet who believes in this way, a poem is not a point of clarification or connection between himself and the world on the one hand and between himself and the reader on the other, nor is it an adventure into any reality or mystery outside himself. It is a seeking of self in words, the making of a word-world in which the word-self may be at home. The poet goes to his poem as other people have gone to the world or to God—for a sense of his own reality. Louis Simpson, for instance, says to an interviewer, "I have a very funny sense of myself in the poem—I'm not talking about me. I'm talking about how the poems make a self for me." Later he says of himself and some of his contemporaries, "We had to be devoted to poetry for its own sake." [1] And Mark Strand says, "I have the feeling that I am a metaphor for my own being." [2]

It may be argued, as Mr. Ransom does, that this emphasis was in some sense forced upon poets by their peculiar isolation in a society dominated by specialists of more practical kinds. But this way of looking at language and at poetry also completes and enforces the isolation of poets, not just within a sort of literary ghetto or subghetto, but within themselves. Mark Strand is evidently not the only poet who would say that "the self in a sense is all we have left."

This feeling is more particularly documented by Philip Levine, who anticipates, beyond the limits of his isolation, a reader—but an ideal reader with whom he may be in touch only by his poetry, with whom he will have no common ground except his poetry. Commenting on his assumption that he has no readers in his native city, he says to his interviewer, "I think it's terrific. I have a Detroit that vanished about 1952 for all I know, when I left. I live it, it's in my head, and it's got nothing to do with what's back there now. It's the life I lived back there and the lives it included, and that's what I'm trying to transform into poetry, and if it could only make it with people living in Detroit it wouldn't be any good anyhow." The world, then, is usable for poetry only after it has been totally subsumed in the self. Mr. Levine goes on to say of a visit to Spain, "By the end of the year the landscape seemed me, seemed like a projection of my own inner being. I felt that when I looked at the Spanish landscape I was looking at a part of myself." [3]

The world that once was mirrored by the poet has become the poet's mirror. This explains, I think, the emphasis upon personal terror and suffering and the fear of death in much recent poetry. When the self is one's exclusive subject and limit, reference and measure, one has no choice but to make a world of words. And this gives to one's own suffering and death the force of cataclysm.

But the difficulties are more than personal. For one thing, the subject of poetry is not words; it is the world, which poets have in common with other people. It has been argued that modern poets were forced to turn inward by the disposition of their materialistic societies to turn outward. But that argument ignores or discounts the traditions that have always bound poetry to the concerns and values of the spirit. This ancient allegiance gives poets the freedom, and perhaps the moral imperative, to turn outward. It is surely no accident that Yeats, perhaps the most spiritual poet in our language in our era, was also perhaps the most political. In relation to the world, the specialization of poetry is exactly analogous to the specialization of religion. Putting exclusive emphasis upon a world of words has the same result as putting exclusive emphasis upon heaven: it leads to, and allows, and abets, the degradation of the world. And it leads ultimately to the degradation of art and religion. Renunciation of the world may sustain religious or artistic fervor for a while, but sooner or later it becomes suicidal.

This exclusive emphasis upon language leads also to the degradation of general literacy. Not so long ago it was generally thought that in order to be a writer a person needed to lead "an exciting life" or that he needed extraordinary knowledge or experience. This, of course, frequently led to some sort of willful absurdity in the life of young writers. But it also suggested a connection — even a responsible connection — between art and experience or art and the world. What we have too frequently now — in the words of hundreds of poetry reviews in the time of my own coming of age — is the notion that what distinguishes a writer from a non-writer is, first and last, a gift and a love of *language.* He is not, that is, distinguished by his knowledge or character or vision or inspiration or the story he has to tell; he is distinguished by his specialty. This is a difference not of degree, but of kind. And the resulting absurdities are greater than before, and more dangerous. The power of such notions among the college-bred is suggested by a statement of Mr. John W. Dean III: "I would still like to be a writer. Maybe I will write a book. I love to play with words and twist phrases. I always play Scrabble." [4] If both writer and reader assume that the writer's gift makes him a person of a radically different kind, then it must follow that writer and reader have nothing to learn from each other. There is no longer any meaningful passage of influence between writer and audience. If the writer acquires a "knack" for language much as one acquires a birthmark, then the reason for reading a book can only be the same as for watching television: to divert one's mind from its concerns. A distinguished writer is of course distinguished by his language, which is certainly his gift and his love. But his language is, after all, the common tongue, to which his gift is uncommon grace and power; without his commonness we could not recognize or value his distinction.

One of the first obligations of poets is certainly to purify the language of the tribe — but *not* merely to write poems with it. The language of the tribe used by a specialist-poet to produce a poem "for its own sake" can only describe the boundaries of an imprisoning and damning selfhood. Joyce Carol Oates says, writing of Sylvia Plath, "When the epic promise of 'One's-self I sing' is mistaken as the singing of a separate self, and not the Universal self, the results can only be tragic." [5] There is a sense of balance that is missing from the atmosphere that now surrounds much of the writing and much of the criticism of poetry. This sense of balance would lead and lead again to the poet's place of responsibility between his readers and his subject — *which is also his readers' subject.* It would see words as fulcrums across which intelligence must endlessly be weighed against experience.

Another common ground is tradition — the awareness and the use of the tradition that poets have in common with all the other sharers of the heritage of literature, writers and readers, living and dead — the tradition that is, moreover, the consciousness of the inheritance conveyed to us, whether we know or acknowledge it or not, in the language we speak. But literary talk nowadays seems remarkable for its lack of interest in tradition. The poets in the interviews are preoccupied with the new, with the modern world and modern times. They speak of very few poets who began to publish before World War II, almost none who lived before this century. Some of these poets seem to relate to the past simply by lack of interest. Others show a sort of vindictiveness against it, typically expressed in extremely generalized condemnations of traditional forms. Mark Strand says that

> we [my emphasis] distrust rhyme because it sounds a little tinny, a little false, a little decorative, and a little unnatural. The point of writing . . . plain-style verse . . . is to affect as much as possible the naturalness of conversation, or plain discourse, not overly excited discourse. Rhyme would get in the way . . . I'm not talking about my own poetry when I say this. I'm sure Galway Kinnell and Robert Mezey . . . would not ever write in meters or rhyme.

Mr. Strand then immediately confuses the issue by saying, "I've rhymed fairly recently, and I find it useful. I don't mind that, and I don't mind meters either. It sometimes seems quite natural to me."

Adrienne Rich apparently feels no such ambivalence. Her interviewer says, "Not many people anymore, not many poets anymore, talk very much, or feel they need to talk much, about form. Right?" And Ms. Rich replies, "Right! Or think very much about it." She calls Yeats "that table-rapping fascist," and says of her inability "to use the literature of the past": "I can't . . . read a poem by Yeats and feel somebody is talking to me whose voice I need to hear." [6]

William Matthews falls into line on the issue of traditional form, but his remarks on the subject are more elaborate, and they may afford some insight into the apparently widespread bias against form, traditional and otherwise. He believes, he says, "that one of the functions of art should be to disarrange patterns of certainty in the psyche . . ." This century has produced "a life that is organized all too well, and . . . we really need . . . to have our certainties shaken up badly." He says that it has never occurred to him to write in traditional forms because "I'm so much a believer in the notion of surprising yourself, and taking risks and preferring disorder to order, that it would be almost temperamentally impossible for me to do it." [7]

There are at least three false assumptions here: (1) that there is no form except "traditional form"; (2) that the employment or the pursuit of form can lead only to what has been predetermined; (3) that organization is necessarily synonymous with order. To the first of these assumptions it can of course be said that, though the interest in form may be traditional, it is certainly possible to invent or to discover forms that are not traditional. The second assumption, it seems to me, is based on a misunderstanding of the nature of form. The third assumption—of the identity of organization and order—is the most serious, because it fails to see the overwhelming disorder inherent in much, perhaps in most, Twentieth Century organization.

The fear of chaos, Mr. Matthews maintains, originates with "people who get up every morning at eight o'clock, teach an Aesthetic theory class at ten, get the department mail at twelve o'clock, give a graduate student exam in the afternoon, go home and have two drinks before dinner." Maybe so. But it seems to me more likely that the *praise* of chaos must come from people whose lives are so safely organized. Mr. Matthews does concede that "there's a kind of chaos which is awful—the moment before civilizations collapse, or when three members of your immediate family or friends are killed." But I do not believe that people who have experienced chaos are apt to praise or advocate any degree or variety of it. And to make these distinctions between kinds and degrees of chaos is both fanciful and dangerous. Formlessness is, after all, neither civilized nor natural. It is a peculiarly human evil, without analogue in nature, caused by the failures of civilization: inattention, irresponsibility, carelessness, ignorance of conse quence. It is the result of the misuse of power. It is neither house nor field nor forest, but rather a war or the spoil bank of a strip mine, where the balance between stability and change has been overthrown. The reason we need to have our certainties shaken is so that we may see the possibility of better orders than we have.

Behind these and other perfunctory dismissals of traditional form there seems to be a feeling that these forms are not "organic." But I have begun to wonder if the distinction between organic and traditional is not false. A better set of terms, I think, would be organic and mechanical. There are some sonnets, for instance, of which the form is organic; others of which it is mechanical. The difference apparently lies in the nature of the poem's conception and in the appropriateness or expressiveness of the form. And I do not see why a traditional verse form might not belong with perfect propriety to what Denise Levertov calls the "constellation" of the experiences that make a poem.[8]

It may be necessary to question how much importance poets assign to statements they make to interviewers. But that Mr. Strand and Ms. Rich and Mr. Matthews spoke so casually and so generally of this matter of tradition and form, knowing that they spoke for publication, seems to imply an assumption that they spoke for many of their contemporaries. And though I am not sure how these statements are meant, they sound compulsively fashionable; they appear to have that eagerness to be contemporary and up to date that identifies the modern cult of originality. That this eagerness to replace the old with the new justifies itself by the alleged uniqueness of the strains and demands of the modern world does not necessarily ennoble it: the modern world is after all largely the product of merchandisers, whose argument has been essentially the same.

Contemporaneity, in the sense of being "up with the times," is of no value. A competent wakefulness to experience — as well as to instruction and example — is another matter. But what we call the modern world is not necessarily, and not often, the real world, and there is no virtue in being up to date in it. It is a false world, based upon economies and values and desires that are fantastical — a world in which millions of people have lost any idea of the resources, the disciplines, the restraints, and the labor necessary to support human life, and who have thus become dangerous to their own lives and to the possibility of life. The job now is to get back to that other perennial and substantial world in which we really do live, in which the foundations of our life will be visible to us, and in which we can accept our responsibilities again within the conditions of necessity and mystery. In that world all competently wakeful and responsible people, dead, living, and unborn, are contemporaries. And that is the only contemporaneity worth having.

What is needed is work of durable value; the time or age of it matters only after the value has been established. That a good poet is our contemporary reassures us of the continuing liveliness of certain possibilities; it is a value. The contemporaneity of a worthless poet is, by the same token, a depressant. But there is much that we need that we cannot get from our contemporaries—even assuming that the work we have from them is the best that is possible: they cannot give us the sense of the longevity of human experience, the sense of the practicable, of *proven* possibility, that we get from older writing. Our past is not merely something to depart from; it is to commune with, to speak with. "Day unto day uttereth speech, and night unto night showeth knowledge." Remove this sense of continuity, and we are left with the thoughtless present tense of machines. If we fail to see that we live in the same world that Homer lived in, then we not only misunderstand Homer; we misunderstand ourselves. The past is our definition. We may strive, with good reason, to escape it, but we will escape it only by adding something better to it.

If, as I believe, one of the functions of tradition is to convey a sense of our perennial nature, and of the necessities and values that are the foundation of our life, then it follows that without a live tradition we are necessarily the prey of fashion: we have no choice but to emulate in the arts the "practical" men of commerce and industry whose mode of life is distraction of spirit and whose livelihood is the outdating of fads.

Isolated by the specialization of their art—by their tendency to make a religion of poetry or to make a world out of words, and by their preoccupation with the present and the new—poets of modern times seem to run extreme occupational risks. James Dickey says, "I think there is a terrible danger in the overcultivation of one's sensibilities, and that's what poets are forced to do in order to become poets." And: "In order to create poetry, you make a monster out of your own mind." He explains that some poets use alcohol or other drugs, first to coax the monster, and then to protect themselves from it. He mentions, as victims, Berryman, Crane, and Dylan Thomas, and calls poetry one of the most dangerous occupations in the world. But he believes that most of the victims have been content with their bargain "because the moments of intensity which do lead to delight and joy and fulfillment are so much better than those that other people have." [9]

The word "monster" is used in a perhaps similar way in the 285th of Berryman's *Dream Songs*. The poem speaks of Henry's struggling and darkness and confusion, and then says that "he took in his stride/more than most monsters can." It ends:

> Henry peered quite alone
> as if the worlds would answer to a code
> just around the corner, down gelid dawn,
> beckoning like a moan.

I think Mr. Dickey's mention of the use of drugs may give too limited a definition to the danger he is talking about, for associated with the possibility of dependence on a drug is the possibility of a dependence on pain, a symbiosis in which a poet's work feeds on a suffering which, in turn, the work elaborates and augments, and again feeds on.

But what I mainly want to question in Mr. Dickey's statement is the assumption that this monstrousness of mind and this suffering are necessary to the art of poetry. There is no denying the evidence that poetry *can* be produced in this way — at least for a while. And history certainly offers examples of unhappy or obsessed or mad poets, but it offers more examples of poets who sang or wrote in the exuberance of sanity, health, wholeness of spirit. And this century's record of poets whose lives have ended in early ruin is probably unique. One instantly credits Anne Sexton's statement that "pain engraves a deeper memory" [10] not because one believes that it invariably does, but because one senses, in the modesty and brevity of the sentence, the probability that it *sometimes* does. But one can only be suspicious of the conclusion of the "afterthought" of Robert Lowell's *Notebook*: "In truth I seem to have felt mostly the joys of living; in remembering, in recording, thanks to the gift of the Muse, it is the pain." [11] One is simply aware of too much joyous poetry that has been the "gift of the Muse," who obviously leaves the ratio of pain and joy to be determined by the poet. To attribute to the Muse a special fondness for pain is to come too close to desiring and cultivating the pain. There is, I believe, some currency to the assumption that a fragmented and diseased people can make a whole and healthy art out of their fragmentation and disease. It has not yet been done. Yeats says that "neither scholars nor the populace have sung or read anything generation after generation because of its pain." [12]

*

The danger may not be so much in the overcultivation of sensibility as in its *exclusive* cultivation. Sensibility becomes the inescapable stock in trade of the isolated poet, who is increasingly cut off from both song and story because the nature of these is communal. And isolation, or the sense of isolation, is moving much of our poetry toward the tone, rhythm, and structure of what Mark Strand calls "not overly excited discourse." This is what Denise Levertov calls "an unexampled production of *notations*: poems which tell of things seen or done, but . . . do not impart a sense of the experiencing of seeing or doing, or of the *value* of such experience . . ." And she says that "the lack of a unifying intelligence, of the implicit presence of an interpreting spirit behind the notation, is associated—and not accidentally—with a lack of music." [13]

I find it impossible to believe that song can come from or lead to a sense of isolation. If a poet says, "I vnto my selfe alone will sing," as Spenser does at the beginning of his "Epithalamion," he can only mean that he does so in anticipation of accompaniment or at least of company. A poet who felt assured that he sang to himself alone would soon find his song lapsing diffidently into a "not overly excited discourse" on the subject of isolation, guilt, suffering, death, and oblivion—the self-exploiting autobiography of disconnected sensibility.

Song is natural; we have it in common with animals. It is also traditional; it has to be sung *to* someone, who will have to recognize it as a song. Rhythm is fundamental to it, and is its profoundest *reference*. The rhythm of a song or a poem rises, no doubt, in reference to the pulse and breath of the poet, as is often said, but that is still too specialized an accounting; it rises also in reference to daily and seasonal—and surely even longer—rhythms in the life of the poet and in the life that surrounds him. The rhythm of a poem resonates with these larger rhythms that surround it; it fills its environment with sympathetic vibrations. Rhyme, which is a function of rhythm, may suggest this sort of resonance; it marks the coincidences of the rhythm of the structure with the rhythm of the lines, or the coincidences of smaller structures with larger ones, as when the day, the month, and the year all end at the same moment. Song, then, is a force opposed to specialty and to isolation. It is the testimony of the singer's inescapable relation to the world, to the human community, and also, I think, to tradition.

But even more suggestive of the specialization of contemporary poets is their estrangement from storytelling. Typically, one can find this debility cited as a virtue and a goal. In an interview that is in general far more carefully spoken and better considered than most, Galway Kinnell says, "I would like a poem to be able to be free of narrative." One needs to know the reasons that lie behind this statement, but the interview does not produce them. Mr. Kinnell says only that "if a poem could be free of narrative altogether, it would at least open the possibility that some truth could be said directly rather than by parable." [14] But he is never asked the two obvious questions: how this might be possible, and why it might be desirable.

(I acknowledge a certain unfairness, here as earlier, in disagreeing with a poet's statement in the absence of his argument. I assume, however, that the general absence, in these interviews, of the questions that would have produced the arguments is, in itself, an implied point. Or, rather, it implies one or the other of two possible points: (1) that the statements are all so widely credited that there is no apparent need to explain or support them; or (2) that specialization imposes an ethic or etiquette which automatically concedes the virtue of anything whatever that a poet says about poetry.)

Though the suppression of narrative has not been directly advocated, there can be no question that the narrative power of poetry has been in decline for generations, until now it is little more than inadvertent. Our century has produced several poems that poets and readers have called "epic," but both character and story, in the old sense of the terms, are absent from them all. ("Epic," as the word is now often used, seems to mean little more than major or ambitious or long.) That so accomplished a poet as Galway Kinnell now speaks of the suppression of narrative as a goal is, it seems to me, a serious matter, especially as it is only the latest in a series of programs to renew or purify poetry by reducing its means. Why is it necessary for poets to believe, like salesmen, that the new inevitably must replace or destroy the old? Why cannot poetry renew itself and advance into new circumstance by *adding* the new to the old? Why cannot the critical faculty, in poets and critics alike, undertake to see that *the best* of the new is grafted to *the best* of the old? Free verse, for instance, is a diminishment of the competence of poetry if it is seen as *replacing* traditional prosody; it is an enlargement only if it is conceived as an addition. Freedom from narrative is a diminishment—it is not even a freedom—unless it is included with the capability of narrative among the live possibilities of poetry. To attempt to advance by more taking away is not to bring into view a renewed and newly powerful art. It heads us instead toward what Mr. Kinnell himself warns against: "the other possibility, that to exist at all poetry will simply give up its old ambitions and adapt itself to what is, that it will simply become the expression of a reality from which all trace of the sacred has been removed."

But this weakening of narrative in poetry—whether by policy, indifference, or debility—may be one of the keys to what is wrong with us, both as poets and as people. It is indicative of a serious lack of interest, first, in action, and second, in *responsible* action. Muir said that "the story, although it is our story, is disappearing from poetry." And he said, "The old story . . . followed some figure—Odysseus, or Ruth, or King David—through time; and it remains the most pure image that we have of temporal life, tracing the journey which we shall take." Narrative poetry records, contemplates, hands down the actions of the past. Poetry has a responsibility to remember and to preserve and reveal the truth about these actions. But it also has a complementary responsibility that is equally public: to help to preserve and to clarify the *possibility* of responsible action. Ezra Pound, perhaps more than anyone else in our time, insisted on this as the social value of "the damned and despised *litterati*. When their work goes rotten . . . when their very medium, the very essence of their work, the application of word to thing goes rotten, i.e. becomes slushy and inexact, or excessive or bloated, the whole machinery of social and of individual thought and order goes to pot." [15] The word *order* as used here, clearly refers to the possibility of responsible *action*, the possibility of good work.

But our malaise, both in our art and in our lives, is that we have lost sight of the possibility of right or responsible action. Publicly, we have delegated our capacity to act to men who are capable of action only because they cannot think. Privately, as in much of our poetry, we communicate by ironic or cynical *allusions* to that debased tale of futility, victimization, and defeat, which we seem to have elected to be our story. The prevailing tendency, in poetry and out, is to see people not as actors, but as sufferers. John Berryman's dream songs, brilliant as they sometimes are, what are they but the mortifications of a splendid intelligence helpless before its salient occasions? To how great an extent is modern poetry the record of highly refined sensibilities that could think or feel but not do? And must not this passiveness of the poetic sensibility *force* its withdrawal into the world of words where, for want of the sustenance of action, it becomes despondent and self-destructive? "Poems," wrote Mrs. Randall Jarrell, "flew at him . . . until just words beat at his head like many wings." [16]

In the last ten years there has been a reaction against this passivity. But for the most part this has produced only protest, which is either a gesture and not an action at all, or a negative action which either repudiates or opposes. The shallowness of protest is in this negativity; it is also in the short-winded righteousness by which it condemns evils for which it accepts no responsibility. In itself, protest implies no discipline and no correction. "A public man," Edwin Muir wrote, "is a man who is entitled to be listened to by the public; a great public man is one who can tell his public on occasion what he thinks of them, knowing that they will listen. This was the position which Yeats achieved, alone among the poets of his time." That we have no poets who are, in that sense, public persons suggests even more forcibly the weakness of our poetry of protest. In his protest the poet is speaking publicly, but not as a spokesman; he is only one outraged citizen *speaking at* other citizens who do not know him, whom he does not know, and with whom he does not identify. The tone of self-righteousness is the inevitable way of accepting and bearing the burden of this circumstance.

*

In "Poets without Laurels," Mr. Ransom holds that the specialization of poetry was "inevitable" because of the specialization of the age, though he ventures that "the modern program, on the whole, is not the one under which men maintain their best health and spirits." Muir, on the other hand, does not look upon the alienation of poets from their audience as inevitable. *The Estate of Poetry* is remarkable for the practicality of its purpose; it faces up to the social and historical context of the problem, and then it argues toward a solution. "Public indifference may be expected to continue, but perhaps the audience will increase when poetry loses what obscurity is left in it by attempting greater themes, for great themes have to be treated clearly. A great theme greatly treated might still put poetry back in its old place." And at the end of his book Muir wrote, "There remains the temptation for poets to turn inward into poetry, to lock themselves into a hygienic prison where they speak only to one another, and to the critic . . . In the end a poet must create his audience and to do that he must turn outward."

*

It may be that poets can make this outward turn and regain the great themes only by taking up again their old interest in action — by renewing the knowledge and meaning of actions known from the past, and by considering the possibility of *right* action now and in the future. Perhaps they will have to repudiate these purely negative actions by which we dissociate ourselves from other people. It is certain that there are better actions. There are actions worthy of the patience and work of whole lives — actions, even, that no whole life can complete — that involve the lives of people in the lives of places and communities. Without such actions, both in life and in art, the consciousness of our people will be fragmentary. How can we explain what Berryman called "the mysterious late excellence" of William Carlos Williams, if not by his community life as a doctor, which carried his art again and again to the test and the renewal of action? And must not the late excellence of Yeats have been indebted to his passionate involvement in the fate of Ireland?

We would be ungrateful and stupid to turn our backs on the work of inward-turned poets. That work contains much of value that we need to cherish and learn from. It is only necessary to understand that that work has flourished upon, and has fostered, a grievous division between life and work, as have virtually all the other specialized disciplines of our time, and that that division has made it possible for work to turn upon and exploit and destroy life.

There is in reality no such choice as Yeats's "Perfection of the life, or of the work." The decision to sacrifice either one for the sake of the other becomes ultimately the fatal disease of both. The division implied by this proposed choice is destructive because it is based upon a misconception of the relation between work and life. The perfections of work rise out of, and commune with and in turn inform, the perfections of life — as Yeats himself knew and as other poems of his testify. The *use* of life to perfect work is an evil of the specialized intellect. It makes of the most humane of disciplines an exploitative industry.

(1975)

Notes

1. *The Ohio Review*, Spring 1973.

2. *The Ohio Review*, Winter 1972.

3. *American Poetry Review*, November–December 1972.

4. Mary McGrory, "The Dean Story," in the Louisville *Courier-Journal*, May 16, 1973.

5. *The Southern Review*, Summer 1973.

6. *The Ohio Review*, Fall 1971.

7. *The Ohio Review*, Spring 1972.

8. "Some Notes on Organic Form," *The Poet in the World*.

9. *Playboy*, November 1973.

10. *The Paris Review*, number 52.

11. Third edition, 1970.

12. "A General Introduction for My Work," *Essays and Introductions*.

13. "Great Possessions," *The Poet in the World*.

14. *The Ohio Review*, Fall 1972.

15. "How to Read," *Literary Essays of Ezra Pound*.

16. "The Group of Two," in Lowell, et al., *Randall Jarrell 1914–1965*.

17. For one reply to this polemic, see Philip Levine, "Letters from a Young Poet," *Antaeus* 30/31 (Spring 1978), pp. 390–93. (Editor's note.)

II. PRACTICE: The Poet's Work

Marianne Moore

Poetry

I, too, dislike it: there are things that are important beyond all
      this fiddle.
  Reading it, however, with a perfect contempt for it, one
      discovers in
  it after all, a place for the genuine.
    Hands that can grasp, eyes
    that can dilate, hair that can rise
      if it must, these things are important not because a

high-sounding interpretation can be put upon them but because
      they are
  useful. When they become so derivative as to become un-
      intelligible,
  the same thing may be said for all of us, that we
    do not admire what
    we cannot understand: the bat
      holding on upside down or in quest of something to

eat, elephants pushing, a wild horse taking a roll, a tireless wolf
      under
  a tree, the immovable critic twitching his skin like a horse that
      feels a flea, the base-
  ball fan, the statistician—
    nor is it valid
      to discriminate against 'business documents and

school-books'; all these phenomena are important. One must make
    a distinction
  however: when dragged into prominence by half poets, the
    result is not poetry,
  nor till the poets among us can be
    'literalists of
    the imagination'—above
      insolence and triviality and can present

for inspection, imaginary gardens with real toads in them, shall we
    have
  it. In the meantime, if you demand on the one hand,
  the raw material of poetry in
    all its rawness and
    that which is on the other hand
      genuine, then you are interested in poetry.

Note

Diary of Tolstoy (Dutton), p. 84. "Where the boundary between prose
and poetry lies, I shall never be able to understand. The question is
raised in manuals of style, yet the answer to it lies beyond me. Poetry is
verse: prose is not verse. Or else poetry is everything with the exception
of business documents and school books."

Antonio Machado

from Notes on Poetry

IN THESE NOTES on poetry which I now publish I am perhaps responding to objections which certain critics have made to my work, or rather, to my intentions, to the aesthetic ideology which is at times latent or implicit in my books, at times explicit. But it is not my purpose to respond to these objections in order to defend my own cause, so much as it is to expound some general notions about lyric poetry which have been with me in the periods of my most intense production.

I am pleased to record—in order to avoid any suspicion on the part of professional critics—that to the literary world of my time I am indebted for praise which outstrips my merits, and that I do not believe I have ever been the target of malicious criticism but, on the contrary, the object of affection and sympathy. For to the extent that I can see into myself, I think that my words must be clear of any rancor toward my literary neighbor, of any resentment or spite, unless there are in my spirit zones of dissatisfaction so deep that they escape a sincere self-inquiry.

Nor will you find in these notes that firmness and certainty of one who, when he thinks, thinks in passing that he thinks the truth. On the contrary, I suspect that if I had a more vigorous mind, gifted with more convolutions and associational paths, greater culture, and habits of greater continuity in discourse, I might have reached conclusions very different from those I offer here. The evidence I have for this has imposed a bit of temerity and laxity on my writing. One would not say that I am myself entirely convinced. Nor do I aspire very much to convince.

"And so?" I will be asked. I well understand that these notes might have remained unpublished. But every artist — every worker, I should say — has a philosophy of work, reflections on the totality of that labor to which, as master or apprentice, he dedicates himself. Why conceal it from the eyes of one's neighbor? This philosophy, like the work itself, is owed to others.

Segovia, August 1, 1924

Vergil

If I were forced to choose a favorite poet, I would choose Vergil. Because of his *Eclogues?* No. His *Georgics?* No. The *Aeneid?* No.

1. Because in his own poems he gave a place to many beautiful lines from other poets, without taking the trouble to disguise them.
2. Because he wanted to destroy that marvel, the *Aeneid.*
3. For his great love of nature.
4. For his great love of books.

On Imagery in the Lyric Poem

(In the margin of a book by Vicente Huidobro)

The objections we may raise against a lyric which is concerned only to create images are so many and come so quickly to mind that I am almost inclined to skip over them, to forgo them entirely, believing that their obviousness will have been apparent with surpassing frequency to the new poets. And, this being so, the decent thing in criticism would be to seek out the new reasons which may justify this pertinacious way of seeing things, so opposed to my own, before taking up the blustering office of a mere repeater of old ideas (which the newest poets know and disdain already).

However, the new reasons cannot be, if they are anything at all, a creation *ex nihilo* of pure reason, but a superseding of the old. Why then not record, without undue tediousness, what twenty-five years ago I thought about the use of metaphor? Thus we may perhaps see the new reasons arise from the old, thanks to the immanent dialectic of all thinking.

My opinion was the following: metaphors are nothing in themselves. They have no value except as a means of indirect expression of that which is missing in the *omnibus* language. If speaking and feeling were perfectly commensurate, the use of metaphors would be not only superfluous, but injurious to expression. Mallarmé glimpsed this truth. He saw rather clearly and put it explicitly: *Parler n'a trait a la réalité des choses que commercialement* (Speech deals with the reality of things only as a business matter); but in his poetry and even in his precepts one notes a superstitious belief in the magic power of enigma. This is the really weak aspect of his work. To create enigmas artificially is as impossible as to attain absolute truths. Yes, one can manufacture mysterious trinkets, little dolls which have, hidden in their bellies, something which will rattle when they are shaken. But enigmas are not of human confection; reality imposes them, and it is there, where they are, that a reflective mind will seek them out in the desire to penetrate them, not to play at amusing itself with them. Only a trivial spirit, an intelligence limited to the radius of its own sensations, can amuse itself by confusing concepts with metaphors, creating obscurities by the suppression of the logical nexus, turning common thought upside down in order to switch wineskins without changing the wine. To suppress the direct names of things when things have direct names—what idiocy! But Mallarmé also knew—and this was his strength—that there are profound realities which lack names, and that the language we employ to understand each other as men expresses only what is conventional, what is objective—by "objective" meaning here "that which is empty of subjectivity," or in other words the abstract terms on which men can agree by eliminating all individual psychic content. In lyric poetry, images and metaphors are therefore proper when they are employed to supply those missing proper names and unique concepts which are required to express the intuitive, never in order to clothe anew the generic and the conventional. Good poets are spare in their use of metaphor; but their metaphors are at times true creations.

In Saint John of the Cross, perhaps the most profound Spanish lyric poet, the metaphor never appears except when feeling overflows logical channels, in deeply emotional moments. For example:

En la noche dichosa,	In that happy night,
en secreto, que nadie me veía,	And secretly, for no one saw me,
ni yo miraba cosa,	Nor did I see any thing,
sin otra luz ni guía	With no light nor guide
sino la que en el corazón ardía	But that which glowed in my heart

The image appears through a sudden increment in the rush of impassioned sentiment, and once created it is in turn creative and engenders, by its emotive content, the following stanza:

Aquesta me guiaba	that [light] guided me
más cierto que la luz del mediodía	More surely than the light of midday

How far we are from the motley imagery of the conceptual and Baroque poets, who appear later, when lyric poetry has in reality already died!

On the Use of Images in the Lyric

In appearance, at least, the new art of poetry in almost all its manifestations seems to have lost that faith in its own importance which it had in earlier centuries. This phenomenon truly began at the inception of the modern age — Ariosto in Italy, Cervantes in Spain and in the entire world. But in the nineteenth century, with the Romantics, and afterward with the symbolist lyric and above all in Wagner's music, art reached, perhaps, the zenith of its illusion of importance. But it can be said that today art itself seeks a subordinate position, that it no longer pretends to be taken very seriously. Perhaps this is an unconscious talent, a wisdom which tries to preserve art at the cost of giving up art's sway. It is worth noting the fact, in any case.

This phenomenon, which can be observed in the most recent writers, is of great importance to lyric poetry. When the poet doubts that the center of the universe lies in his own heart, that his spirit is an overflowing fountain, a focus which irradiates creative energy capable of informing and even of deforming the world around him, then the spirit of the poet wanders disoriented again among objects. He doubts their emotive value, and with this lack of esteem for the subject he falls into the fetishism of things. Images no longer attempt to express the poet's intimate feelings, because he himself holds the latter in low esteem, indeed is almost ashamed of them. Images pretend to be trans-subjective, to have the value of things themselves. But if this devaluation of the internal allows the poet any introspection, he will understand that, at the same time, the world of things has itself been devalued, because it was those very sentiments, already absent or declining, which had imparted all magic to the exterior world. Things materialize, disperse, are freed from the cordial link which beforehand had tamed them, and now seem to invade and beseige the poet, to lose their respect for him, to laugh in his face. In the midst of his image-bazaar, the poet senses his inner failure, laughs at himself, and, as a consequence, lends his creations no other value but that of mechanical toys — good, at best, for alleviating childish ennui.

The deeper fact worth noting, of which the latest writing is only an external sign, is simply the evolution of affective values. We are living in a period of profound crisis. Hearts are disoriented, which means that they are searching for their bearings. The art of this epoch, its lyric poetry above all, will be at least in appearance a subordinate or retarded activity.

On Poetry

When Homer says "the hollow ship," he is not describing any given ship, but simply presenting us with a definition of a ship and at the same time a way of looking at ships, whether they are propelled by oars, steam, or ultraviolet rays. Is the Homeric ship beyond space and time? As you wish. For me, it is only important to establish that any sailor will recognize it as his own. Phoenicians, Greeks, Normans, Venetians, Portuguese, and Spaniards have sailed in the hollow ship to which Homer referred, and in it all the peoples of the earth will continue to sail.

When modern art does away with the defining adjective or the generic scheme, in order to give us the living sensation of a unique object or the momentary trembling of an unusual soul, it makes too great a sacrifice. Too great a sacrifice because the enterprise is bound to fail. Let us not forget that the generic image has an esthetic value. Simply because it is an image, its logical aspect, which is of a truncated nature, is no obstacle to its speaking directly to our feelings, if in fact not quite as acutely as the direct vision of the unique object.

The psychologically immediate—intuition itself—whose expression tempts the lyric poet of all epochs, is certainly something unique which wanders restlessly as long as it cannot find a logical frame in our spirit in which to inscribe itself. But in order to be recognized as the poetic *sine qua non* which it is, it requires the ghostly background of familiar, generic images against which its uniqueness can stand out.

And let these words not be taken as a precept of merely sensational effects. That our interior world might contain a few living blossoms among all the dried ones is nothing but a philosopher's metaphor, as imprecise as a poet's theorem. Imprecise and, in part, erroneous, because nothing in our psyche reminds us of an herbarium. But let us accept whatever truth it has. Let us not try to be either more original or more childish than in fact we are.

*

The anecdotal, the documentary of the human, is not poetic in itself. This was precisely my judgment twenty years ago. In my "Los cantos de los niños," written in 1898 (published in 1904 in *Soledades*), I proclaim the right of the lyric to *relate* pure emotion, eliminating the totality of the human anecdote. *Soledades* was the first Spanish book in which the anecdotal was entirely proscribed. Thus, in anticipation, I agreed with the most recent aesthetic. But the coincidence of my then purpose went no farther than this abolition of the anecdotal.

I am very far from those poets who try to manipulate pure images (free from any concept [!] and also free of emotion) by subjecting them to a mechanical and capricious hustle and bustle, without allowing any emotion to enter in.

*

Beneath the motley imagery of the newest poets one senses an arbitrary game of concepts, not of intuitions. This may all be very new (if indeed it is) and very ingenious, but it is not lyric poetry. The most absurd fetishism into which a poet can fall is the cult of metaphors.

166   ANTONIO MACHADO

El adjetivo y el nombre,	The adjective and the noun,
remansos del agua limpia,	Clear pools of still water,
son accidentes del verbo	Are accidents of the verb
en la gramática lírica,	In the poetic grammar,
del Hoy que será Mañana,	Of the Today that will be Tomorrow,
y el Ayer que es Todavía.	And the Yesterday that is still to be.

That was my aesthetic in 1902. It has nothing to do with the poetics of Verlaine. It was simply an attempt to place the lyric inside time and, as far as possible, outside the spatial.

Del pretérito imperfecto	From the imperfect preterite
brotó el romance en Castilla.	Sprang the Castilian *romance.*

Classical poetry in an eternal present — that is, outside time — is essentially substantive and adjectival. Classical images are definitions, concepts. But on the other hand, Hellenic verse, always defining, has nothing to do, as many geese opine, with the academic and the Neoclassical.

The diamond is cold, but it is a work of fire, and of its experience there would be much to say.

June 15, 1914

Problems of the Lyric

We do not say much, nor do we say nearly enough, when we hold that it is sufficient for the poet to feel strongly and deeply, and to express his feeling clearly. In affirming this we are assuming, without even having mentioned them, that a great many problems are already resolved.

Feelings are not the creation of the individual subject, a sincere [*cordial*] elaboration of the "I" out of materials from the exterior world. They always contain a collaboration with a "You" — that is, with other subjects. One cannot arrive at this simple formula: my heart, confronting a landscape, produces a feeling; and once it is produced, I communicate it to my neighbor by means of language. My heart, confronting a landscape, would barely be able to feel cosmic terror, because even this elemental feeling requires the anguish of other hearts caught in the middle of a natural world not fully understood. My feeling in the face of the exterior world, which I am here calling a landscape, does not arise without an invigorating atmosphere. My feeling, in sum, is not exclusively mine, but rather *ours*. Without going out of myself, I note that in my feeling other feelings are vibrating as well, and that my heart is always singing in a chorus, although its own voice may be, for me, the best. That it also be the best for others — *that* is the problem of lyrical expression.

A second problem: in order to express my feelings I have language. But language is already much *less mine* than are my feelings. For after all I have had to acquire it, learn it from others. Before being *ours* — because it will never be *mine* alone — it was theirs; it belonged to that world which is neither subjective nor objective, to that third world to which psychology has not yet paid sufficient attention, the world of *other I's*.

Juan Ramón Jiménez, that great Andalusian poet, is following a path which must eventually attenuate the fervor of his early admirers. His lyrics are more and more Baroque; that is, more conceptual and at the same time less instinctual. Criticism has not pointed this out. In his latest book, *Estío*, images abound, but they are the cloak of concepts.

Madrid, May 1, 1917

On Poetry

Every poet should create for himself a metaphysics which he need not expound, but which will lie implicit in his work. This metaphysics need not be that which he expresses in his most profound thoughts, but rather that which properly frames his poetry. But it should not therefore be false, much less arbitrary. Speculative metaphysical thought is by nature antinomic; but action — and poetry is action — obliges one to choose provisionally one of the terms of the antinomy. On one of these terms — imposed rather than freely chosen — the poet constructs his metaphysics.

In a philosophy there is no right to postulate either the homogeneity or the heterogeneity of being; rather, a recognition of the Kantian antinomy imposes itself. But the poet, whose thinking is deeper than that of the mere speculative philosopher, cannot see, in what logically is pure antinomy, only the play of reason —

which is necessarily contradictory when it functions in a void of intuitions—but rather discovers in himself an invigorating* faith, a deep belief, which is never simply a perfect balance of equal weights of thesis and antithesis, but is weighed down on one side or the other. The poet understands that behind the logical antinomy the heart has taken sides. Once he knows this, it is proper for him to choose either thesis or antithesis, according to which one agrees with his sincere* orientation, in order to make of the chosen side the postulate of his metaphysics.

Segovia, 1923

Translated by Reginald Gibbons

---

* In both instances Machado uses the word *"cordial,"* which aside from suggesting pleasantness and affection, is a pun on Latin *cor* (Spanish *corazón*). "Sincere" is an admittedly weak stab at this constellation of associations, but "cordial" in English has lost all association with "heart." Machado earlier says that "things materialize, disperse, are freed from the cordial link which beforehand had tamed them."

from *Notes on Poetry*   169

Paul Valéry

A Poet's Notebook

POETRY. Is it impossible, given time, care, skill, and desire, to proceed in an orderly way to arrive at poetry?

To end by *hearing* exactly what one wished to hear by means of a skillful and patient management of that same desire?

You want to write a particular poem, with a certain effect, more or less, on a particular subject: first of all, you have images of various *orders.*

Some are people, landscapes, points of view, attitudes; others are undefined voices, notes . . .

So far, words are only placards.

Other words or scraps of phrases have no particular use, but want to be used; meanwhile they drift.

I see everything and I see nothing.

Other images make me see quite different conditions. They seem to show the states of mind of an individual undergoing the poem, his attention, his suspense, his expectations, his presentiments, all of which must be created, played with, disarmed, or satisfied.

I have, therefore, several levels of ideas, some of result, others of execution; and the idea of uncertainty dominates them all; and, finally, there is the idea of my own expectation, ready to seize on the already realized, writable elements that are or will be offered, even those not confined to the subject.

It can happen, then, that the germ is no more than a word or a fragment of a sentence, a line that seeks and toils to create its own justification and so gives rise to a context, a subject, a man, etc.

What does reflection draw from the subject or the germ?

Reflection is a restraint on chance, a chance to which one adapts a *convention*. And what is a play of chance if not that addition which creates an expectation, gives a *different* importance to the various faces of dice?

These faces are equal from one point of view, unequal from another . . . Where one loses, another wins. This idea or that expression which came into the mind of Racine and was rejected by him as a loss was seized on by Hugo as a gain.

*

So the poet at work is an expectation. He is a transition within a man—which makes him sensitive to certain terms of his own development: those which reward this expectation by conforming with the convention. He reconstructs what he desired. He reconstructs *quasi-mechanisms capable of giving back to him the energy they cost him and more* (for here the principles are apparently violated). *His ear speaks to him.*

We wait for the unexpected word—which cannot be foreseen but must be awaited. We are the first to hear it.

To hear? But that means *to speak.* One understands what one hears only if one has said it oneself from another motive.

To speak is to hear.

What is concerned, then, is a *twofold* attention. The state of being able to produce what is perceived admits of more or of less by reason of the number of elementary functions involved.

And this is on account of memory. This demonstrates that memory and understanding—and imagining—are intimately linked.

If a difficult discourse is addressed to us, we can repeat the words rather than the sentences; we retain the propositions rather than their order, and understanding is therefore memory in action. It implies a maximum that can only be a maximum of memory.

Understanding is a *closed* thing. To understand A is to be able to reconstruct A.

And to imagine is only to understand oneself.

One gets the idea of a reversible apparatus, like a telephone or a dynamo.

It is as though the auditive current reached a point where the waves would be thrown back onto the interruption of, the broken end of, the transmitting line.

"Off" and "On" cannot coexist.

Silence and attention are incompatible. The circuit must be closed.

The aim, then, is to create the kind of silence to which the *beautiful* responds. Or the pure line of verse, or the luminous idea . . . Then the line seems to be born of itself, born of necessity—which is precisely my state—and finds that it is memory. Or rather, is at once the uniting element of memory, act, and perception, a fixed novelty and yet an organized, repeatable function; an energy and a generator of energy. At once astonishment and function . . . Exception, chance, *and* act.

*

The passage from prose to verse, from speech to song, from walking to dancing—a moment that is at once action and dream.

The aim of the dance is not to transport me from one point to another; nor of pure verse, nor of song.

But they exist to make me more present to myself, more entirely given up to myself, expending my energy to no useful end, replacing myself—and all things and sensations have no other value. A particular movement sets them free, and infinitely mobile, infinitely present, they hasten to serve as fuel to a fire. Hence metaphors, those stationary movements!

Song is more real than level speech, for the latter is of value only by a substitution and a deciphering operation, whereas the former stirs and provokes imitation, arouses desire, causes a vibration as though its variation and substance were the law and matter of my being. It stands in my stead; but level speech is on the surface, it sets out external things, divides and labels them.

One can get a wonderful conception of this difference by observing the efforts and inventions of those who have tried to make music speak and language sing or dance.

*

If you want to write verse and you begin with thoughts, you begin with prose.

In prose one can draw up a plan and *follow* it!

*

Poetry. Those ideas which cannot be put into prose are put into verse. If one finds them in prose, they demand verse and have the air of verse that has not yet been able to take shape. What ideas are these?

They are ideas that are possible only in very lively, rhythmic, or spontaneous movements of thought.

Metaphor, for example, marks in its naïve principle a *groping*, a hesitation between several different expressions of one thought, an explosive incapacity that surpasses the *necessary* and *sufficient* capacity. Once one has gone over and made the thought rigorously precise, restricted it to a single object, then the metaphor will be effaced, and prose will reappear.

These procedures, observed and cultivated for their own sake, have become the object of a study and an employment: poetry. The result of this analysis is that poetry's special aim and own true sphere is the expression of what cannot be expressed in the finite functions of words. The proper object of poetry is what has no single name, what in itself provokes and demands more than one expression. That which, for the expression of its unity, arouses a plurality of expressions.

*

The habit of long labor at poetry has accustomed me to consider all speech and all writing as work in progress that can nearly always be taken up again and altered; and I consider *work itself* as having its own value, generally much superior to that which the crowd attaches only to the *product*.

No doubt the product is the thing that lasts and has, or should have, a meaning of itself and an independent existence; but the acts from which it proceeds, in so far as they *react* on their author, form within him another *product*, which is a man more skillful and more in possession of his domain of memory.

A work is never necessarily *finished*, for he who made it is never complete, and the power and agility he has drawn from it confer on him just the power to improve it, and so on . . . *He draws from it what is needed to efface and remake it.* This is how a *free* artist, at least, should regard things. And he ends by considering as satisfactory only those works which have taught him something more.

This point of view is not that of ordinary art lovers. It could never suit them.

But I have written all this by following, from the beginning, a different road from the one I thought to take from that beginning.

I meant to talk of philosophers—and to philosophers.

I wanted to show that it would be of the greatest profit to them to practice this labor of poetry which leads insensibly to the study of word combinations, not so much through the conformity of the meanings of these groups to an idea or thought that one thinks should be *expressed,* as, on the contrary, through their effects once they are formed, from which one chooses.

Generally one tries to "express one's thought," that is, to pass from an *impure* form, a mixture of all the resources of the mind, to a *pure* form, that is, one solely verbal and organized, amounting to a system of arranged acts or contrasts.

But the art of poetry is alone in leading one to envisage pure forms in themselves.

*

Any man might see "poetry" in what he does, feels, etc. . . . It does not reside in any particular objects. And many men feel poetically what they encounter in their life and their business.

But this does not make them poets. Those who think it does are merely confusing effects produced with producing effects, the unique or intense vision and the means of provoking or reproducing it. The engineer is not strong like his machine. He is strong differently, quite differently.

From this point, it is easy to understand that if the poetic impression is not linked to any special object, at least poetic fabrication can be. Not in any absolute way, but each literary age and each *fabricator* relies upon certain ideas or forms poetically ready-made, whose use at once simplifies the poetic problem, allowing him combinations of greater complexity and of a higher order, like a language he knows well. Etc. . . .

*

Stupidity and poetry. There are subtle relations between these two categories. The category of stupidity and that of poetry.

*

Thought must be hidden in verse like the nutritive essence in fruit. It is nourishing but seems merely delicious. One perceives pleasure only, but one receives a substance. Enchantment, that is the nourishment it conveys. The passage is sweet.

*

Obscurity, a product of two factors. If my mind is richer, more rapid, freer, more disciplined than yours, neither you nor I can do anything about it.

*

Not the least of the pleasures of rhyme is the rage it inspires in those poor people who think they know something more important than a *convention.* They hold the naïve belief that a thought *can* be more profound, more organic . . . than any mere convention.

*

Prose is the kind of work that permits of beginning with the thought of things, with their image or idea, and of ending with *words.* Every time the game begins with language, whenever the mind attacks with words or sentences, prose is born rhythmical, as in oratory. Prose is born without rhythm when it results from a deciphering; it then admits an indefinite series of inner interruptions. All writing that is *rhythmical* and *deliberate* is *artificial;* that is, the apparent spontaneity due to the rhythm has been constructed later, out of a substance incompatible with it during its generation. The words and the music are not by the same author. I mean not of the same moment.

*

"X—— is more poet than artist."
    Does this mean that X—— has more *energy* at his disposal than operations or machines for using it?

*

X—— would like one to believe that a metaphor is a communication from heaven.

A metaphor is *what happens* when one *looks in a certain way*, just as a sneeze is what happens when one looks at the sun.

In what way?—You can feel it. One day, perhaps one will be able to *say* it precisely.

Do this and do that—and behold all the metaphors in the world . . .

*

A poem's worth is its content of *pure poetry*, that is, of extraordinary truth; of perfect adaptation in the sphere of perfect uselessness; of apparent and convincing probability in the production of the improbable.

*

The poet has essentially the "intuition" of a special order of combinations. A certain combination of objects (of thought) which has no value for a normal man, has for him an existence and *makes itself noticed.* It strikes him in the way that a relationship of sounds, separately perceived by an ordinary ear, strikes a musical ear as a relationship—like a contrast of colors, etc.

Sometimes it is a combination of *things,* and this must be *translated;* sometimes one of *words* that will possess the quality already mentioned, and this must be *justified.*

1. Combination of things. He sees figures of a particular order where anyone else sees only what interests a man picked at random.

For this poet a "subject" is that set of relations which can receive or furnish the maximum of things of this kind.

2. Combination of sounds. It must not be forgotten that the poet, unlike the musician, does not start from an existing and already pure collection, which is sound. His scale must be reconstructed each time.

*

In what would the artist's special position consist if he did not consider certain details inviolable? For example, the alternation of masculine and feminine rhymes. No inspiration must be allowed to ignore them. *This* is irritating, *this* is nonsense, but without *this*, everything falls apart, and the poet corrupts the artist, and the arbitrariness of the moment overcomes the arbitrariness of an order superior to the moment.

*

Eternal glory to the inventor of the sonnet. However, although so many beautiful sonnets have been written, the most beautiful is still to be done: it will be the one whose four parts will each fulfill a quite different function from the others, and this progression of differences in the strophes will be well justified by the structure of the discourse as a whole. Sonnets must be written. It is astonishing how much one learns by writing sonnets and poems in set form.

The fruit of these labors is not in them alone. (But poets in general let the best of their efforts go to waste.)

I have always written my verses while observing myself write them, in which respect, perhaps, I have never been exclusively a poet.

—I learned very quickly to distinguish clearly between the reality of thought and the reality of effects.

But without this confusion, is one a poet?

*

Literature is the instrument neither of a whole thought nor of an organized thought.

*

The great interest of classic art is perhaps in the series of transformations it requires to express things while respecting the imposed conditions *sine qua non*.

Problems of putting into verse. This obliges one to consider from a great height what one wishes or is compelled to say.

*

One must not aim at originality, particularly in our time; for everything original is the object of a concentrated aim and a very avid attention that is anxious to exploit the slightest means for distinguishing itself. The result is that what was original in the morning is copied the same evening; and the more conspicuous and new it was in the morning, the more conspicuous and intolerable in the evening is the repetition of the effect one had created. — Despise the old and the new.

*

Synthesis and novelty. One of Virgil's *Eclogues* would be nothing new to present to the reader (although I am not so sure!); but if an eclogue were obtained by methods very different from those of the first century, that might be new. The scent of the rose has been known since there were roses, but to reconstruct it from the molecules COH — that is fairly novel.

I confess once again that work interests me far more than the product of that work.

*

An epic poem is a poem that can be told.

When one *tells* it, one has a bilingual text.

*

Literature. What is "form" for anyone else is "content" for me.

*

Poet. Your kind of verbal materialism.

You can *look down* on novelists, philosophers, and all who are enslaved to words by credulity — who *must* believe that their speech is *real* by its content and signifies some reality. But as for you, you know that the reality of a discourse is only the words and the forms.

(1933)
Translated by Denise Folliot

Hart Crane

General Aims and Theories

WHEN I STARTED WRITING "Faustus and Helen" it was my inten-
tion to embody in modern terms (words, symbols, metaphors) a
contemporary approximation to an ancient human culture or my-
thology that seems to have been obscured rather than illumined
with the frequency of poetic allusions made to it during the last
century. The name of Helen, for instance, has become an all too
easily employed crutch for evocation whenever a poet felt a stitch
in his side. The real evocation of this (to me) very real and abso-
lute conception of beauty seemed to consist in a reconstruction in
these modern terms of the basic emotional attitude toward beauty
that the Greeks had. And in so doing I found that I was really
building a bridge between so-called classic experience and many
divergent realities of our seething, confused cosmos of today,
which has no formulated mythology yet for classic poetic refer-
ence or for religious exploitation.

So I found "Helen" sitting in a street car; the Dionysian revels
of her court and her seduction were transferred to a Metropolitan
roof garden with a jazz orchestra; and the *katharsis* of the fall of
Troy I saw approximated in the recent World War. The impor-
tance of this scaffolding may easily be exaggerated, but it gave me
a series of correspondences between two widely separated worlds
on which to sound some major themes of human speculation—
love, beauty, death, renascence. It was a kind of grafting process
that I shall doubtless not be interested in repeating, but which is

consistent with subsequent theories of mine on the relation of tradition to the contemporary creating imagination.

It is a terrific problem that faces the poet today — a world that is so in transition from a decayed culture toward a reorganization of human evaluations that there are few common terms, general denominators of speech that are solid enough or that ring with any vibration or spiritual conviction. The great mythologies of the past (including the Church) are deprived of enough façade to even launch good raillery against. Yet much of their traditions are operative still — in millions of chance combinations of related and unrelated detail, psychological reference, figures of speech, precepts, etc. These are all a part of our common experience and the terms, at least partially, of that very experience when it defines or extends itself.

The deliberate program, then, of a "break" with the past or tradition seems to me to be a sentimental fallacy . . . The poet has a right to draw on whatever practical resources he finds in books or otherwise about him. He must tax his sensibility and his touchstone of experience for the proper selections of these themes and details, however — and that is where he either stands, or falls into useless archaeology.

I put no particular value on the simple objective of "modernity." The element of the temporal location of an artist's creation is of very secondary importance; it can be left to the impressionist or historian just as well. It seems to me that a poet will accidentally define his time well enough simply by reacting honestly and to the full extent of his sensibilities to the states of passion, experience, and rumination that fate forces on him, firsthand. He must, of course, have a sufficiently universal basis of experience to make his imagination selective and valuable. His picture of the "period," then, will simply be a by-product of his curiosity and the relation of his experience to a postulated "eternity."

I am concerned with the future of America, but not because I think that America has any so-called par value as a state or as a group of people . . . It is only because I feel persuaded that here are destined to be discovered certain as yet undefined spiritual quantities, perhaps a new hierarchy of faith not to be developed so completely elsewhere. And in this process I like to feel myself as a potential factor; certainly I must speak in its terms and what discoveries I may make are situated in its experience.

But to fool oneself that definitions are being reached by merely referring frequently to skyscrapers, radio antennae, steam whistles, or other surface phenomena of our time is merely to paint a photograph. I think that what is interesting and significant will emerge only under the conditions of our submission to, and examination and assimilation of the organic effects on us of, these and other fundamental factors of our experience. It can certainly not be an organic expression otherwise. And the expression of such values may often be as well accomplished with the vocabulary and blank verse of the Elizabethans as with the calligraphic tricks and slang used so brilliantly at times by an impressionist like Cummings.

It may not be possible to say that there is, strictly speaking, any "absolute" experience. But it seems evident that certain aesthetic experience (and this may for a time engross the total faculties of the spectator) can be called absolute, inasmuch as it approximates a formally convincing statement of a conception or apprehension of life that gains our unquestioning assent, and under the conditions of which our imagination is unable to suggest a further detail consistent with the design of the aesthetic whole.

I have been called an "absolutist" in poetry, and if I am to welcome such a label it should be under the terms of the above definition. It is really only a *modus operandi*, however, and as such has been used organically before by at least a dozen poets, such as Donne, Blake, Baudelaire, Rimbaud, etc. I may succeed in defining it better by contrasting it with the impressionistic method. The impressionist is interesting as far as he goes — but his goal has been reached when he has succeeded in projecting certain selected factual details into his reader's consciousness. He is really not interested in the *causes* (metaphysical) of his materials, their emotional derivations, or their utmost spiritual consequences. A kind of retinal registration is enough, along with a certain psychological stimulation. And this is also true of your realist (of the Zola type), and to a certain extent of the classicist, like Horace, Ovid, Pope, etc.

Blake meant these differences when he wrote:

> We are led to believe in a lie
> When we see *with* not *through* the eye.

The impressionist creates only with the eye and for the readiest surface of the consciousness, at least relatively so. If the effect has been harmonious or even stimulating, he can stop there, relinquishing entirely to his audience the problematic synthesis of the details into terms of their own personal consciousness.

It is my hope to go *through* the combined materials of the poem, using our "real" world somewhat as a springboard, and to give the poem *as a whole* an orbit or predetermined direction of its own. I would like to establish it as free from my own personality as from any chance evaluation on the reader's part. (This is, of course, an impossibility, but it is a characteristic worth mentioning.) Such a poem is at least a stab at a truth, and to such an extent may be differentiated from other kinds of poetry and called "absolute." Its evocation will not be toward decoration or amusement, but rather toward a state of consciousness, an "innocence" (Blake) or absolute beauty. In this condition there may be discoverable under new forms certain spiritual illuminations, shining with a morality essentialized from experience directly, and not from previous precepts or preconceptions. It is as though a poem gave the reader as he left it a single, new *word*, never before spoken and impossible to actually enunciate, but self-evident as an active principle in the reader's consciousness henceforward.

As to technical considerations: the motivation of the poem must be derived from the implicit emotional dynamics of the materials used, and the terms of expression employed are often selected less for their logical (literal) significance than for their associational meanings. Via this and their metaphorical interrelationships, the entire construction of the poem is raised on the organic principle of a "logic of metaphor," which antedates our so-called pure logic, and which is the genetic basis of all speech, hence consciousness and thought-extension.

These dynamics often result, I'm told, in certain initial difficulties in understanding my poems. But on the other hand I find them at times the only means possible for expressing certain concepts in any forceful or direct way whatever. To cite two examples: when, in "Voyages" (II), I speak of "adagios of islands," the reference is to the motion of a boat through islands clustered thickly, the rhythm of the motion, etc. And it seems a much more direct and creative statement than any more logical employment of words such as "coasting slowly through the islands," besides ushering in a whole world of music. Similarly in "Faustus and Helen" (III) the speed and tense altitude of an aeroplane are much better suggested by the idea of "nimble blue plateaus" — *implying* the aeroplane and its speed against a contrast of stationary elevated earth. Although the statement is pseudo in relation to formal logic — it *is* completely logical in relation to the truth of the imagination, and there is expressed a concept of speed and space that could not be handled so well in other terms.

In manipulating the more imponderable phenomena of psychic motives, pure emotional crystallizations, etc., I have had to rely even more on these dynamics of inferential mention, and I am doubtless still very unconscious of having committed myself to what seems nothing but obscurities to some minds. A poem like "Possessions" really cannot be technically explained. It must rely (even to a large extent with myself) on its organic impact on the imagination to successfully imply its meaning. This seems to me to present an exceptionally difficult problem, however, considering the real clarity and consistent logic of many of the other poems.

I know that I run the risk of much criticism by defending such theories as I have, but as it is part of a poet's business to risk not only criticism — but folly — in the conquest of consciousness, I can only say that I attach no intrinsic value to what means I use beyond their practical service in giving form to the living stuff of the imagination.

New conditions of life germinate new forms of spiritual articulation. And while I feel that my work includes a more consistent extension of traditional literary elements than many contemporary poets are capable of appraising, I realize that I am utilizing the gifts of the past as instruments principally; and that the voice of the present, if it is to be known, must be caught at the risk of speaking in idioms and circumlocutions sometimes shocking to the scholar and historians of logic. Language has built towers and bridges, but itself is inevitably as fluid as always.

(1937)

Dylan Thomas

Poetic Manifesto

The following are the poet's replies to five questions asked him by a research student in the summer of 1951.

YOU WANT TO KNOW why and how I first began to write poetry, and which poets or kind of poetry I was first moved and influenced by.

To answer the first part of this question, I should say I wanted to write poetry in the beginning because I had fallen in love with words. The first poems I knew were nursery rhymes, and before I could read them for myself I had come to love just the words of them, the words alone. What the words stood for, symbolized, or meant, was of very secondary importance; what mattered was the *sound* of them as I heard them for the first time on the lips of the remote and incomprehensible grownups who seemed, for some reason, to be living in my world. And these words were, to me, as the notes of bells, the sounds of musical instruments, the noises of wind, sea, and rain, the rattle of milk carts, the clopping of hooves on cobbles, the fingering of branches on a windowpane, might be to someone, deaf from birth, who has miraculously found his hearing. I did not care what the words said, overmuch, nor what happened to Jack & Jill & the Mother Goose rest of them; I cared for the shapes of sound that their names, and the words describing their actions, made in my ears; I cared for the colors the words cast on my eyes. I realize that I may be, as I think back all that way, romanticizing my reactions to the simple and beautiful words of those pure poems; but that is all I can honestly remember, however much time might have falsified my memory. I fell in love — that is the only expression I can think of — at once, and am still at the mercy of words, though sometimes now, knowing a little of their behavior very well, I think I can influence them slightly and have even learned to beat them now and then, which they appear to enjoy. I tumbled for words at once. And, when I began to read the nursery rhymes for myself, and, later, to read other verses and ballads, I knew that I had discovered the most important things, to me, that could be ever. There they were, seemingly lifeless, made only of black and white, but out of them, out of their own being, came love and terror and pity and pain and wonder and all the other vague abstractions that make our ephemeral lives dangerous, great, and bearable. Out of them came the gusts and grunts and hiccups and heehaws of the common fun of the earth; and though what the words meant was, in its own way, often deliciously funny enough, so much funnier seemed to me, at that almost forgotten time, the shape and shade and size and noise of the words as they hummed, strummed, jigged, and galloped along. That was the time of innocence; words burst upon me, unencumbered by trivial or portentous association; words were their springlike selves, fresh with Eden's dew, as they flew out of the air. They made their own original associations as they sprang and shone. The words "Ride a cockhorse to Banbury Cross" were as haunting to me, who did not know then what a cockhorse was nor cared a damn where Banbury Cross might be, as, much later, were such lines as John Donne's "Go and catch a falling star, Get with child a mandrake root," which also I could not understand when I first read them. And as I read more and more, and it was not all verse, by any means, my love for the real life of words increased until I knew that I must live *with* them and *in* them, always. I knew, in fact, that I must be a writer of words, and nothing else. The first thing was to feel and know their sound and substance; what I was going to do with those words, what use I was going to make of them, what I was going to *say* through them, would come later. I knew I had to know them most intimately in all their forms and moods, their ups and downs, their chops and changes, their needs and demands. (Here, I am afraid, I am beginning to talk too vaguely. I do not like writing *about* words, because then I often use bad and wrong and stale and woolly words. What I like to do is to treat words as a craftsman does his wood or stone or what-have-you, to hew, carve, mold, coil, polish, and plane them into patterns, sequences, sculptures, fugues of sound expressing some lyrical impulse, some spiritual doubt or conviction, some dimly realized truth I must try to reach and realize.) It was when I was very young, and just at school, that, in my father's study, before homework that was never done, I began to know one kind of writing from another, one kind of goodness, one kind of badness. My first, and greatest, liberty was that of being able to read everything and anything I cared to. I read indiscriminately, and with my eyes hanging out. I could never have dreamt that there were such goings-on in the world between the covers of books, such sandstorms and ice blasts of words, such slashing of humbug, and humbug too, such staggering peace, such enormous laughter, such and so many blinding bright lights breaking across the just-awaking wits and splashing all over the pages in a million bits and pieces all of which were words, words, words, and each of which was alive forever in its own delight and glory and oddity and light. (I must try not to make these supposedly helpful notes as confusing as my poems themselves.) I wrote endless imitations, though I never thought them to be imitations but, rather, wonderfully original things, like eggs laid by tigers. They were imitations of anything I happened to be reading at the time: Sir Thomas Browne, de Quincey, Henry Newbolt, the Ballads, Blake, Baroness Orczy, Marlowe, Chums, the Imagists, the Bible, Poe, Keats, Lawrence, Anon., and Shakespeare. A mixed lot, as you see, and randomly remembered. I tried my callow hand at almost every poetical form. How could I learn the tricks of a trade unless I tried to do them myself? I learned that the bad tricks come easily; and the good ones, which help you to say what you think you wish to say in the most meaningful, moving way, I am still learning. (But in earnest company you must call these tricks by other names, such as technical devices, prosodic experiments, etc.)

The writers, then, who influenced my earliest poems and stories were, quite simply and truthfully, all the writers I was reading at the time, and, as you see from a specimen list higher up the page, they ranged from writers of schoolboy adventure yarns to incomparable and inimitable masters like Blake. That is, when I began, bad writing had as much influence on my stuff as good. The bad influences I tried to remove and renounce bit by bit, shadow by shadow, echo by echo, through trial and error, through delight and disgust and misgiving, as I came to love words more and to hate the heavy hands that knocked them about, the thick tongues that had no feel for their multitudinous tastes, the dull and botching hacks who flattened them out into a colorless and insipid paste, the pedants who made them moribund and pompous as themselves. Let me say that the things that first made me love language and want to work *in* it and *for* it were nursery rhymes and folk tales, the Scottish Ballads, a few lines of hymns, the most famous Bible stories and the rhythms of the Bible, Blake's *Songs of Innocence*, and the quite incomprehensible magical majesty and nonsense of Shakespeare heard, read, and near-murdered in the first forms of my school.

*

You ask me, next, if it is true that three of the dominant influences on my published prose and poetry are Joyce, the Bible, and Freud. (I purposely say my "published" prose and poetry, as in the preceding pages I have been talking about the primary influences upon my very first and forever unpublishable juvenilia.) I cannot say that I have been "influenced" by Joyce, whom I enormously admire and whose *Ulysses* and earlier stories I have read a great deal. I think this Joyce question arose because somebody once, in print, remarked on the closeness of the title of my book of short stories, *Portrait of the Artist As a Young Dog* to Joyce's title, *Portrait of the Artist as a Young Man*. As you know, the name given to innumerable portrait paintings by their artists is "Portrait of the Artist as a Young Man"—a perfectly straightforward title. Joyce used the painting title for the first time as the title of a literary work. I myself made a bit of doggish fun of the *painting* title and, of course, intended no possible reference to Joyce. I do not think that Joyce has had any hand at all in my writing; certainly his *Ulysses* has not. On the other hand, I cannot deny that the shaping of some of my *Portrait* stories might owe something to Joyce's stories in the volume *Dubliners*. But then *Dubliners* was a pioneering work in the world of the short story, and no good story writer since can have failed, in some way, however little, to have benefited by it.

The Bible, I have referred to in attempting to answer your first question. Its great stories of Noah, Jonah, Lot, Moses, Jacob, David, Solomon, and a thousand more, I had, of course, known from very early youth; the great rhythms had rolled over me from the Welsh pulpits; and I read, for myself, from Job and Ecclesiastes; and the story of the New Testament is part of my life. But I have never sat down and studied the Bible, never consciously echoed its language, and am, in reality, as ignorant of it as most brought-up Christians. All of the Bible that I use in my work is remembered from childhood, and is the common property of all who were brought up in English-speaking communities. Nowhere, indeed, in all my writing, do I use any knowledge which is not commonplace to any literate person. I *have* used a few difficult words in early poems, but they are easily looked up and were, in any case, thrown into the poems in a kind of adolescent showing-off which I hope I have now discarded.

And that leads me to the third "dominant influence": Sigmund Freud. My only acquaintance with the theories and discoveries of Dr. Freud has been through the work of novelists who have been excited by his casebook histories, of popular newspaper scientific-potboilers who have, I imagine, vulgarized his work beyond recognition, and of a few modern poets, including Auden, who have attempted to use psychoanalytical phraseology and theory in some of their poems. I have read only one book of Freud's, *The Interpretation of Dreams*, and do not recall having being influenced by it in any way. Again, no honest writer today can possibly avoid being influenced by Freud through his pioneering work into the Unconscious and by the influence of those discoveries on the scientific, philosophic, and artistic work of his contemporaries; but not, by any means, necessarily through Freud's own writing.

*

To your third question—do I deliberately utilize devices of rhyme, rhythm, and word-formation in my writing—I must, of course, answer with an immediate yes. I am a painstaking, conscientious, involved, and devious craftsman in words, however unsuccessful the result so often appears; and to whatever wrong uses I may apply my technical paraphernalia, I use everything and anything to make my poems work and move in the directions I want them to: old tricks, new tricks, puns, portmanteau words, paradox, allusion, paranomasia, paragram, catachresis, slang, assonantal rhymes, vowel rhymes, sprung rhythm. Every device there is in language is there to be used if you will. Poets have got to enjoy themselves sometimes, and the twistings and convolutions of words, the inventions and contrivances, are all part of the joy that is part of the painful, voluntary work.

*

Your next question asks whether my use of combinations of words to create something new, "in the Surrealist way," is according to a set formula or is spontaneous.

There is a confusion here, for the Surrealists' set formula was to juxtapose the unpremeditated.

Let me make it clearer if I can. The Surrealists (that is, super-realists, or those who work *above* realism) were a coterie of painters and writers in Paris, in the nineteen twenties, who did not believe in the conscious selection of images. To put it in another way: they were artists who were dissatisfied with both the realists (roughly speaking, those who tried to put down in paint and words an actual representation of what they imagined to be the real world in which they lived) and the impressionists, who, roughly speaking again, were those who tried to give an impression of what they imagined to be the real world. The Surrealists wanted to dive into the subconscious mind, the mind below the conscious surface, and dig up their images from there without the aid of logic or reason, and put them down, illogically and unreasonably, in paint and words. The Surrealists affirmed that, as three quarters of the mind was submerged, it was the function of the artist to gather his material from the greatest submerged mass of the mind rather than from that quarter of the mind which, like the tip of an iceberg, protruded from the subconscious sea. One method the Surrealists used in their poetry was to juxtapose words and images that had no rational relationship; and out of this they hoped to achieve a kind of subconscious, or dream, poetry that would be truer to the real, imaginative world of the mind, mostly submerged, than is the poetry of the conscious mind, which relies upon the rational and logical relationship of ideas, objects, and images.

This is, very crudely, the credo of the Surrealists, and one with which I profoundly disagree. I do not mind from where the images of a poem are dragged up: drag them up, if you like, from the nethermost sea of the hidden self; but before they reach paper, they must go through all the rational processes of the intellect. The Surrealists, on the other hand, put their words down together on paper exactly as they emerge from chaos; they do not shape these words or put them in order; to them, chaos is the shape and order. This seems to me to be exceedingly presumptuous; the Surrealists imagine that whatever they dredge from their subconscious selves and put down in paint or in words must, essentially, be of some interest or value. I deny this. One of the arts of the poet is to make comprehensible and articulate what might emerge from subconscious sources; one of the great main uses of the intellect is to *select*, from the amorphous mass of subconscious images, those that will best further his imaginative purpose, which is to write the best poem he can.

*

And question five is, God help us, what is my definition of Poetry?

I, myself, do not read poetry for anything but pleasure. I read only the poems I like. This means, of course, that I have to read a lot of poems I don't like before I find the ones I do, but when I *do* find the ones I do, then all I can say is "Here they are," and read them to myself for pleasure.

Read the poems you like reading. Don't bother whether they're "important" or if they'll live. What does it matter what poetry *is*, after all? If you want a definition of poetry, say, "Poetry is what makes me laugh or cry or yawn, what makes my toenails twinkle, what makes me want to do this or that or nothing," and let it go at that. All that matters about poetry is the enjoyment of it, however tragic it may be. All that matters is the eternal movement behind it, the vast undercurrent of human grief, folly, pretension, exaltation, or ignorance, however unlofty the intention of the poem.

You can tear a poem apart to see what makes it technically tick, and say to yourself, when the works are laid out before you, the vowels, the consonants, the rhymes or rhythms, "Yes, this is *it*. This is why the poem moves me so. It is because of the craftsmanship." But you're back again where you began.

You're back with the mystery of having been moved by words. The best craftsmanship always leaves holes and gaps in the works of the poem so that something that is *not* in the poem can creep, crawl, flash, or thunder in.

The joy and function of poetry is, and was, the celebration of man, which is also the celebration of God.

William Carlos Williams

Projective Verse *and* The Practice

Projective Verse

Until we have reorganized the basis of our thinking in any category, we cannot understand our errors. An advance of estimable proportions is made by looking at the poems as a field rather than an assembly of more or less ankylosed lines—well illustrated by Charles Olson in the following:

> PROJECTIVE VERSE
> (projectile
> (percussive
> (prospective
>
> vs.
>
> The NON-Projective
> *Charles Olson*
>
> (or what a French critic calls "closed" verse, that verse which print bred and which is pretty much what we have had, in English and American, and have still got, despite the work of Pound & Williams:
> it led Keats, already a hundred years ago, to see it (Wordsworth's, Milton's) in the light of "the Egotistical Sublime"; and it persists, at this latter day, as what you might call the private-soul-at-any-public-wall)
> Verse now, 1950, if it is to go ahead, if it is to be of *essential* use, must, I take it, catch up and put into itself certain laws and possi-

bilities of the breath, of the breathing of the man who writes as well as of his listenings. (The revolution of the ear, 1910, the trochee's heave, asks it of the younger poets.) . . .

First, some simplicities that a man learns, if he works in OPEN, or what can also be called COMPOSITION BY FIELD, as opposed to inherited line, stanza, over-all form, what is the "old" base of the non-projective.

(1) the *kinetics* of the thing. A poem is energy transferred from where the poet got it (he will have some several causations), by way of the poem itself to, all the way over to, the reader. Okay. Then the poem itself must, at all points, be a high energy-construct and, at all points, an energy-discharge. So: how is the poet to accomplish same energy, how is he, what is the process by which a poet gets in, at all points, energy at least the equivalent of the energy which propelled him in the first place, yet an energy which is peculiar to verse alone and which will be, obviously, also different from the energy which the reader, because he is a third term, will take away?

This is the problem which any poet who departs from closed form is specially confronted by. And it involves a whole series of new recognitions. From the moment he ventures into FIELD COMPOSITION—puts himself in the open—he can go by no track other than the one the poem under hand declares for itself. Thus he has to behave, and be, instant by instant, aware of some several forces just now beginning to be examined. (It is much more, for example, this push, than simply such a one as Pound put, so wisely, to get us started: "the musical phrase," go by it, boys, rather than by the metronome.)

(2) is the *principle*, the law which presides conspicuously over such composition, and, when obeyed, is the reason why a projective poem can come into being. It is this: FORM IS NEVER MORE THAN AN EXTENSION OF CONTENT. (Or so it got phrased by one, R. Creeley, and it makes absolute sense to me, with this possible corollary, that right form, in any given poem, is the only and exclusively possible extension of content under hand.) There it is, brothers, sitting there, for USE.

Now (3) the *process* of the thing, how the principle can be made so to shape the energies that the form is accomplished. And I think it can be boiled down to one statement (first pounded into my head by Edward Dahlberg); ONE PERCEPTION MUST IMMEDIATELY AND DIRECTLY LEAD TO A FURTHER PERCEPTION. It means exactly what it says, is a matter of, at *all* points (even, I should say, of our management of daily reality as of the daily work) get on with it, keep moving, keep in, speed, the nerves, their speed, the perceptions, theirs, the acts, the split-second acts, the whole business, keep it moving as fast as you can, citizen. And if you also set up as a poet, USE USE USE the process at all points, in any given poem always, always one perception must must must MOVE, INSTANTER, ON ANOTHER! . . .

Let's start from the smallest particle of all, the syllable. It is the king and pin of versification, what rules and holds together the lines, the larger forms, of a poem. I would suggest that verse here and in England dropped this secret from the late Elizabethans to Ezra Pound, lost it, in the sweetness of meter and rime, in a honey-head. (The syllable is one way to distinguish the original success of blank verse, and its falling off, with Milton.) . . .

It would do no harm, as an act of correction, to both prose and verse as now written, if both rime and meter, and, in the quantity words, both sense and sound, were less in the forefront of the mind than the syllable, if the syllable, that fine creature, were more allowed to lead the harmony on. With this warning, to those who would try: to step back here to this place of the elements and minims of language, is to engage speech where it is least careless — and least logical. Listening for the syllables must be so constant and so scrupulous, the exaction must be so complete, that the assurance of the ear is purchased at the highest — forty-hour-a-day — price . . .

But the syllable is only the first child of the incest of verse (always, that Egyptian thing, it produces twins!). The other child is the LINE. And together, these two, the syllable *and* the line, they make a poem, they make that thing, the — what shall we call it, the Boss of all, the "Single Intelligence." And the line comes (I swear it) from the breath, from the breathing of the man who writes, at the moment that he writes, and thus is, it is here that, the daily work, the WORK, gets in, for only he, the man who writes, can declare, at every moment, the line, its metric and its ending — where its breathings shall come to, termination.

The trouble with most work, to my taking, since the breaking away from the traditional lines and stanzas, and from such wholes, as, say, Chaucer's *Troilus* or S's *Lear*, is: contemporary workers go lazy RIGHT HERE WHERE THE LINE IS BORN.

Let me put it baldly, The two halves are:

the HEAD, by way of the EAR, to the SYLLABLE

the HEART, by way of the BREATH, to the LINE

. . . I am dogmatic, that the head shows in the syllable. The dance of the intellect is there, among them, prose or verse. Consider the best minds you know in this here business: where does the head show, is it not, precise, here, in the swift currents of the syllable? It is true, what the master says he picked up from Confusion: all the thoughts men are capable of can be entered on the back of a postage stamp. So, is it not the PLAY of a mind we are after, is not that that shows whether a mind is there at all? . . .

In presenting the reconstruction of the poem as one of the major occupations of the intelligence in our day, take the following example:

After nine years Charles Sheeler had married again. His bride was Musya Sokolova, a dancer who at the age of fifteen had been driven from Russia by the Revolutionists.

He abandoned the place at Ridgefield, where he had taken her, and came to live in the Hudson River Valley near New York. He had got hold of the gardener's cottage of the former Lowe estate, a miniature mansion of gray stone, mansard-roof style, deep-set French windows, that was perfect to his purpose.

We have the location: a willfully destroyed Hudson River estate, a former home of the "aristocracy" of American Colonial history with subsequent wealth engrafted upon it to make it lovelier, Washington Irving's country, the country of the early Dutch and English—the Livingstons, the Phillipses, the woman who might have married George Washington and made him a New York State instead of a Virginia planter, with all that is implied in that.

The main building of sixty or more rooms had been torn down, out of very spite, it seemed, toward Franklin Roosevelt, leaving only the small cottage, the voluminous barns, and the remains of as beautiful a grove of trees, maples, purple beeches, basswoods, Japanese ginkos, to be found in the eastern part of the country. Many of them were over seventy years old when Charles and Musya moved in.

The poem is our objective, the secret at the heart of the matter—as Sheeler's small house, reorganized, is the heart of the gone estate of the Lowes—the effect of a fortune founded on tobacco or chicle or whatever it was.

Charles Sheeler, artist, has taken the one rare object remaining more or less intact (I omit the spacious wooden barn), a stone unit of real merit stylistically, and proceeded to live in it—with Musya, a Russian of a tragic past but vigorous integrities, and make a poem (a painting) of it; made it a cell, a seed of intelligent and feeling security. It is ourselves we organize in this way not against the past or for the future or even for survival but for integrity of understanding to insure persistence, to give the mind its stay.

The poem (in Charles's case the painting) is the construction in understandable limits of his life. That is Sheeler; that, lucky for him, partial or possible, is also music. It is called also a marriage. All these terms have to be redefined; a marriage has to be seen as a thing. The poem is made of things—on a field.

The poem, the small house (gray stone, a wisteria vine big around as a leg, the association of the broken-down estate peopled by the perfect trees) has been seized by Charles difficultly, not easily, and made into an expression—as well as he can, which he paints—as well as he can! (Not realistically.)

But the thing, the make-up of their house, is a continuation of the earlier life, of Sheeler the artist, of his old Welsh father, his Pennsylvania background, even of the fact that his uncle planned when he was a boy to make him a pitcher for the old Athletics and took him to the field to induce him to go in that direction.

The house that they have set up (I continue to refer to the construction, the reconstitution of the poem as my major theme) is the present-day necessity.

Charles admires his friends like the Greens and others for their tastes and abilities against which he places his own valid reasons, consciously, appraising what they offer and offering his own values. If they are friends they will see that against the advantages of Paris, of Italy, of whatever place it may be, he must lay his own poem, fully conscious of their Brancusis, their Picassos, their Cézannes, to which I add their Lorcas, even their British.

And what has he had to give? Bucks County barns? How shall we in this region of the mind which is all we can tactically, sensually know, organize our history other than as Shaker furniture is organized? It is a past, totally uninfluenced by anything but the necessity, the total worth of the thing itself, the relationship of the parts to the whole. The Shakers made furniture for their own simple ritualistic use, of white pine, applewood, birch—what they had. Sheeler has a remarkable collection of this furniture. He has quilts, rugs, glass, early paintings in use about him.

Musya, his wife, has the solid Russian sense of a present-day quality not overshadowed by an overwhelming western European past. She has been able with Sheeler's assistance to transfer herself to this environment—like her great, really great friend and admiration, the daughter of Leo Tolstoy, who also lives in the Hudson River Valley just across the river.

That is a feat of the intelligence, to transfer an understanding from an aristocratic past and from another context of thoughts to this context, the context of Shaker pieces, a New York Modern Museum, bad as it can be at times. To transfer values into a new context, to make a poem again.

I have seen men and women run off from the pressing necessity of making a new construction. This woman, full of strong qualities, has come bringing qualities for a new construction here. It is of great value to me to have these factors before me when I come to composition. They are the essentials of my work in making the poem.

Once, after Willie Hansen had been let go from the now-despoiled Lowe estate, he took a job as gardener for the Princesse de Talleyrand, née Gould, who had a much larger place at Tarrytown, which we were privileged to visit. (In the orchard houses, hardly a soul cuts a flower.) One never knows what is of use in rebuilding the poem. One uses what one finds. Willie didn't last long there.

Nothing can grow unless it taps into the soil.

The Practice

It's the humdrum, day-in, day-out, everyday work that is the real satisfaction of the practice of medicine; the patients a man has seen on his daily visits over a forty-year period of weekdays and Sundays that make up his life. I have never had a money practice; it would have been impossible for me. But the actual calling on people, at all times and under all conditions, the coming to grips with the intimate conditions of their lives, when they were being born, when they were dying, watching them die, watching them get well when they were ill, has always absorbed me.

I lost myself in the very properties of their minds: for the moment at least I actually became *them*, whoever they should be, so that when I detached myself from them at the end of a half hour of intense concentration over some illness which was affecting them, it was as though I were reawakening from a sleep. For the moment I myself did not exist; nothing of myself affected me. As a consequence I came back to myself, as from any other sleep, rested.

Time after time I have gone out into my office in the evening feeling as if I couldn't keep my eyes open a moment longer. I would start out on my morning calls after only a few hours' sleep, sit in front of some house waiting to get the courage to climb the steps and push the front-door bell. But once I saw the patient, all that would disappear. In a flash the details of case would begin to formulate themselves into a recognizable outline, the diagnosis would unravel itself or would refuse to make itself plain, and the hunt was on. Along with that, the patient himself would shape up into something that called for attention, his peculiarities, her reticences or candors. And though I might be attracted or repelled, the professional attitude which every physician must call on would steady me, dictate the terms on which I was to proceed. Many a time a man must watch the patient's mind as it watches him, distrusting him, ready to fly off at a tangent at the first opportunity; sees himself distrusted, sees the patient turn to someone else, rejected.

More than once we have all seen ourselves rejected, seen some hard-pressed mother or husband go to some other adviser when we know that the advice we have given him has been correct. That, too, is part of the game. But in general it is the rest, the peace of mind that comes from adopting the patient's condition as one's own to be struggled with toward a solution during those few minutes or that hour or those trying days when we are searching for causes, trying to relate this to that to build a reasonable basis for action which really gives us our peace. As I say, often after I have gone into my office harassed by personal perplexities of whatever sort, fatigued physically and mentally, after two hours of intense application to the work, I came out at the finish completely rested (and I mean rested), ready to smile and to laugh as if the day were just starting.

That is why as a writer I have never felt that medicine interfered with me but rather that it was my very food and drink, the very thing which made it possible for me to write. Was I not interested in man? There the thing was, right in front of me. I could touch it, smell it. It was myself, naked, just as it was, without a lie telling itself to me in its own terms. Oh, I knew it wasn't for the most part giving me anything very profound, but it was giving me terms, basic terms with which I could spell out matters as profound as I cared to think of.

I knew it was an elementary world that I was facing, but I have always been amazed at the authenticity with which the simple-minded often face that world when compared with the tawdriness of the public viewpoint exhibited in reports from the world at large. The public view which affects the behavior of so many is a very shabby thing when compared with what I see every day in my practice of medicine. I can almost say it is the interference of the public view of their lives with what I see which makes the difficulty, in most instances, between sham and a satisfactory basis of thought.

I don't care much about that, however. I don't care a rap what people are or believe. They come to me. I care for them and either they become my friends or they don't. That is their business. My business, aside from the mere physical diagnosis, is to make a different sort of diagnosis concerning them as individuals, quite apart from anything for which they seek my advice. That fascinates me. From the very beginning, that fascinated me even more than I myself knew. For no matter where I might find myself, every sort of individual that it is possible to imagine in some phase of his development, from the highest to the lowest, at some time exhibited himself to me. I am sure I have seen them all. And all have contributed to my pie. Let the successful carry off their blue ribbons, I have known the unsuccessful, far better persons than their more lucky brothers. One can laugh at them both, whatever the costumes they adopt. And when one is able to reveal them to themselves, high or low, they are always grateful as they are surprised that one can so have revealed the inner secrets of another's private motives. To do this is what makes a writer worth heeding: that somehow or other, whatever the source may be, he has gone to the base of the matter to lay it bare before us in terms which, try as we may, we cannot in the end escape. There is no choice then but to accept him and make him a hero.

All day long the doctor carries on this work, observing, weighing, comparing values of which neither he nor his patients may know the significance. He may be insensitive. But if in addition to actually being an accurate craftsman and a man of insight, he has the added quality of — some distress of mind, a restless concern with the . . . If he is not satisfied with mere cures, if he lacks ambition, if he is content to . . . If there is no content in him and likely to be none; if, in other words, without wishing to force it, since that would interfere with his lifelong observation, he allows himself to be called a name! What can one think of him?

He is half-ashamed to have people suspect him of carrying on a clandestine, a sort of underhand piece of spying on the public at large. They naïvely ask him, "How do you do it? How can you carry on an active business like that and at the same time find time to write? You must be superhuman. You must have at the very least the energy of two men." But they do not grasp that one occupation complements the other, that they are two parts of a whole, that it is not two jobs at all, that one rests the man when the other fatigues him. The only person to feel sorry for is his wife. She practically becomes a recluse. His only fear is that the source of his interest, his daily going about among human beings of all sorts, all ages, all conditions, will be terminated. That he will be found out.

As far as the writing itself is concerned, it takes next to no time at all. Much too much is written every day of our lives. We are overwhelmed by it. But when at times we see through the welter of evasive or interested patter, when by chance we penetrate to some moving detail of a life, there is always time to bang out a few pages. The thing isn't to find the time for it—we waste hours every day doing absolutely nothing at all—the difficulty is to catch the evasive life of the thing, to phrase the words in such a way that stereotype will yield a moment of insight. That is where the difficulty lies. We are lucky when that underground current can be tapped and the secret spring of all our lives will send up its pure water. It seldom happens. A thousand trivialities push themselves to the front, our lying habits of everyday speech and thought are foremost, telling us that *that* is what "they" want to hear. Tell them something else. You know you want to be a successful writer. This sort of chit-chat the daily practice of medicine tends drastically to cure.

Forget writing; it's a trivial matter. But day in, day out, when the inarticulate patient struggles to lay himself bare for you, or with nothing more than a boil on his back is so caught off balance that he reveals some secret twist of a whole community's pathetic way of thought, a man is suddenly seized again with a desire to speak of the underground stream which for a moment has come up just under surface. It is just a glimpse, an intimation of all that which the daily print misses or deliberately hides, but the excitement is intense and the rush to write is on again. It is then we see, by this constant feeling for a meaning, from the unselected nature of the material, just as it comes in over the phone or at the office door, that there is no better way to get an intimation of what is going on in the world.

We catch a glimpse of something, from time to time, which shows us that a presence has just brushed past us, some rare thing—just when the smiling little Italian woman has left us. For a moment we are dazzled. What was that? We can't name it; we know it never gets into any recognizable avenue of expression; men will be long dead before they can have so much as ever approached it. Whole lives are spent in the tremendous affairs of daily events without even approaching the great sights that I see every day. My patients do not know what is about them among their very husbands and children, their wives and acquaintances. But there is no need for us to be such strangers to each other, saving alone laziness, indifference, and age-old besotted ignorance.

So for me the practice of medicine has become the pursuit of a rare element which may appear at any time, at any place, at a glance. It can be most embarrassing. Mutual recognition is likely to flare up at a moment's notice. The relationship between physician and patient, if it were literally followed, would give us a world of extraordinary fertility of the imagination, which we can hardly afford. There's no use trying to multiply cases; it is there, it is magnificent, it fills my thoughts, it reaches to the farthest limits of our lives.

What is the use of reading the common news of the day, the tragic deaths and abuses of daily living, when for over half a lifetime we have known that they must have occurred just as they have occurred, given the conditions that cause them? There is no light in it. It is trivial fill-gap. We know the plane will crash, the train be derailed. And we know why. No one cares; no one can care. We get the news and discount it; we are quite right in doing so. It is trivial. But the hunted news I get from some obscure patients' eyes is not trivial. It is profound: whole academies of learning, whole ecclesiastical hierarchies are founded upon it and have developed what they call their dialectic upon nothing else, their lying dialectics. A dialectic is any arbitrary system, which, since all systems are mere inventions, is necessarily in each case a false premise, upon which a closed system is built, shutting those who confine themselves to it from the rest of the world. All men one way or another use a dialectic of some sort into which they are shut, whether it be an Argentina or a Japan. So each group is maimed. Each is enclosed in a dialectic cloud, incommunicado, and for that reason we rush into wars and prides of the most superficial natures.

Do we not see that we are inarticulate? That is what defeats us. It is our inability to communicate to another how we are locked within ourselves, unable to say the simplest thing of importance to one another, any of us, even the most valuable, that makes our lives like those of a litter of kittens in a woodpile. That gives the physician, and I don't mean the high-priced psychoanalyst, his opportunity; psychoanalysis amounts to no more than another dialectic into which to be locked.

The physician enjoys a wonderful opportunity actually to witness the words being born. Their actual colors and shapes are laid before him carrying their tiny burdens, which he is privileged to take into his care with their unspoiled newness. He may see the difficulty with which they have been born and what they are destined to do. No one else is present but the speaker and ourselves; we have been the words' very parents. Nothing is more moving.

But after we have run the gamut of the simple meanings that come to one over the years, a change gradually occurs. We have grown used to the range of communication which is likely to reach us. The girl who comes to me breathless, staggering into my office, in her underwear a still breathing infant, asking me to lock her mother out of the room; the man whose mind is gone—all of them finally say the same thing. And then a new meaning begins to intervene. For under that language to which we have been listening all our lives a new, a more profound language underlying all the dialectics offers itself. It is what they call poetry. That is the final phase.

It is that, we realize, which beyond all they have been saying is what they have been trying to say. They laugh (for are they not laughable?); they can think of nothing more useless (what else are they but the same?); something made of words (have they not been trying to use words all their lives?). We begin to see that the underlying meaning of all they want to tell us and have always failed to communicate is the poem, the poem which their lives are being lived to realize. No one will believe it. And it is the actual words, as we hear them spoken under all circumstances, which contain it. It is actually there, in the life before us, every minute that we are listening, a rarest element—not in our imaginations but there, there in fact. It is that essence which is hidden in the very words which are going in at our ears and from which we must recover underlying meaning as realistically as we recover metal out of ore.

The poem that each is trying actually to communicate to us lies in the words. It is at least the words that make it articulate. It has always been so. Occasionally that named person is born who catches a rumor of it, a Homer, a Villon, and his race and the world perpetuate his memory. Is it not plain why? The physician, listening from day to day, catches a hint of it in his preoccupation. By listening to the minutest variations of the speech, we begin to detect that today, as always, the essence is also to be found, hidden under the verbiage, seeking to be realized.

But one of the characteristics of this rare presence is that it is jealous of exposure and that it is shy and revengeful. It is not a name that is bandied about in the marketplace, no more than it is something that can be captured and exploited by the academy. Its face is a particular face; it is likely to appear under the most unlikely disguises. You cannot recognize it from past appearances— in fact it is always a new face. It knows all that we are in the habit of describing. It will not use the same appearance for any new materialization. And it is our very life. It is we ourselves, at our rarest moments, but inarticulate for the most part except when in the poem one man, every five or six hundred years, escapes to formulate a few gifted sentences.

The poem springs from the half-spoken words of such patients as the physician sees from day to day. He observes it in the peculiar, actual conformations in which its life is hid. Humbly he presents himself before it, and by long practice he strives as best he can to interpret the manner of its speech. In that the secret lies. This, in the end, comes perhaps to be the occupation of the physician after a lifetime of careful listening.

(1951)

Louise Bogan

The Pleasures of Formal Poetry

BEFORE I TRY to analyze out certain basic virtues of formal poetry, I should like to state, and to analyze, certain modern objections to form. The first objection to form that rises in our minds is that form binds. The second objection to the use of form in modern poetry is that poetic form has become exhausted.

The main tendency in poetry since Baudelaire, Rimbaud, and Whitman would seem to be bound up with efforts to free poetry from formal restrictions. This tendency has been central, but it has never been, as a matter of fact, steady. Baudelaire, whom we now name the great ancestor of modern poetry, wrote in a form that was so strict that it was often Racinian. Rimbaud, who smashed the French alexandrine and wrote the first French *vers libre*, was continually going back to form; he wrote exquisitely balanced sonnets and, even in the late *Saison en enfer*, the most delicate and evanescent sort of formal lyric. Mallarmé, of course, was a tremendous formalist up to and including *Un Coup de dés*, for in this late and seemingly experimental work Mallarmé (according to Thibaudet) "wished to produce a visual and typographic aesthetic, built on the difference between the kinds of type, the largeness of the white spaces between, the dimension of the lines—[on] the entire architecture of the page." The subtlety of the language and of the inner rhymes and echoes in this poem certainly bring it over to the side of form. Mallarmé is adding another "formality" to verse.

This alternate and gradual loosening and tightening of form continues, through Laforgue, who could write in the most precise "light-verse" style, through Pound, Apollinaire, and Eliot. As a matter of fact, as we look back on "modern" poetry as a whole, we find as much experimentation *in* form as out of it.

One cannot deny, however, that certain set forms in the verse of all European languages now seem to the modern poet either pedantic or trivial. Certain formal verse patterns, therefore, seem to have been exhausted. Certain modern poets cannot function, for example, in the sonnet form. Others cannot function in any form which has regular stress, or which is pointed up by any sort of rhyme. It is interesting to remember in what way, and for what reasons, this exhaustion came about. For the dislike of form, in many young writers, amounts to actual fear and revulsion. The matter of form as opposed to non-form or free form sometimes slips over from the field of aesthetics into the moral plane. Nowadays young poets avoid form as they would avoid some stupid or reprehensible action.

The exhaustion of formal poetry goes back to a complex of reasons, and some of these reasons are closely meshed in with the history of morals in the nineteenth century. In France, at the height of the French Romantic movement, poets (notably Victor Hugo) began to load their form with fantastic emotion and with cloying music. The middle-class revolution in taste was bound closely in with all this, as well as patriotic fervor, political conviction, and so on. In France, however, an anti-Romantic reaction occurred early, in 1857, the year of publication of *Les Fleurs du Mal* and *Madame Bovary*, to be exact. So that it was quite natural for Verlaine, years later, to demand that poets wring the neck of rhetoric, even while he made, at the same time, poetry into pure music. In England, poetry was taken over bodily by the middle-class assumptions, and there was no adequate facing up to the situation by any major poet known in the Victorian era. (Hopkins was not published until 1916.) And the more that serious poets became absorbed into the society which surrounded them, the more complicated and unfitting forms they devised. Poetry was *used:* as a means of consolation, to bolster up flagging spirits, to cheer on, to cheer up, to create optimism where optimism was cheaply applied or out of place, to back up middle-class social ideals as well as certain philosophical ideals concerning human perfectibility. And a split occurred between "serious" and "light" verse. The quick and varied meters and the witty rhymes which Byron had devised as carriers for satire were siphoned off from the main stream of serious poetry. Within serious poetry, poets like Tennyson, meanwhile, doggedly experimented with unsuitable (to English) meters, in order to give some show of variety to their repetitive and tiresome subject matter. These experiments reached a dead end in Robert Bridges' — a true upholder of Victorian tradition — experiments with quantitative verse. These experiments were dead because the breath of life did not exist in the poets themselves or in the material with which they were attempting to deal.

"Light verse" took up the entire satiric burden, and lost caste because of its involvement with *opéra bouffe* (as used by William Gilbert in combination with Arthur Sullivan's music); or because of its (to the Victorian mind) even sillier relationship to the nonsense rhymes of Lewis Carroll and Edward Lear. These are the two limits to which poets in English pushed form: dull imitation of Greek and Roman poetry on the one hand, and gay and complicated satirical "patter songs" and nonsense verse on the other. Both limits are unusable, in modern poetry. But the best nineteenth-century poets soon realized that a reunion of these two streams was not only important but imperative. For complicated rhythmic patterns and light and limber and dancing rhythms have existed in serious poetry since the Greeks. When Gilbert Murray wishes to give an example of a rhythmic pattern used in Greek comedy, he is forced to quote a Gilbert stanza. It is a breach in culture when such rhythmic effects are lost, and French poets realized this fact before English ones did. Rimbaud goes back to folk song, Laforgue goes back to "light verse," whenever they sensed some tone of emotion which demanded these meters; neither was too proud or too inflexible not to make use of any meter that successfully carried his thought and feeling.

It is still the task of modern poets to bridge the division between serious and light forms; to refresh the drooping and weary rhythms of serious poetry with the varied, crisp, and fresh qualities of light verse. In English, Pound and Eliot have performed miracles of deflation and revivification. Auden, as well, has worked to break down artificial barriers of form and tone, between the lively and the grave subject and treatment.

What is formal poetry? It is poetry written in form. And what is *form?* The elements of form, so far as poetry is concerned, are meter and rhyme. Are these elements merely mold and ornaments that have been impressed upon poetry from without? Are they indeed restrictions which bind and fetter language and the thought and emotion behind, under, within language in a repressive way? Are they arbitrary rules which have lost all validity since they have been broken to good purpose by "experimental poets," ancient and modern? Does the breaking up of form, or its total elimination, always result in an increase of power and of effect; and is any return to form a sort of relinquishment of freedom, or retreat to old fogeyism?

Let us examine meter. Meter is rhythm. In the words of the Scots professor who, in the nineteenth century, edited, with a preface, Walker's eighteenth-century *Rhyming Dictionary*: "A little consideration will lead to the conclusion, that verse, in most languages, differs from prose in the *return* of certain number of syllables that have a peculiar relation to one another as *accented* and *unaccented,* or as long and short. It is universally felt that a degree of *pleasure* arises from this definite arrangement, and the origin of that pleasure is to be traced back to the sense of time with which men are generally endowed." (You will remember Yeats saying of himself, "I have the poet's exact time-sense.") Now, when I asked a group of students, recently, to name some definite bodily rhythm which might illustrate mankind's sense of time, and with which a definite pleasure might be said to be connected, they could think only of the dance. This answer is interesting, because it shows how many rhythmic habits and rhythmic effects have become rare either as observed phenomena, or as direct experience, with the advent of the machine. Students in a former century would think immediately, I believe, of the rhythmic principles underlying the actions which the Scottish professor at once brings forward as examples. "It is this principle which regulates," he goes on to say, "the step of a man or the stroke of an oar; and hence the pleasure we experience in beholding the regular step of a company of soldiers in their march, and the simultaneous sweep of the oars of a well-manned boat." Marching as a sort of everyday ritual — as seen in the changing of a guard, in a religious procession, or in a funeral cortège — is now a fairly rare sight, and so is the spectacle of rowers in "a well-manned boat." The Scotch professor then illustrates his point by the *time,* as distinguished from the tune, in music, but I do not want to bring rhythm in music (or in language) into the discussion at this point. I want to keep on emphasizing the pleasure to be found in bodily rhythm as such. What else formerly went to rhythm? We think of certain tasks, the rhythm of which has become set. Sowing, reaping, threshing, washing clothes, rowing, and even milking cows go to rhythm. The variety of rhythm in sea shanties depends upon the variety of tasks on board a sailing ship, with the doing of which a sailor was confronted. Hauling up sail or pulling it down, coiling rope, pulling and pushing and climbing and lifting, all went to different rhythms; and these rhythms are preserved for us, fast or slow, smooth or rough, in sailors' songs.

How far back can we push this sense of time? It appears everywhere in the most primitive cultures. It certainly springs from the fact that a living man has rhythm built into him, as it were. His heart beats. He has a pulse. A pulse of some sort exists in all living creatures — in plants as well, I think scientists have proved — and man shares with the animals not only a pulse, but an attendant rhythm: his breathing.

So we see man, long before he has much of a "mind," celebrating and extending and enjoying the rhythms of his heartbeat and of his breath. He is still at the point, let us say, where he performs these extensions without speech, or with the most rudimentary form of speech. Even without speech, a great many rhythmic effects can be produced by a human being. He can clap his hands rhythmically and he can stamp his feet rhythmically. Here is the beginning of the dance, of ritual, of drama. Then artifacts began to increase the pleasure of rhythm. The first aids and abettors of human rhythm were undoubtedly percussion instruments. A beaten hollow log must have been a great aid. The clicking together of the chestnut shells from which castanets take their name was another.

Eliot has said that poetry goes back to a savage beating a tom-tom in a jungle. That is, it goes back to reiterative beat. The Greeks have no god of the drum, no muse of the drum, it is true. The Muses, when we first hear of them, are three only: one of study, one of memory, and one of song. But Greek poetry, when we first come upon it, is a highly sophisticated and complex affair: the fruit of centuries of trial and error, of matching rhythm to language and language to rhythm, of a complicated and civilized relationship between dance and song. When we come upon the epics of Homer, written in the infinitely resonant and infinitely variable dactylic hexameter; or, later, when we read the no less fixed yet no less variable Sapphics or Alcaics of the Greek lyric, we have passed far beyond a Stone Age. Man has become a worker in metals; the cymbal and the bell have been added to the castanet and the drum; man is now a musician as well as a dancer.

One Greek word combines dance and song, the word *molpe*; and the word constantly applied to the *effect* of all good singing and harping (for the lyre was the purely Greek instrument, since the wind instrument, the *aulos*, was always considered of Asiatic origin) was *himeroeis*, meaning "not merely beautiful, but possessing that sort of beauty which makes the heart yearn." "*Himeros* and *rhythmos*—longing and rhythm—are the two special elements which the voice finds strengthened in the movement of the body. *Metron* means measurement; and the things measured are the *feet* or *steps* on which the words of the song move. For the words had to dance with the dancers..."

Why are Greek rhythms now unusable? Why does the Greek hexameter, which managed to pass over into Latin poetry, remain forever outside any feasible use in English? The chief reason is that both Greek and Latin, being inflected languages, are nearer to each other than either of them can ever be to English. "A highly inflected language," Gilbert Murray says in his valuable study *The Classical Tradition in Poetry*, "must have each syllable clearly spoken, because each syllable up to the last may seriously alter the meaning. This is perhaps the reason why, in Latin and Greek pronunciation, *quantity* was the chief variable; while modern uninflected languages have fallen back more and more on the easy careless method of stress." (And we should remember here that certain rhythmic effects in modern poetry do indeed stem from Greek rhythms. Gerard Manley Hopkins was saturated in Greek. He was one of Jowett's brilliant young men at Balliol, and many of the effects in Hopkins which we think of as triumphs of "modern" compression are actually models of Greek compression, as transformed into English verse by the hands of a master.)

I want to quote, at this point—before I quote some incisive remarks by Eliot on the limits of freedom in verse—another passage from Gilbert Murray, a passage concerned with the inner meaning of the Greek term *molpe*. Murray says:

Love, Strife and Death and that which is beyond Death; an atmosphere formed by the worship of Nature and the enchantment of Memory; a combination of dance and song like the sweep of a great singing bird; all working toward an ecstasy or a transcending of personality, a "standing outside" of the prison of the material present, to be merged in some life that is the object of adoration or desire: these seem to be the subjects, and this the spirit and setting of that primitive MOLPE which is the foundation of ancient classical poetry. The tradition, if there is a tradition, rises there.

And this tradition, let us remember, goes back to *rhythm*, the effect of which attracted the adjective *himeroeis*: "not merely beautiful, but possessing that sort of beauty which makes the heart yearn."

Here, perhaps, I should make a few remarks on that other element of formal poetry as we know it today: rhyme. Rhyme becomes necessary in poetry as rhythm weakens. The Greeks of the great period scorned rhyme; and so did Latin writers, although certain internal rhymes can be detected in Ovid and later Latin versifiers. Rhyme has probably always been present in folk song and folk poetry (we know how pleased children are when they strike upon two words that rhyme); but high formal art for a long time dismissed and ignored it. But as rhythm began to break down, and when what we now think of as "monkish Latin" began to appear, rhyme appears as well. As soon as the ordinary speech of the people — the so-called vulgar tongues — began to build up a body of formal literature, rhyme became usual. The Provençal poets elaborated and extended the use of rhyme to a remarkable degree, so that by the time Dante began to write in Italian, his native vulgar tongue — having had as his master the Provençal poet Arnaut Daniel — he had at his disposal a great variety of rhymed forms, the sonnet among them; and Dante used the sonnet and, later, *terza rima* as a *rhymed* carrier of his long poem, *The Divine Comedy*.

Greek and Latin could do without rhyme because they had clear meters. Rhyme is needed to mark clearly the end of the line, and to provide the ear with fixed resting places. Without such divisions the metrical form would become dull and obscure. The

> hearer would not be sure where one line ended and the other began; he might not even be sure whether he was listening to prose or to verse. It is worth noticing that Latin took to rhyme when it had begun to lose the sense of quantity. Chinese insists on rhyme because it has no meter.

This is still Murray, who says a little farther on, "The renewed popularity of rhyme in the time of Dryden followed upon an increasing looseness of the treatment of blank verse by the later Jacobean dramatists, and was part of a general reaction toward severity of form."

Every language seems to seek its own large meter—its own dramatic carrier, capable of long breaths, capable of bearing weights, capable of projecting maximum emotional power and yet allowing for delicate variation, capable of assuming various speeds, and capable of letting through intricacy of thought and sharpness of wit—a meter suited to the syntax and the rhythm of any given language, to the preponderance within that language of actual vowels and consonantal sounds. The vulgar tongues have more light vowels and fewer massive clusters of consonants than the classical languages. A spoken language, from Dante on, seems to fall most naturally into an iambic line of one length or another. English poetry has for a long time been based on the iamb—a short followed by a long beat—an unaccented syllable followed by an accented one; and the classic and large carrier of English poetry has for centuries been the iambic pentameter or five beat line (sometimes with an additional syllable at the end, as in "To be or not to be, that is the question"): blank verse.

Now, it was a tremendous task to smash the Alexandrine, as Rimbaud smashed it, when it had been recently charged with music and feeling by the Romantics. To smash iambic pentameter has not been such a tremendous task; for all during the nineteenth century, as we have seen, the line was becoming more and more feeble, since no strong talent had taken hold of it and filled it with refreshing power. (Browning's innovations were not strong enough.) The line continued to dwindle, and when it was finally smashed, it was already at its last gasp, as it were. Now, a dominant formal meter cannot become absolutely enfeebled if the common language which surrounds it continues to feed it. If the common, everyday language itself changes, the dominant meter must also change. If the accent shifts in the common tongue, then the accent in the dominant meter must shift, too.

Certain Victorian poets sensed this shift—Browning particularly—and in Bridges and in Swinburne, the iambic beat is broken by the introduction of trochaic, dactylic, anapestic, and spondaic feet. These innovations went back, in part, to Milton, who, in his later works, had introduced a consistent trochaic variation; and to Coleridge, who counted *only* the accented syllables in a line. It was the introduction of a sense of rhythms foreign to classical English, in three English-speaking "foreigners," that finally broke the iambic hold. These poets—William Butler Yeats, Ezra Pound, and T. S. Eliot—by their experiments changed the iambic line so that it again became flexible and vigorous. The trochaic foot—a long followed by a short—had become dominant in ordinary speech. It has also become dominant in the formal poetry of our day.

How far can this mingling of meters go? Soon we come upon a mingling of meters—in sections of Pound's *Cantos*, for example—that is nearer the beat of prose than of verse, that *is* prose. Prose has its own rhythm, certainly. But is not something lost to us, being, as we are, rhythmic creatures, in the disappearance of many "rich and exquisite" poetic meters? Free verse is valuable only when it continues to broaden and enrich, and it becomes as hampering as any rigid meter when it rules out *any* return to form.

"It seems to be almost a necessity in good verse that the ear should subconsciously expect a certain pattern, and have its hope, alternately or varyingly, suspended and fulfilled." There speaks the student of classical meters. But we hear very much the same dictum in Eliot's remark that "the ghost of some simple meter should lurk behind the arras in even the 'freest' verse; to advance menacingly as we doze, and withdraw as we rouse." A failure in any discoverable beat is a failure in tension.

Eliot himself, one of the greatest English metrists, has made other remarks on modern versification. He says, for example, "that no *vers* is *libre* for the man who wants to do a good job."

> The term [he goes on] which fifty years ago [he was writing in 1928] had an exact meaning in relation to the French Alexandrine, now means too much to mean anything at all. The *vers libre* of Jules Laforgue, who if not quite the greatest poet after

Baudelaire, was certainly the most important technical innovator, is *free verse* in much the same way that the latter verse of Shakespeare, Webster and Tourneur is *free verse:* that is to say, it stretches, contracts and distorts the traditional French measure as later Elizabethan and Jacobean poetry stretches, contracts and distorts the blank verse measure. But the term is applied to several types of verse which have developed in English *without relation* to Laforgue, Corbière and Rimbaud, or to each other. To be more precise, there are, for instance, my own type of verse, that of Pound, and that of the disciples of Whitman. I will not say that subsequently there have not appeared traces of reciprocal influence of several types upon one another, but I am here speaking of origins. My own verse is, so far as I can judge, nearer to the original meaning of *vers libre* than is any of the other types: at least the form in which I began to write, in 1908 or 1909, was directly drawn from the study of Laforgue together with the later Elizabethan drama; and I do not know anyone who started from exactly that point. I did not read Whitman until much later in life, and had to conquer an aversion to his form, as well as much of his matter, to do so. I am equally certain that Pound owes nothing to Whitman.* This is an elementary observation; but when dealing with popular conceptions of *vers libre* one must still be as simple and elementary as fifteen years ago.

Eliot, in this passage (from his introduction to Pound's *Selected Poems*) goes on to list Pound's Victorian "influences." "Technically," he adds, "these influences were all good; for they combine to insist upon the importance of *verse as speech* while from more antiquarian studies Pound was learning the importance of *verse as song*."

"Verse as speech" and "verse as song": these are the two attitudes toward formal poetry — or rather in formal poetry — that die out first, and perennially need to be renewed. Formal poetry should continually remain in contact with the speech and the life around it, but this it does not do, and this division is made easier by the fact that poetry has for centuries been encased — one might almost say embalmed — in print. The technique becomes rigidified, and poets begin to write by the rules that scholars have de-

---

* Eliot has come to speak "more respectfully" of Whitman; and Pound has paid homage to Whitman's power both directly (in a poem addressed to his forerunner) and indirectly (in prose comments).

duced from this or that poetic canon. Poets become frightened of emotion and of the Sublime (young poets today, I have found, are particularly terrified of the Sublime; they want no part of it!). In this situation, we have the keepers of the canon, and we have the breakers of the canon. Let us listen to Eliot a little longer, as he fruitfully defines originality.

> Poets may be divided into those who develop technique, those who imitate technique and those who invent technique. When I say "invent," I should use inverted commas, for invention would be irreproachable if it were possible. "Invention" is wrong only because it is impossible. I mean that the difference between the "development" and the "sport" is, in poetry, a capital one. There are two kinds of "sports" in poetry, in the floricultural sense. One is the imitation of development, and the other is the imitation of some idea of originality. The former is commonplace, a waste product of civilization. The latter is contrary to life. The poem which is absolutely original is absolutely bad; it is, in the bad sense, "subjective," with no relation to the world to which it appeals.
>
> Originality, in other words, is by no means a simple idea in the criticism of poetry. True originality is merely development; and if it is the right development it may appear in the end so inevitable that we almost come to the point of view of denying all "original" virtue to the poet. He simply did the next thing.

Eliot then says that spurious originality usually gives the public a greater shock than true originality, and ends by stating that Pound's originality is genuine in that his versification is a logical development of the verse of his English predecessors.

The technical tradition, then, runs on unbroken. We now know more of the linkages which connect any art to human function, and this knowledge should make us take more pleasure, rather than less, in *form*. I again quote Murray.

> The regular or irregular rhythm of verse [corresponds], as we now are told, to the various physiological rhythms of the living body, and derives therefrom a mysterious power over the emotions. There is also a quality of rhythm or architecture in the composition itself which is quite different from mere plot-interest and corresponds, I think, to the real rhythms of life, as revealed in one part or another of the Tragic Pattern. All these elements, and

doubtless others also, combine to make the felt but indefinable contrast with reality or truth, conveyed by the poem ... Poetry tries to convey truth concerning those subjects about which we care most and know least, or at any rate are least able to make explicit statements. These mysteries were the subjects with which the Greek MOLPE was concerned — Love, Strife, Death and that which is beyond Death.

We still celebrate these subjects and face these mysteries, and formal art — art in which the great tradition is still alive and by which it still functions — is as modern as this moment, and as ancient as the farthest antiquity. This is the formal art fragments of which we should not only as readers "shore against our ruins," but keep as a directing influence in whatever we manage to build — to create.

(1953)

Marianne Moore

Idiosyncrasy and Technique

I. Technique

IN HIS INAUGURAL lecture as Professor of Poetry at Oxford,[1] Mr. Auden said, "There is only one thing that all poetry must do; it must praise all it can for being as for happening." He also said, "Every poem is rooted in imaginative awe." These statements answer, or imply an answer, to the question: Why does one write?

I was startled, indeed horrified, when a writing class in which I have an interest was asked, "Is it for money or fame?" as though it must be one or the other—and writing were not for some a felicity, if not a species of intellectual self-preservation. Gorgeously remunerated as I am for being here, it would seem both hypocritical and inappropriate to feign that a love of letters renders money irrelevant. Still, may I say, and with emphasis, that I do not write for money or fame. To earn a living is needful, but it can be done in routine ways. One writes because one has a burning desire to objectify what it is indispensable to one's happiness to express, a statement which is not at variance with the fact that Sir Walter Scott, driven by a fanatically sensitive conscience, shortened his life writing to pay what was not a personal debt. And Anthony Trollope, while writing to earn a living, at the same time was writing what he very much loved to write.

Amplifying the impression which Bernard Shaw, as music critic, himself gives of his "veracity, catholicity, and pugnacity," [2]

Hesketh Pearson says of him as stage manager of his plays, "No author could be more modest than Shaw. He did not regard his text as sacrosanct. He laughed over his own lines as if they were jokes by somebody else and never could repeat them accurately. Once, when an actor apologized for misquoting a passage, he remarked, 'What you said is better than what I wrote. If you can always misquote so well, keep on misquoting—but remember to give the right cues!' " [3] Writing was resilience. Resilience was an adventure. Is it part of the adventure to revise what one wrote? Professor Ewing has suggested that something be said about this. My own revisions are usually the result of impatience with unkempt diction and lapses in logic, together with an awareness that for most defects, to delete is the instantaneous cure.

The rhythms of the King James Version of the Bible stand forever as writing, although certain emendations as to meaning seem obligatory. The King James Epistle of Paul to the Philippians, 3:20, reads: "For our conversation is in heaven"; the Revised Standard Version reads: "We are a heavenly body"; each a mistranslation, according to Dr. Alvin E. Magary, who feels that Dr. Moffat got it right: " 'We are a colony of heaven'—a Roman outpost as it were, in which people conformed their lives to the life of Rome—an interpretation which makes sense as applied to Christianity"; Dr. Magary also emphasizes that the beatitude "Blessed are the meek" should have no connotation of subservience, since if rendered more strictly, the word would be not the "meek," but the "begging."

The revisions by Henry James of his novels are evidently in part the result of an insistent desire to do justice to first intention. Reverting to pronouncements on Milton and Goethe made previously, T. S. Eliot seems to feel that after-judgment cannot merely be taken for granted, and when accepting the Goethe Prize in 1954, he said, "As one's reading is extended [one begins] to develop that critical ability, that power of self-criticism without which the poet will do no more than repeat himself . . ."; then, farther on: "To understand what Wisdom is, is to be wise oneself: and I have only the degree of understanding that can be attained by a man who knows that he is not wise, yet has some faith that he is wiser than he was twenty years ago. I say twenty years ago, because I am under the distressing necessity of quoting a sentence I printed in

1933. It is this: 'Of Goethe perhaps it is truer to say that he dabbled in both philosophy and poetry and made no great success at either; his true role was that of a man of the world and sage, a La Rochefoucauld, a La Bruyère, a Vauvenargues.' "

Mr. Eliot says he ". . . never re-read the passage in which this sentence is buried [and had] discovered it not so very long ago in Mr. Michael Hamburger's introduction to his edition and translation of the text of Hölderlin's poems." He then goes on to say of Goethe, "It may be that there are areas of wisdom that he did not penetrate: but I am more interested in trying to understand the wisdom he possessed than to define its limitations. When a man is a good deal wiser than oneself, one does not complain that he is no wiser than he is." [4]

Since writing is not only an art but a trade embodying principles attested by experience, we would do well not to forget that it is an expedient for making oneself understood, and that what is said should at least have the air of having meant something to the person who wrote it—as is the case with Gertrude Stein and James Joyce. Stewart Sherman one time devised a piece of jargon which he offered as indistinguishable from work by Gertrude Stein, which gave itself away at once as lacking any private air of interest. If I may venture to say again what I have already said when obscurity was deplored, one should be as clear as one's natural reticence allows one to be. Laurence Binyon, reflecting on the state of letters after completing his Dante, said, "How indulgent we are to infirmity of structure . . ." [5] and structural infirmity truly has, under surrealism, become a kind of horticultural verbal blight threatening firmness at the core; a situation met long ago in *The Classic Anthology Defined by Confucius:*

> Enjoy the good yet sink not in excess.
> True scholar stands by his steadfastness.[6]
> . . .
>
> Lamb-skin for suavity, trimmed and ornate,
> But a good soldier who will get things straight.[7]

In attaining this noble firmness, one must have clarity, and clarity depends on precision; not that intentional ambiguity cannot be an art. Reinhold Niebuhr is not famed as easy reading, but is at times a study in precision, as when he says, "The self does not realize itself most fully when self-realization is its conscious aim"; and of conscience, says, "We will define it provisionally at least as capacity to view itself and judge obligation in contrast with inclination." [8] It is not "the purpose [but] the function of roots to absorb water," Dr. Edmund Sinnott notes in his book *The Biology of the Spirit*, in which he discusses the self-regulating properties of protoplasm — digressing, with a shade of outrage, to deplore untidiness in the use of terms. One is corrected when referring to certain African tribes for saying they worship the devil; they propitiate the devil; and if precise, one weeds text of adjective, adverbs, and unnecessary punctuation. As an instance of such concision, we have Mr. Francis Watson's account of Edwin Arnold, "the traveller, linguist, and semi-mystic, with whom Matthew Arnold did not like to be confused." [9] Informing us that Edwin Arnold had been married three times and that two of his wives had died — a lackluster kind of statement which few of us perhaps would avoid — Mr. Watson says, "After being twice bereaved, he found a third wife from Japan, a land whose culture he extolled in articles..." Paramount as a rule for any kind of writing — scientific, commercial, informal, prose, or verse — we dare not be dull. Finding Akira Kurosawa's film *The Magnificent Seven* too reiterative, Bosley Crowther says that "the director shows so many shots of horses' feet tromping in the mud that we wonder if those horses have heads." [10]

In his "Advice to a Young Critic" (Golding Bright),[11] Bernard Shaw says, "Never strike an attitude, national, moral, or critical" — an axiom he did not observe too fanatically if judged by the telegram he is said to have sent to an actress with a leading part in one of his plays: "... wonderful, marvelous, superb..." to which the actress replied, "Undeserving such praise"; and he: "I meant the play"; and she: "So did I."

I have a mania for straight writing — however circuitous I may be in what I myself say of plants, animals, or places; and although one may reverse the order of words for emphasis, it should not be to rescue a rhyme. There are exceptions, of course, as when Mr. Oliver Warner, speaking of Captain Cook, the explorer, in commending the remarkable drawings made by members of the Captain's staff, says, "None of Cook's artists worked to preconceived notions. They drew what they saw and wonderful it was." [12] To say "and it was wonderful" would have been very flat. We have literature, William Archer said, when we impart distinctiveness to ordinary talk and make it still seem ordinary.

Like dullness, implausibility obscures the point; so, familiar though we are with "Fenimore Cooper's Literary Offenses," by Mark Twain,[13] allow me to quote a line or two. "It is a rule of literary art in the domain of fiction," Mark Twain says, "that always the reader shall be able to tell the corpses from the others. But this detail often has been overlooked in the *Deerslayer* tale. [Cooper] bends 'a sapling' to the form of an arch over [a] narrow passage, and conceals six Indians in its foliage." Then, ". . . one of his acute Indian experts, Chingachgook (pronounced Chicago, I think), has lost the trail of a person he is tracking . . . turned a running stream out of its course, and there, in the slush of its old bed, were that person's moccasin-tracks . . ." Even the laws of nature take a vacation when Cooper is practicing "the delicate art of the forest."

What has been said pertains to technique (*teknikos*, from the Greek, akin to *tekto*: to produce or bring forth — as art, especially the useful arts). And, indeed, if technique is of no interest to a writer, I doubt that the writer is an artist.

What do I mean by straight writing, I have been asked. I mean, in part, writing that is not mannered, overconscious, or at war with common sense, as when a reviewer of *The Evolution of Cambridge Publishing*, by S. C. Roberts, refers to "a demure account of Cambridge's flirtation with the *Encyclopaedia Britannica*." [14] At the risk of seeming to find every virtue in certain authors and these authors in a certain few books or critiques, let me contrast with the unreal manner, W. D. Howells' *My Mark Twain* and a similar uninfected retrospect by the Duke of Windsor.

> Of all the literary men I have known [Howells says of Mark Twain], he was the most unliterary in his make and manner . . . His style was what we know, for good or for bad, but his manner, if I may difference the two, was as entirely his own as if no one had ever written before. [He] despised the avoidance of repetitions out of fear of tautology. If a word served his turn better than a substitute, he would use it as many times on a page as he chose . . . [There] never was a more biddable man in things you could show him a reason for . . . If you wanted a thing

changed, very good, he changed it; if you suggested that a word or a sentence or a paragraph had better be struck out, very good, he struck it out. His proof sheets came back each a veritable "mush of concession," as Emerson says . . . He was always reading some vital book . . . which gave him life at first hand. It is in vain that I try to give a notion of the intensity with which he compassed the whole world . . .

The other instance of straight writing to which I referred is "My Garden," by the Duke of Windsor.[15] Prosperity and royalty are always under suspicion. "Of course they had help," people say. "Someone must have written it for them"; as they said of the shepherd made judge, in the fable of the shepherd and the king, ". . . he is given the credit; we did the work; he has amassed riches; we are poor." [16] So let me say, I have in the following narrative an impression of individuality, conviction, and verbal selectiveness.

"I think my deep enjoyment of gardening must be latent," the Duke begins. "At least it was not inherited . . . The gardens at Sandringham and Windsor . . . made a fine show in summertime [a word with flavor, for me], but people did not really live with them. A garden is a mood, as Rousseau said, and my mood was one of intimacy, not splendor." Of his present gardening at The Mill, not far from Paris, he says, "French gardens can be remarkably beautiful things. They look like continuations of the Savonnerie of Aubusson carpets in the great chateaus rolled outside the the windows onto the lawns, perfectly patterned and mathematically precise . . . I wanted an English type of garden, which means green grass and seemingly casual arrangement of flowers, and here I had the perfect framework." Commenting on one of the color photographs which supplement the account, he says, "The main entrance to the property has an old covered gateway with ancient oak doors and a cobbled drive which leads to the main building. There is a big sundial above the front door, put there when The Mill was restored about 1732. In the foreground is Trooper, one of our four pugs." Technically an oversight, perhaps—the f-o-r-e ground and f-o-u-r pugs in close proximity—this clash lends authenticity, has the charm of not too conscious writing. Unmistakably, all along, the article embodies a zeal for the subject, a deep affection for flowers as seen in the complaint "The mildest stone-mason turns scourge when it comes to plant life." The piece smiles, whereas saturninity is a bad omen. "We do not praise God by dispraising man." [17]

II. Idiosyncrasy

In considering technique, I tried to say that writing can be affirmative and that we must, as Dr. Nathan Scott says, "reject the attitude of philosophic distrust." The writer should have "a sense of upthrusting vitality and self-discovery" [18] without thinking about the impression made, except as one needs to make oneself understood.

We are suffering from too much sarcasm, I feel. Any touch of unfeigned gusto in our smart press is accompanied by an arch word implying, "Now to me, of course, this is a bit asinine." Denigration, indeed, is to me so disaffecting that when I was asked to write something for the Columbia Chapter of Phi Beta Kappa Class Day exercises, I felt that I should not let my sense of incapacity as an orator hinder me from saying what I feel about the mildew of disrespect and leave appreciation to Mr. Auden, to salute "literary marines landing in little magazines." I then realized that what I was so urgent to emphasize is reduced in the First Psalm to a sentence: Blessed is the man who does not sit in the seat of the scoffer.

Odd as it may seem that a few words of overwhelming urgency should be a mosaic of quotations, why paraphrase what for maximum impact should be quoted verbatim? I borrowed, at all events, Ambassador Conant's title The Citadel of Learning, taken for his book from Stalin: "[Facing us] stands the citadel of learning. This citadel we must capture at any price. This citadel must be taken by our youth, if they wish to be the builders of a new life, if they wish, in fact, to take the place of the old guard." [19]

> Blessed is the man
>
> who does not sit in the seat of the scoffer—
>   the man who does not denigrate, depreciate, denunciate;
>   who is not "characteristically intemperate,"
> who does not "excuse, retreat, equivocate; and will be heard."

(Ah, Giorgione! there are those who mongrelize
and those who heighten anything they touch; although it
may well be
that if Giorgione's self-portrait were not said to be he,
it might not take my fancy. Blessed the geniuses who know

that egomania is not a duty.)
"Diversity, controversy; tolerance" — in that "citadel
of learning" we have a fort that ought to armor us well.
Blessed is the man who "takes the risk of a decision" — asks

himself the question: "Would it solve the problem?
Is it right as I see it? Is it in the best interests of all?"
Alas. Ulysses' companions are now political —
living self-indulgently until the moral sense is drowned,

having lost all power of comparison,
thinking license emancipates one, "slaves whom they
themselves have bound."
Brazen authors, downright soiled and downright spoiled,
as if sound
and exceptional, are the old quasi-modish counterfeit,

mitin-proofing conscience against character.
Affronted by "private lies and public shame," blessed is the
author
who favors what the supercilious do not favor —
who will not comply. Blessed, the unaccommodating man.

Blessed the man whose faith is different
from possessiveness — of a kind not framed by "things which
do appear" —
who will not visualize defeat, too intent to cower;
whose illumined eye has seen the shaft that gilds the sultan's
tower.

I had written these lines about denigration as treason, and was
assembling advice for some students of verse, when I found that
Rolfe Humphries, in his little treatise entitled "Writing the
Lyric," [20] has thrown light on the use of consonants. "Take the let-
ter *s*," he says, "one of the most insidious sounds in the language,
one which will creep in, in a sibilant reptilian fashion like the
original serpent in the garden, and if you are not careful, not only
drive you out of Paradise, but hiss you off the stage; . . . see if you
cannot write a quatrain without using it at all." Pondering my

"Blessed is the man who does not sit in the seat of the scoffer," I could only say that another's expertise might save one considerable awkwardness. Initiate John Barry came to my rescue by citing the *Aeneid* (II, 8):

> . . . *Et iam nox umida caelo*
> *praecipitat suadentque cadentia sidera somnos.*

Convinced that denigration is baneful, one readily sanctions the attack prompted by affection. In fact, nothing is more entertaining than the fraternal accolade in reverse, as when *The London News Chronicle* of November 16, 1954, published a cartoon, and lines entitled "Winniehaha," [21] concerning Mr. Churchill — prime minister then — after a cousin of his, Captain Lionel Leslie, had referred to the drop of Indian blood inherited by Sir Winston through his grandmother Clara Jerome. The complimentary cast of the sally — a parody of Longfellow's *Hiawatha* — which was written before Mr. Churchill had been knighted, when the date of his retirement was a subject of speculation, is apparent from even a line or two.

> In the center of the village
> In the wigwam of the wise ones,
> Where the head men of the nation
> Come to talk in solemn council,
> Squats the old chief, Winniehaha,
> Also known as Sitting Bulldog . . .
>
> Some there are with minds that wander
> From the purpose of the powwow;
> Minds that wonder will he give us
> Just an inkling, to be candid,
> Of the date of his retirement?
> Not that we would wish to rush him,
> Wish to rush old Winniehaha,
> Rush our splendid Sitting Bulldog
> From the headship of the head men
> In the center of the village,
> In the wigwam of the wise ones.
> Still, it's just a bit unsettling
> Not to know when Winniehaha
> Will give place to handsome Pinstripe.
> Will he tell us? Will he tell us?

In connection with personality, it is a curiosity of literature how often what one says of another seems descriptive of oneself. Would-be statesmen who spike their utterances with malice should bear this in mind and take fright as they drive home the moral of the Lion, the Wolf, and the Fox: "Slander flies home faster than rumor of good one has done." [22] In any case, Sir Winston Churchill's pronouncement on Alfred the Great does seem appropriate to himself—his own defeats, triumphs, and hardihood: "This sublime power to rise above the whole force of circumstances, to remain unbiased by the extremes of victory or defeat, to greet returning fortune with a cool eye, to have faith in men after repeated betrayals, raises Alfred far above the turmoil of barbaric wars to his pinnacle of deathless glory." [23]

Walter de la Mare found "prose worthy of the name of literature ... tinged with that erratic and unique factor, the personal ..." reminding one of the statement by Mr. F. O. Matthiessen, in his study of Sarah Orne Jewett, that "style means that the author has fused his material and his technique with the distinctive quality of his personality ..." and of the word "idiolect" used by Professor Harry Levin as meaning "the language of a speaker or writer who has an inflection of his own." In saying there is no substitute for content, one is partly saying there is no substitute for individuality—that which is peculiar to the person (the Greek *idioma*). One also recalls the remark by Henry James: "A thing's being one's own will double the use of it." Discoveries in art, certainly, are personal before they are general.

Goya—in *The Taste of Our Time* series,[24] reviewed by Pierre Gassier somewhat as follows—should afford us creative impetus. After surviving a lethal threat, severe illness at Cádiz in 1792, Goya was left with his right side paralyzed, with dizzy spells, a buzzing in his head, and partial blindness. He recovered, only to find himself irremediably deaf. On returning to Madrid, he began work at once, painted eleven pictures for the Academy of San Fernando, and sent them with a letter to the director, Don Berbardo Iriarte. "In order to occupy an imagination mortified by the contemplation of my sufferings," he said, "and recover, partially at all events, the expenses incurred by illness, I fell to painting a set of pictures in which I have given observation a place usually denied it in works made to order, in which little scope is left for fancy and invention." Fancy and invention—not made to order—perfectly describe the work; the *Burial of the Sardine*, say: a careening throng in which one can identify a bear's mask and paws, a black monster wearing a horned hood, a huge turquoise quadricorn, a goblin mouth on a sepia fish-tailed banner, and twin dancers in filmy gowns with pink satin bows in their hair. Pieter Bruegel, the Elder, an observer as careful and as populous as Goya, "crossed the Alps and travelled the length of Italy, returning in 1555 to paint as though Michelangelo had never existed," so powerful was predilective intention.[25] In a television interview after receiving the National Book Award for *Ten North Frederick*, John O'Hara was asked if he might not have to find, as a background for fiction, something different from small-town life in Pennsylvania, to which he replied, "There is in one room in one day of one man's life, material for a lifetime." The artist does not—as we sometimes hear—"seek fresh sources of inspiration." A subject to which he is susceptible entices him to it; as we see in the epics of Marko Marulíc (1450–1524), the fifth centenary of whose birth Yugoslavia has celebrated, in honor largely of his Latin epic *Judita* (1501), enhanced by woodcuts such as *The Muster at Dubrovnik*: trumpeters, men at arms in an elephant-castle, dog, king, queen, and attendants. The New York Yugoslav Information Center says, "What is important is that in following the classics, Marulíc did not transplant . . . mechanically . . . but depended on his own poetic abilities," his novelty consisting in "comparisons taken from his own field of experience, in language abounding in speech forms of the people." An author, that is to say, is a fashioner of words, stamps them with his own personality, and wears the raiment he has made, in his own way.

Psychoanalysis can do some harm "taking things to pieces that it cannot put together again," as Mr. Whit Burnett said in a discourse entitled "Secrets of Creativeness." It has also been of true service, sharpening our faculties and combating complacence. Mr. Burnett drew attention to the biography of Dr. Freud by Ernest Jones, and to what is said there of genius as being not a quality but qualitative—a combination of attributes which differs with the person—three of which are honesty, a sense of the really significant, and the power of concentration.

Curiosity seems to me connected with this sense of significance. Thoreau, you may recall, demurred when commended for originality and said that it was curiosity. "I am curiosity from top to toe." I think I detect curiosity in the work of Sybille Bedford—in her novel *A Legacy*—in the statement "No one in the house was supposed to handle *used* notes [banknotes]. Everybody was paid straight off the press: The problem of change was not envisaged"; sententiousness in the writing, being offset by the unstereotyped juxtaposing of a word or two such as "querulous" and "placid." Grandma Merz, for instance, "was a short bundle of a woman swaddled in stuffs and folds . . . stuck with brooches of rather gray diamonds. Her face was a round, large, indeterminate expanse . . . with features that escaped attention and an expression that was at once querulous and placid." [26]

In Marguerite Yourcenar's "Author's Note" to her *Memoirs of Hadrian* [27]—a study which does "border on the domain of fiction and sometimes of poetry," as has been said—one sees what concentration editorially can be. And Paul Delarue's "Sources and Commentary" appended to the *Borzoi Book of French Folk Tales* [28] are similarly impressive—besides affording an exciting knowledge of variants. In "The White Dove" (the story of Bluebeard, abridged by Perrault), the ninth victim's pretexts for delay become specific—in this early version—"to put on my petticoat, my wedding-gown, my cap, my bouquet." And we learn that "The Ass's Skin," enshrined for us by La Fontaine in "The Power of Fable," [29] is "The Story of Goldilocks," and of Madame d'Aulnoy's "Beauty and the Beast" (1698). The presentment here of obscure minutiae, demonstrating that tales of all nations have a common fabric, makes the most artful of detective stories seem tame.

Creative secrets; are they secrets? Impassioned interest in life, that burns its bridges behind it and will not contemplate defeat, is one, I would say. Discouragement is a form of temptation, but paranoia is not optimism. In an essay entitled "Solitude" (the theme chosen by the *Figaro* for an essay contest), Maxime Bennebon, a boy seventeen, visualizes "Michelangelo's *Moses*, head in hands, the attitude of the child who prays with eyes closed; of the pianist—his back to the audience; they must be alone that they may offer what is most treasurable, themselves."

The master secret may be steadfastness, that of Nehemiah, Artaxerxes' cupbearer, as it was of the three youths in the fiery furnace, who would not bow down to the image which the King had set up. "Why is thy countenance sad, seeing that thou art not sick?" the King asked. Nehemiah requested that he be allowed to rebuild the wall of Jerusalem, and the King granted his request, gave him leave of absence and a letter to the keeper of the forest that he might have timber for the gates of the palace — subject to sarcasm while building, such as Sanballet's "If a fox go up, he shall break down their wall." Summoned four times to a colloquy, Nehemiah sent word: "I am doing a great work and I cannot come down." Then, when warned that he would be slain, he said, "Should such a man as I flee?" "So the wall was finished." [30] A result which is sensational is implemented by what to the craftsman was private and unsensational. Tyrone Guthrie, in connection with the theater, made a statement which sums up what I have been trying to say about idiosyncrasy and technique: "It is one of the paradoxes of art that a work can only be universal if it is rooted in a part of its creator which is most privately and particularly himself." [31]

Thomas Mann, fending off eulogy, rendered a service when he said, "Praise will never subdue skepticism." We fail in some degree — and know that we do, if we are competent; but can prevail; and the following attributes, applied by a London journal to Victor Gollancz, the author and publisher, I adopt as a prescription: we can in the end prevail if our attachment to art is sufficiently deep; "unpriggish, subtle, perceptive, and consuming." [32]

(1956)

Notes

Inaugurating the Ewing Lectures at the University of California, October 3 and 5, 1956; published as a pamphlet by University of California Press, Berkeley and Los Angeles, in 1958

1. *Making, Knowing and Judging: An Inaugural Lecture by W. H. Auden Delivered before the University of Oxford on 11 June 1956* (Oxford at the Clarendon Press).

2. Michael Tippett, "An Irish Basset-Horn," *The Listener*, July 26, 1956.

3. Hesketh Pearson, "Bernard Shaw as Producer," *The Listener*, August 16, 1956.

4. "Discourse in Praise of Wisdom," re-entitled "Goethe as the Sage."

5. *The Dalhousie Review*, January 1943.

6. Translated by Ezra Pound (Cambridge: Harvard University Press, 1954), p. 55.

7. Ibid., p. 80.

8. *The Self and the Dramas of History* (New York: Scribner, 1955).

9. "Edwin Arnold and 'The Light of Asia,' " *The Listener*, June 14, 1956.

10. *The New York Times*, November 20, 1957.

11. *The Listener*, June 14, 1956.

12. "In Honour of James Cook," *The Listener*, June 14, 1956.

13. *The Shock of Recognition*, ed. by Edmund Wilson (New York: Doubleday, 1943).

14. Unsigned review in *The Times Literary Supplement*, London, March 2, 1956.

15. *Life*, July 16, 1956.

16. *The Fables of La Fontaine*, trans. by Marianne Moore (New York: Viking, 1954), Book Ten, IX.

17. Dr. Alvin E. Magary.

18. Maxwell Geismar, *The Nation*, April 14, 1956.

19. As "freely translated" by Charles Poore, reviewing James B. Conant, *The Citadel of Learning* (New Haven: Yale University Press, 1956), in *The New York Times*, April 7, 1956.

20. In *Writers on Writing*, ed. by Herschel Brickell (New York: Doubleday, 1949).

21. Anonymous. Reprinted in *The New York Times*, November 17, 1954.

22. *The Fables of La Fontaine*, Book Eight, III.

23. *A History of the English-Speaking Peoples*, vol. I: *The Birth of Britain* (New York: Dodd, Mead, 1956).

24. "Essay on Prose," *The National and English Review* (in three sections, concluded in March 1955), quoted by *Arts* (New York).

25. Fritz Grossmann, *The Paintings of Bruegel* (New York: Phaidon Press, 1955).

26. Sybille Bedford, *A Legacy* (New York: Simon and Schuster, 1957).

27. Translated from the French by Grace Frick (New York: Farrar, Straus and Cudahy, 1954).

28. Translated by Austin E. Fife (New York: Knopf, 1956).

29. *The Fables of La Fontaine*, Book Eight, IV: "The moment The Ass's Skin commences, Away with appearances; I am enraptured, really am."

30. Nehemiah 2, 4, and 6.

31. *The New York Times* magazine, November 27, 1955.

32. *The Observer*, March 11, 1956.

Randall Jarrell

The Woman at the Washington Zoo

CRITICS *fairly often write essays about how some poem was writ-ten; the poet who wrote it seldom does. When Robert Penn War-ren and Cleanth Brooks were making a new edition of* Under-standing Poetry, *they asked several poets to write such essays. I no longer remembered much about writing* The Woman at the Washington Zoo—*a poem is, so to speak, a way of making you forget how you wrote it*—*but I had almost all the sheets of paper on which it was written, starting with a paper napkin from the Methodist Cafeteria. If you had asked me where I had begun the poem I'd have said, "Why, Sir, at the beginning"; it was a surprise to me to see that I hadn't.*

As I read, arranged, and remembered the pages, it all came back to me. I went over them for several days, copying down most of the lines and phrases and mentioning some of the sights and cir-cumstances they came out of; I tried to give a fairly good idea of the objective process of writing the poem. You may say, "But isn't a poem a kind of subjective process, like a dream? Doesn't it come out of unconscious wishes of yours, childhood memories, parts of your own private emotional life?" It certainly does: part of them I don't know about and the rest I didn't write about. Nor did I write about or copy down something that begins to appear on the last two or three pages: lines and phrases from a kind of counter-poem, named Jerome, in which Saint Jerome is a psychoanalyst and his lion is at the zoo.

230

*If after reading·this essay the reader should say, "You did all
that you could to the things, but the things just came," he would
feel about it as I do.*

LATE IN THE SUMMER of 1956 my wife and I moved to Washing-
ton. We lived with two daughters, a cat, and a dog in Chevy
Chase; every day I would drive to work through Rock Creek Park,
past the zoo. I worked across the street from the Capitol, at the Li-
brary of Congress. I knew Washington fairly well but had never
lived there; I had been in the army, but except for that had never
worked for the government.

Some of the new and some of the old things there — I was often
reminded of the army — had a good deal of effect on me: after a
few weeks I began to write a poem. I have most of what I wrote,
though the first page is gone; the earliest lines are

                any color
My print, that has clung to its old colors
Through many washings; this dull null
Navy I wear to work, and wear from work, and so
~~*And so to bed*~~   *To bed*
With no complaint, no comment — neither from my
   chief,
                     nor
The Deputy Chief Assistant, ~~from~~ his chief,
Nor   *nor*
~~*From*~~*Congressmen, ~~from~~ their constituents —*
                  ~~*thin*~~
Only I complain; this ~~poor~~ worn serviceable . . .

The woman talking is a near relation of women I was seeing
there in Washington — some at close range, at the Library — and a
distant relation of women I had written about before, in "The End
of the Rainbow" and "Cinderella" and "Seele im Raum." She is a
kind of aging machine-part. I wrote, as they say in suits, "acting as
next friend"; I had for her the sympathy of an aging machine-part.
(If I was also something else, that was just personal; and she also
was something else.) I felt that one of these hundreds of thousands
of government clerks might feel all her dresses one dress, a faded
navy blue print, and that dress her body. This work- or life-uni-

form of hers excites neither complaint, nor comment, nor the me-
chanically protective *No comment* of the civil servant; excites
them neither from her "chief," the Deputy Chief Assistant, nor
from his, nor from any being on any level of that many-leveled
machine: all the system is silent, except for her own cry, which
goes unnoticed just as she herself goes unnoticed. (I had met a
Deputy Chief Assistant, who saw nothing remarkable in the title.)
The woman's days seem to her the going-up-to-work and coming-
down-from-work of a worker; each ends in *And so to bed*, the dia-
rist's conclusive unvarying entry in the daybook of his life.

These abruptly opening lines are full of duplications and ech-
oes, like what they describe. And they are wrong in the way in
which beginnings are wrong: either there is too much of some-
thing or it is not yet there. The lines break off with *this worn serv-
iceable* — the words can apply either to her dress or to her body,
but anything so obviously suitable to the dress must be intended
for the body. *Body that no sunlight dyes, no hand suffuses*, the
page written the next day goes on; then after a space there is
*Dome-shadowed, withering among columns,/ Wavy upon the
pools of fountains, small beside statues . . .* No sun colors, no hand
suffuses with its touch, this used, still-useful body. It is subdued to
the element it works in; is shadowed by the domes, grows old and
small and dry among the columns, of the buildings of the capital;
becomes a reflection, its material identity lost, upon the pools of
the fountains of the capital; is dwarfed beside the statues of the
capital — as year by year it passes among the public places of this
city of space and trees and light, city sinking beneath the weight
of its marble, city of graded, voteless workers.

The word *small*, as it joins the reflections in the pools, the trips
to the public places, brings the poem to its real place and subject —
to its title, even: next, there is *small and shining*, then (with the
star beside it that means "use, don't lose") *small, far-off, shining
in the eyes of animals*; the woman ends at the zoo, looking so in-
tently into its cages that she sees her own reflection in *the eyes of
animals, these wild ones trapped/ As I am trapped but not, them-
selves, the trap . . .* The lines have written above them *The
Woman at the Washington Zoo.*

The next page has the title and twelve lines:

This print, that has kept the memory of color

Alive through many cleanings; this dull null
Navy I wear to work, and wear from work, and so
To bed (with no complaints, no comment: neither from my chief,
The Deputy Chief Assistant, nor her chief,
Nor his, nor Congressmen, nor their constituents
                           ~~wan~~
— Only I complain); this ~~plain,~~ worn, serviceable
             sunlight
Body that no ~~sunset~~ dyes, no hand suffuses
But, dome-shadowed, withering among columns,
Wavy beneath fountains — small, far-off, shining
                           ~~wild~~
In the eyes of animals, these beings trapped
As I am trapped but not, themselves, the trap . . .

Written underneath this, in the rapid, ugly, disorganized handwriting of most of the pages, is *bars of my body burst blood breath breathing* — *lives aging but without knowledge of age/ Waiting in their safe prisons for death, knowing not of death*. Immediately, this is changed into two lines: *Aging, but without knowledge of their age,/ Kept safe here, knowing not of death, for death* — and out at the side, scrawled heavily, is *O bars of my own body, open, open!* She recognizes herself in the animals — and recognizes herself, also, in the cages.

Written across the top of this page is *2nd and 3rd alphabet*. Streets in Washington run through a one-syllable, a two-syllable, and a three-syllable (Albemarle, Brandywine, Chesapeake . . .) alphabet, so that people say about an address, "Let's see, that's in the second alphabet, isn't it?" It made me think of Kronecker's "God made the integers; all else is the work of man"; but it seemed right for Washington to have alphabets of its own — I made up the title of a detective story, *Murder in the Second Alphabet*. The alphabets were a piece of Washington that should have fitted into the poem, but didn't; but the zoo was a whole group of pieces, a little Washington, into which the poem itself fitted.

Rock Creek Park, with its miles of heavily wooded hills and valleys, its rocky stream, is like some National Forest dropped into Washington by mistake. Many of the animals of the zoo are in unroofed cages back in its ravines. My wife and I had often visited the zoo, and now that we were living in Washington we went to it a great deal. We had made friends with a lynx that was very like our cat that had died the spring before, at the age of sixteen. We would feed the lynx pieces of liver or scraps of chicken and turkey; we fed liver, sometimes, to two enormous white timber wolves that lived at the end of one ravine. Eager for the meat, they would stand up against the bars on their hind legs, taller than a man, and stare into our eyes; they reminded me of Akela, white with age, in *The Jungle Books*, and of the wolves who fawn at the man Mowgli's brown feet in *In the Rukh*. In one of the buildings of the zoo there was a lioness with two big cubs; when the keeper came she would come over, purring her bass purr, to rub her head against the bars, almost as our lynx would rub his head against the turkey-skin, in rapture, before he finally gulped it down. In the lions' building there were two black leopards; when you got close to them you saw they had not lost the spots of the ordinary leopards—were the ordinary leopards, but spotted black on black, dingy somehow.

On the way to the wolves one went by a big unroofed cage of foxes curled up asleep; on the concrete floor of the enclosure there would be scattered two or three white rats—stiff, quite untouched—that the foxes had left. (The wolves left their meat, too—big slabs of horse meat, glazing, covered with flies.) Twice when I came to the foxes' cage there was a turkey-buzzard that had come down for the rats; startled at me, he flapped up heavily, with a rat dangling underneath. (There are usually vultures circling over the zoo; nearby, at the tennis courts of the Sheraton Park, I used to see vultures perched on the tower of WTTG, above the court on which Defense Secretary McElroy was playing doubles— so that I would say to myself, like Peer Gynt, "Nature is witty.") As a child, coming around the bend of a country road, I had often seen a turkey-buzzard, with its black wings and naked red head, flap heavily up from the mashed body of a skunk or possum or rabbit.

A good deal of this writes itself on the next page, almost too rapidly for line-endings or punctuation: *to be and never know I am   when the vulture buzzard comes for the white rat that the foxes left   May he take off his black wings, the red flesh of his head, and step to me as man—a man at whose brown feet the white wolves fawn—to whose hand of power/ The lioness stalks, leaving her cubs playing/ and rubs her head along the bars as he strokes it.* Along the side of the page, between these lines, two or three words to a line, is written *the animals who are trapped but are not themselves the trap black leopards spots, light and darkened, hidden except to the close eyes of love, in their life-long darkness, so I in decent black, navy blue.*

As soon as the zoo came into the poem, everything else settled into it and was at home there; on this page it is plain even to the writer that all the things in the poem come out of, and are divided between, color and colorlessness. Colored women and colored animals and colored cloth — all that the woman sees as her own opposite — come into the poem to begin it. Beside the typed lines are many hurried phrases, most of them crossed out: *red and yellow as October maples   rosy, blood seen through flesh in summer   colors wild and easy natural   leaf-yellow cloud-rose leopard-yellow, cloth from another planet the leopards look back at their wearers, hue for hue   the women look back at the leopard.* And on the back of the vulture's page there is a flight of ideas, almost a daydream, coming out of these last phrases: *we have never mistaken you for the others   among the legations one of a different architecture women, saris of a different color envoy impassive   clear bullet-proof glass   lips, through the clear glass of a rose sedan   color of blood   you too are represented on this earth . . .*

One often sees on the streets of Washington — fairly often sees at the zoo — what seem beings of a different species: women from the embassies of India and Pakistan, their sallow skin and black hair leopardlike, their yellow or rose or green saris exactly as one imagines the robes of Greek statues before the statues had lost their colors. It was easy for me to see the saris as cloth from another planet or satellite; I have written about a sick child who wants "a ship from some near star/ To land in the yard and beings to come out/ And think to me: 'So this is where you are!' " and about an old man who says that it is his ambition to be the pet of visitors from another planet; as an old reader of science fiction, I am used to looking at the sun red over the hills, the moon white over the ocean, and saying to my wife in a sober voice, "It's like another planet." After I had worked a little longer, the poem began as it begins now.

> *The saris go by me from the embassies.*
>
> *Cloth from the moon. Cloth from another planet.*

They look back at the leopard like the leopard.

And I . . . This print of mine, that has kept its color
Alive through so many cleanings; this dull null
Navy I wear to work, and wear from work, and so
To my bed, so to my grave, with no
Complaints, no comment: neither from my chief,
The Deputy Chief Assistant, nor his chief—
Only I complain; this serviceable
Body that no sunlight dyes, no hand suffuses
But, dome-shadowed, withering among columns,
Wavy beneath fountains — small, far-off, shining
In the eyes of animals, these beings trapped
As I am trapped but not, themselves, the trap,
Aging, but without knowledge of their age,
Kept safe here, knowing not of death, for death
— Oh, bars of my own body, open, open!

It is almost as if, once all the materials of the poem were there, the middle and end of the poem made themselves, as the beginning seemed to make itself. After the imperative *open, open!* there is a space, and the middle of the poem begins evenly — since her despair is beyond expression — in a statement of accomplished fact: *The world goes by my cage and never sees me.* Inside the mechanical official cage of her life, her body, she lives invisibly; no one feeds this animal, reads out its name, pokes a stick through the bars at it — the cage is empty. She feels that she is even worse off than the other animals of the zoo: they are still wild animals — since they do not know how to change into domesticated animals, beings that are their own cages — and they are surrounded by a world that does not know how to surrender them, still thinks them part of itself. This natural world comes through or over the bars of the cages, on its continual visits to those within: to those who are not machine-parts, convicts behind the bars of their penitentiary, but wild animals — the free beasts come to their imprisoned brothers and never know that they are not also free. Written on the back of one page, crossed out, is *Come still, you free;* on the next page this becomes

> *The world goes by my cage and never sees me.*
> *And there come not to me, as come to these,*

> *The wild* ~~ones~~ *beasts, sparrows pecking the llamas' grain,*
> *Pigeons* ~~fluttering to~~ *settling on the bear's bread, turkey-buzzards*
> ~~Coming with grace first, then with horror — Vulture seizing~~
> *Tearing the meat the flies have clouded . . .*

In saying mournfully that the wild animals do not come to her as they come to the animals of the zoo, she is wishing for their human equivalent to come to her. But she is right in believing that she has become her own cage—she has changed so much, in her manless, childless, fleshless existence, that her longing wish has inside it an increasing repugnance and horror: the innocent sparrows *pecking* the llamas' grain become larger in the pigeons *settling on* (not *fluttering to*) the bears' bread; and these grow larger and larger, come (with grace first, far off in the sky, but at last with horror) as turkey-buzzards seizing, no, *tearing* the meat the flies have clouded. She herself is that stale leftover flesh, nauseating just as what comes to it is horrible and nauseating. The series *pecking, settling on,* and *tearing* has inside it a sexual metaphor: the stale flesh that no one would have is taken at last by the turkey-buzzard with his naked red neck and head.

Her own life is so terrible to her that, to change, she is willing to accept even this, changing it as best she can. She says: *Vulture* [it is a euphemism that gives him distance and solemnity], *when you come for the white rat that the foxes left* [to her the rat is so plainly herself that she does not need to say so; the small, white, untouched thing is more accurately what she is than was the clouded meat—but, also, it is euphemistic, more nearly bearable], *take off the red helmet of your head* [the bestiality, the obscene sexuality of the flesh-eating death bird is really—she hopes or pretends or desperately is sure—merely external, *clothes*, an intentionally frightening war garment like a Greek or Roman helmet], *the black wings that have shadowed me* [she feels that their inhuman colorless darkness has always, like the domes of the inhuman city, shadowed her; the wings are like a black parody of the wings the Swan Brothers wear in the fairy tale, just as the whole costume is like that of the Frog Prince or the other beastprinces of the stories] *and step* [as a human being, not fly as an animal] *to me as* [what you really are under the disguising clothing of red flesh and black feathers] *man*—not the machine-part,

the domesticated animal that is its own cage, but man as he was
first, still must be, is: the animals' natural lord,

> The wild brother at whose feet the white wolves fawn,
> To whose hand of power the great lioness
> Stalks, purring . . .

And she ends the poem when she says to him

> You know what I was,
> You see what I am: change me, change me!

Here is the whole poem:

The Woman at the Washington Zoo

> The saris go by me from the embassies.
>
> Cloth from the moon. Cloth from another planet.
> They look back at the leopard like the leopard.
>
> And I . . .
>   This print of mine, that has kept its color
> Alive through so many cleanings; this dull null
> Navy I wear to work, and wear from work, and so
> To my bed, so to my grave, with no
> Complaints, no comment: neither from my chief,
> The Deputy Chief Assistant, nor his chief—
> Only I complain; this serviceable
> Body that no sunlight dyes, no hand suffuses
> But, dome-shadowed, withering among columns,
> Wavy beneath fountains—small, far-off, shining
> In the eyes of animals, these beings trapped
> As I am trapped but not, themselves, the trap,
> Aging, but without knowledge of their age,
> Kept safe here, knowing not of death, for death
> —Oh, bars of my own body, open, open!
>
> The world goes by my cage and never sees me.
> And there come not to me, as come to these,
> The wild beasts, sparrows pecking the llamas' grain,
> Pigeons settling on the bears' bread, buzzards
> Tearing the meat the flies have clouded . . .

                                        Vulture,
When you come for the white rat that the foxes left,
Take off the red helmet of your head, the black
Wings that have shadowed me, and step to me as man,
The wild brother at whose feet the white wolves fawn,
To whose hand of power the great lioness
Stalks, purring . . .
                        You know what I was,
You see what I am: change me, change me!

                                        (1961)

W. H. Auden

Writing

It is the author's aim to say once and emphatically, "He said."

— H. D. THOREAU

The art of literature, vocal or written, is to adjust the language so that it embodies what it indicates.

— A. N. WHITEHEAD

ALL THOSE whose success in life depends neither upon a job which satisfies some specific and unchanging social need, like a farmer's, nor, like a surgeon's, upon some craft which he can be taught by others and improve by practice, but upon "inspiration," the lucky hazard of ideas, live by their wits, a phrase which carries a slightly pejorative meaning. Every "original" genius, be he an artist or a scientist, has something a bit shady about him, like a gambler or a medium.

Literary gatherings, cocktail parties and the like, are a social nightmare because writers have no "shop" to talk. Lawyers and doctors can entertain each other with stories about interesting cases, about experiences, that is to say, related to their professional interests but yet impersonal and outside themselves. Writers have no impersonal professional interests. The literary equivalent of talking shop would be writers reciting their own work at each other, an unpopular procedure for which only very young writers have the nerve.

No poet or novelist wishes he were the only one who ever lived, but most of them wish they were the only one alive, and quite a number fondly believe their wish has been granted.

In theory, the author of a good book should remain anonymous, for it is to his work, not to himself, that admiration is due. In practice, this seems to be impossible. However, the praise and public attention that writers sometimes receive do not seem to be as fatal to them as one might expect. Just as a good man forgets his deed the moment he has done it, a genuine writer forgets a work as soon as he has completed it and starts to think about the next one; if he thinks about his past work at all, he is more likely to remember its faults than its virtues. Fame often makes a writer vain, but seldom makes him proud.

Writers can be guilty of every kind of human conceit but one, the conceit of the social worker: "We are all here on earth to help others; what on earth the others are here for, I don't know."

When a successful author analyzes the reasons for his success, he generally underestimates the talent he was born with, and overestimates his skill in employing it.

Every writer would rather be rich than poor, but no genuine writer cares about popularity as such. He needs approval of his work by others in order to be reassured that the vision of life he believes he has had is a true vision and not a self-delusion, but he can only be reassured by those whose judgment he respects. It would only be necessary for a writer to secure universal popularity if imagination and intelligence were equally distributed among all men.

When some obvious booby tells me he has liked a poem of mine, I feel as if I had picked his pocket.

Writers, poets especially, have an odd relation to the public because their medium, language, is not, like the paint of the painter or the notes of the composer, reserved for their use but is the common property of the linguistic group to which they belong. Lots of people are willing to admit that they don't understand painting or music, but very few indeed who have been to school and learned to read advertisements will admit that they don't understand English. As Karl Kraus said, "The public doesn't understand German, and in Journalese I can't tell them so."

How happy the lot of the mathematician! He is judged solely by his peers, and the standard is so high that no colleague or rival can ever win a reputation he does not deserve. No cashier writes a letter to the press complaining about the incomprehensibility of Modern Mathematics and comparing it unfavorably with the good old days when mathematicians were content to paper irregularly shaped rooms and fill bathtubs without closing the waste pipe.

To say that a work is inspired means that, in the judgment of its author or his readers, it is better than they could reasonably hope it would be, and nothing else.

All works of art are commissioned in the sense that no artist can create one by a simple act of will but must wait until what he believes to be a good idea for a work "comes" to him. Among those works which are failures because their initial conceptions were false or inadequate, the number of self-commissioned works may well be greater than the number commissioned by patrons.

The degree of excitement which a writer feels during the process of composition is as much an indication of the value of the final result as the excitement felt by a worshiper is an indication of the value of his devotions, that is to say, very little indication.

The Oracle claimed to make prophecies and give good advice about the future; it never pretended to be giving poetry readings.

If poems could be created in a trance without the conscious participation of the poet, the writing of poetry would be so boring or even unpleasant an operation that only a substantial reward in money or social prestige could induce a man to be a poet. From the manuscript evidence, it now appears that Coleridge's account of the composition of "Kubla Khan" was a fib.

It is true that when he is writing a poem, it seems to a poet as if there were two people involved, his conscious self and a Muse whom he has to woo or an Angel with whom he has to wrestle, but, as in an ordinary wooing or wrestling match, his role is as important as Hers. The Muse, like Beatrice in *Much Ado*, is a spirited girl who has as little use for an abject suitor as she has for a vulgar brute. She appreciates chivalry and good manners, but she despises those who will not stand up to her, and takes a cruel delight in telling them nonsense and lies, which the poor little things obediently write down as "inspired" truth.

> When I was writing the chorus in G Minor, I suddenly dipped my pen into the medicine bottle instead of the ink; I made a blot, and when I dried it with sand (blotting paper had not been invented then) it took the form of a natural, which instantly gave me the idea of the effect which the change from G minor to G major would make, and to this blot all the effect—if any—is due.
> —Rossini to Louis Engel

Such an act of judgment, distinguishing between Chance and Providence, deserves, surely, to be called an inspiration.

To keep his errors down to a minimum, the internal Censor to whom a poet submits his work in progress should be a Censorate. It should include, for instance, a sensitive only child, a practical housewife, a logician, a monk, an irreverent buffoon, and even, perhaps, hated by all the others and returning their dislike, a brutal, foul-mouthed drill sergeant who considers all poetry rubbish.

In the course of many centuries a few labor-saving devices have been introduced into the mental kitchen—alcohol, coffee, tobacco, Benzedrine, etc.—but these are very crude, constantly breaking down, and liable to injure the cook. Literary composition in the twentieth century A.D. is pretty much what it was in the twentieth century B.C.: nearly everything has still to be done by hand.

Most people enjoy the sight of their own handwriting as they enjoy the smell of their own farts. Much as I loathe the typewriter, I must admit that it is a help in self-criticism. Typescript is so impersonal and hideous to look at that if I type out a poem, I immediately see defects which I missed when I looked through it in manuscript. When it comes to a poem by somebody else, the severest test I know of is to write it out in longhand. The physical tedium of doing this ensures that the slightest defect will reveal itself; the hand is constantly looking for an excuse to stop.

Most artists are sincere and most art is bad, though some insincere (sincerely insincere) works can be quite good. (STRAVINSKY.) Sincerity is like sleep. Normally, one should assume that, of course, one will be sincere, and not give the question a second thought. Most writers, however, suffer occasionally from bouts of insincerity as men do from bouts of insomnia. The remedy in both cases is often quite simple: in the case of the latter, to change one's diet; in the case of the former, to change one's company.

The schoolmasters of literature frown on affectations of style as silly and unhealthy. Instead of frowning, they ought to laugh indulgently. Shakespeare makes fun of the Euphuists in *Love's Labor's Lost* and in *Hamlet,* but he owed them a great deal and he knew it. Nothing, on the face of it, could have been more futile than the attempt of Spenser, Harvey, and others to be good little humanists and write English verse in classical meters, yet, but for their folly, many of Campion's most beautiful songs and the choruses in *Samson Agonistes* would never have been written. In literature, as in life, affectation, passionately adopted and loyally persevered in, is one of the chief forms of self-discipline by which mankind has raised itself by its own bootstraps.

A mannered style, that of Góngora or Henry James, for example, is like eccentric clothing: very few writers can carry it off, but one is enchanted by the rare exception who can.

When a reviewer describes a book as "sincere," one knows immediately that it is (a) insincere (insincerely insincere) and (b) badly written. Sincerity in the proper sense of the word, meaning authenticity, is, however, or ought to be, a writer's chief preoccupation. No writer can ever judge exactly how good or bad a work of his may be, but he can always know, not immediately perhaps, but certainly in a short while, whether something he has written is authentic—in his handwriting—or a forgery.

The most painful of all experiences to a poet is to find that a poem of his which he knows to be a forgery has pleased the public and got into the anthologies. For all he knows or cares, the poem may be quite good, but that is not the point; *he* should not have written it.

The work of a young writer—*Werther* is the classic example—is sometimes a therapeutic act. He finds himself obsessed by certain ways of feeling and thinking of which his instinct tells him he must be rid before he can discover his authentic interests and sympathies, and the only way by which he can be rid of them forever is by surrendering to them. Once he has done this, he has developed the necessary antibodies which will make him immune for the rest of his life. As a rule, the disease is some spiritual malaise of his generation. If so, he may, as Goethe did, find himself in an embarrassing situation. What he wrote in order to exorcise certain feelings is enthusiastically welcomed by his contemporaries because it expresses just what they feel, but, unlike him, they are perfectly happy to feel in this way; for the moment they regard him as their spokesman. Time passes. Having gotten the poison out of his system, the writer turns to his true interests which are not, and never were, those of his early admirers, who now pursue him with cries of "Traitor!"

The intellect of man is forced to choose
Perfection of the life or of the work. (YEATS.)
This is untrue; perfection is possible in neither. All one can say is that a writer who, like all men, has his personal weaknesses and limitations, should be aware of them and try his best to keep them out of his work. For every writer, there are certain subjects which,

because of defects in his character and his talent, he should never touch.

What makes it difficult for a poet not to tell lies is that, in poetry, all facts and all beliefs cease to be true or false and become interesting possibilities. The reader does not have to share the beliefs expressed in a poem in order to enjoy it. Knowing this, a poet is constantly tempted to make use of an idea or a belief, not because he believes it to be true, but because he sees it has interesting poetic possibilities. It may not, perhaps, be absolutely necessary that he *believe* it, but it is certainly necessary that his emotions be deeply involved, and this they can never be unless, as a man, he takes it more seriously than as a mere poetic convenience.

The integrity of a writer is more threatened by appeals to his social conscience, his political or religious convictions, than by appeals to his cupidity. It is morally less confusing to be goosed by a traveling salesman than by a bishop.

Some writers confuse authenticity, which they ought always to aim at, with originality, which they should never bother about. There is a certain kind of person who is so dominated by the desire to be loved for himself alone that he has constantly to test those around him by tiresome behavior; what he says and does must be admired, not because it is intrinsically admirable, but because it is *his* remark, *his* act. Does not this explain a good deal of avant-garde art?

Slavery is so intolerable a condition that the slave can hardly escape deluding himself into thinking that he is choosing to obey his master's commands when, in fact, he is obliged to. Most slaves of habit suffer from this delusion and so do some writers, enslaved by an all too "personal" style.

> "Let me think: was I the same when I got up this morning? . . . But if I'm not the same, the next question is 'Who in the world am I?' . . . I'm sure I'm not Ada . . . for her hair goes in such long ringlets and mine doesn't go in ringlets at all; and I'm sure I can't be Mabel, for I know all sorts of things, and she, oh! she knows such a very little! Beside she's she and I'm I and — oh dear, how

puzzling it all is! I'll try if I know all the things I used to know..." Her eyes filled with tears... "I must be Mabel after all, and I shall have to go and live in that poky little house, and have next to no toys to play with, and oh! — ever so many lessons to learn! No, I've made up my mind about it: if I'm Mabel, I'll stay down here!"

(Alice in Wonderland.)

At the next peg the Queen turned again and this time she said: "Speak in French when you can't think of the English for a thing — turn your toes out as you walk — and remember who you are."

(Through the Looking-Glass.)

Most writers, except the supreme masters who transcend all systems of classification, are either Alices or Mabels. For example:

Alice	*Mabel*
Montaigne	Pascal
Marvell	Donne
Burns	Shelley
Jane Austen	Dickens
Turgenev	Dostoevski
Valéry	Gide
Virginia Woolf	Joyce
E. M. Forster	Lawrence
Robert Graves	Yeats

"Orthodoxy," said a real Alice of a bishop, "is reticence."

Except when used as historical labels, the terms "Classical" and "Romantic" are misleading terms for two poetic parties, the Aristocratic and the Democratic, which have always existed and to one of which every writer belongs, though he may switch his party allegiance or, on some specific issue, refuse to obey his Party Whip.

The Aristocratic Principle as regards subject matter:
   No subject matter shall be treated by poets which poetry cannot digest. It defends poetry against didacticism and journalism.
The Democratic Principle as regards subject matter:
   No subject matter shall be excluded by poets which poetry is ca-

pable of digesting. It defends poetry against limited or stale conceptions of what is "poetic."

The Aristocratic Principle as regards treatment:

No irrelevant aspects of a given subject shall be expressed in a poem which treats it. It defends poetry against barbaric vagueness.

The Democratic Principle as regards treatment:

No relevant aspect of a given subject shall remain unexpressed in a poem which treats it. It defends poetry against decadent triviality.

Every work of a writer should be a first step, but this will be a false step unless, whether or not he realize it at the time, it is also a further step. When a writer is dead, one ought to be able to see that his various works, taken together, make one consistent *oeuvre*.

It takes little talent to see clearly what lies under one's nose, a good deal of it to know in which direction to point that organ.

The greatest writer cannot see through a brick wall but, unlike the rest of us, he does not build one.

Only a minor talent can be a perfect gentleman; a major talent is always more than a bit of a cad. Hence the importance of minor writers—as teachers of good manners. Now and again, an exquisite minor work can make a master feel thoroughly ashamed of himself.

The poet is the father of his poem; its mother is a language: one could list poems as race horses are listed—*out of L by P.*

A poet has to woo not only his own Muse but also Dame Philology, and, for the beginner, the latter is the more important. As a rule, the sign that a beginner has a genuine original talent is that he is more interested in playing with words than in saying something original; his attitude is that of the old lady, quoted by E. M. Forster—"How can I know what I think till I see what I say?" It is only later, when he has wooed and won Dame Philology, that he can give his entire devotion to his Muse.

Rhymes, meters, stanza forms, etc., are like servants. If the master is fair enough to win their affection and firm enough to command their respect, the result is an orderly, happy household. If he is too tyrannical, they give notice; if he lacks authority, they become slovenly, impertinent, drunk, and dishonest.

The poet who writes "free" verse is like Robinson Crusoe on his desert island: he must do all his cooking, laundry, and darning for himself. In a few exceptional cases, this manly independence produces something original and impressive, but more often the result is squalor—dirty sheets on the unmade bed and empty bottles on the unswept floor.

There are some poets, Kipling, for example, whose relation to language reminds one of a drill sergeant: the words are taught to wash behind their ears, stand properly at attention, and execute complicated maneuvers, but at the cost of never being allowed to think for themselves. There are others, Swinburne, for example, who remind one more of Svengali: under their hypnotic suggestion, an extraordinary performance is put on, not by raw recruits, but by feeble-minded schoolchildren.

Due to the Curse of Babel, poetry is the most provincial of the arts, but today, when civilization is becoming monotonously the same all the world over, one feels inclined to regard this as a blessing rather than a curse: in poetry, at least, there cannot be an "International Style."

My language is the universal whore whom I have to make into a virgin. (KARL KRAUS.) It is both the glory and the shame of poetry that its medium is not its private property, that a poet cannot invent his words, and that words are products, not of nature, but of a human society which uses them for a thousand different purposes. In modern societies where language is continually being debased and reduced to nonspeech, the poet is in constant danger of having his ear corrupted, a danger to which the painter and the composer, whose media are their private property, are not exposed. On the other hand, he is more protected than they from another modern peril, that of solipsist subjectivity; however esoteric a poem may be, the fact that all its words have meanings which can be looked up in a dictionary makes it testify to the existence of other people. Even the language of *Finnegans Wake* was not created by Joyce *ex nihilo*; a purely private verbal world is not possible.

The difference between verse and prose is self-evident, but it is a sheer waste of time to look for a definition of the difference between poetry and prose. Frost's definition of poetry as the untranslatable element in language looks plausible at first sight but, on closer examination, will not quite do. In the first place, even in the most rarefied poetry, there are some elements which are translatable. The sound of the words, their rhythmical relations, and all meanings and association of meanings which depend upon sound, like rhymes and puns, are, of course, untranslatable, but poetry is not, like music, pure sound. Any elements in a poem which are not based on verbal experience are, to some degree, translatable into another tongue; for example, images, similes, and metaphors which are drawn from sensory experience. Moreover, because one characteristic that all men, whatever their culture, have in common is uniqueness—every man is a member of a class of one—the unique perspective on the world which every genuine poet has survives translation. If one takes a poem by Goethe and a poem by Hölderlin and makes literal prose cribs of them, every reader will recognize that the two poems were written by two different people. In the second place, if speech can never become music, neither can it ever become algebra. Even in the most "prosy" language, in informative and technical prose, there is a personal element because language is a personal creation. *Ne pas se pencher au dehors* has a different feeling tone from *Nichthinauslehnen*. A purely poetic language would be unlearnable, a purely prosaic not worth learning.

Valéry bases his definitions of poetry and prose on the difference between the gratuitous and the useful, play and work, and uses as an analogy the difference between dancing and walking. But this will not do, either. A commuter may walk to his suburban station every morning, but at the same time he may enjoy the walk for its own sake; the fact that his walk is necessary does not exclude the possibility of its also being a form of play. Vice versa, a dance does not cease to be play if it is also believed to have a useful purpose, like promoting a good harvest.

If French poets have been more prone than English to fall into the heresy of thinking that poetry ought to be as much like music as possible, one reason may be that in traditional French verse sound effects have always played a much more important role than they have in English verse. The English-speaking peoples have always felt that the difference between poetic speech and the conversational speech of everyday should be kept small, and whenever English poets have felt that the gap between poetic and ordinary speech was growing too wide, there has been a stylistic revolution to bring them closer again. In English verse, even in Shakespeare's grandest rhetorical passages, the ear is always aware of its relation to everyday speech. A good actor must—alas, today he too seldom does—make the audience hear Shakespeare's lines as verse not prose, but if he tries to make the verse sound like a different language, he will make himself ridiculous.

But French poetry, both in the way it is written and the way it is recited, has emphasized and gloried in the difference between itself and ordinary speech; in French drama, verse and prose *are* different languages. Valéry quotes a contemporary description of Rachel's powers of declamation; in reciting, she could and did use a range of two octaves, from F below middle C to F in alt. An actress who tried to do the same with Shakespeare as Rachel did with Racine would be laughed off the stage.

One can read Shakespeare to oneself without even mentally *hearing* the lines and be very moved; indeed, one may easily find a performance disappointing because almost anyone with an understanding of English verse can speak it better than the average actor and actress. But to read Racine to oneself, even, I fancy, if one is a Frenchman, is like reading the score of an opera when one can hardly play or sing; one can no more get an adequate notion of *Phèdre* without having heard a great performance than one can of *Tristan und Isolde* if one has never heard a great Isolde like Leider or Flagstad.

(Monsieur St. John Perse tells me that when it comes to everyday speech, it is French which is the more monotonous, and English which has the wider range of vocal inflection.)

I must confess that French classical tragedy strikes me as being opera for the unmusical. When I read the *Hippolytus*, I can recognize, despite all differences, a kinship between the world of Euripides and the world of Shakespeare, but the world of Racine, like the world of opera, seems to be another planet altogether. Euripides' Aphrodite is as concerned with fish and fowl as she is with human beings; Racine's Venus is not only unconcerned with animals, she takes no interest in the Lower Orders. It is impossible to imagine any of Racine's characters sneezing or wanting to go to the bathroom, for in his world there is neither weather nor nature. In consequence, the passions by which his characters are consumed can only exist, as it were, on stage, the creation of the magnificent speech and the grand gestures of the actors and actresses who endow them with flesh and blood. This is also the case in opera, but no speaking voice, however magnificent, can hope to compete, in expressiveness through sound, with a great singing voice backed by an orchestra.

Whenever people talk to me about the weather, I always feel certain that they mean something else. (OSCAR WILDE.) The only kind of speech which approximates to the symbolist's poetic ideal is polite tea-table conversation, in which the meaning of the banalities uttered depends almost entirely upon vocal inflections.

Owing to its superior power as a mnemonic, verse is superior to prose as a medium for didactic instruction. Those who condemn didacticism must disapprove *a fortiori* of didactic prose; in verse, as the Alka-Seltzer advertisements testify, the didactic message loses half its immodesty. Verse is also certainly the equal of prose as a medium for the lucid exposition of ideas; in skillful hands, the form of the verse can parallel and reinforce the steps of the logic. Indeed, contrary to what most people who have inherited the Romantic conception of poetry believe, the danger of argument in verse — Pope's *Essay on Man* is an example — is that the verse may make the ideas *too* clear and distinct, more Cartesian than they really are.

On the other hand, verse is unsuited to controversy, to proving some truth or belief which is not universally accepted, because its formal nature cannot but convey a certain skepticism about its conclusions.

> Thirty days hath September,
> April, June, and November

is valid because nobody doubts its truth. Were there, however, a party who passionately denied it, the lines would be powerless to convince him, because, formally, it would make no difference if the lines ran:

> Thirty days hath September,
> August, May, and December.

Poetry is not magic. Insofar as poetry, or any other of the arts, can be said to have an ulterior purpose, it is, by telling the truth, to disenchant and disintoxicate.

"The unacknowledged legislators of the world" describes the secret police, not the poets.

Catharsis is properly effected, not by works of art, but by religious rites. It is also effected, usually improperly, by bullfights, professional football matches, bad movies, military bands, and monster rallies at which ten thousand girl guides form themselves into a model of the national flag.

The condition of mankind is, and always has been, so miserable and depraved that if anyone were to say to the poet, "For God's sake, stop singing and do something useful like putting on the kettle or fetching bandages," what just reason could he give for refusing? But nobody says this. The self-appointed unqualified nurse says, "You are to sing the patient a song which will make him believe that I, and I alone, can cure him. If you can't or won't, I shall confiscate your passport and send you to the mines." And the poor patient in his delirium cries, "Please sing me a song which will give me sweet dreams instead of nightmares. If you succeed, I will give you a penthouse in New York or a ranch in Arizona."

(Published 1962, partly compiled from earlier essays)

Denise Levertov

Some Notes on Organic Form

FOR ME, back of the idea of organic form is the concept that there is a form in all things (and in our experience) which the poet can discover and reveal. There are, no doubt, temperamental differences between poets who use prescribed forms and those who look for new ones — people who need a tight schedule to get anything done, and people who have to have a free hand — but the difference in their conception of "content" or "reality" is functionally more important. On the one hand is the idea that content, reality, experience, is essentially fluid and must be given form; on the other, this sense of seeking out inherent, though not immediately apparent, form. Gerard Manley Hopkins invented the word "inscape" to denote intrinsic form, the pattern of essential characteristics both in single objects and (what is more interesting) in objects in a state of relation to each other, and the word "instress" to denote the experiencing of the perception of inscape, the apperception of inscape. In thinking of the process of poetry as I know it, I extend the use of these words, which he seems to have used mainly in reference to sensory phenomena, to include intellectual and emotional experience as well; I would speak of the inscape of an experience (which might be composed of any and all of these elements, including the sensory) or of the inscape of a sequence or constellation of experiences.

A partial definition, then, of organic poetry might be that it is a method of apperception, that is, of recognizing what we perceive, and is based on an intuition of an order, a form beyond forms, in which forms partake, and of which man's creative works are analogies, resemblances, natural allegories. Such poetry is exploratory.

How does one go about such a poetry? I think it's like this: first there must be an experience, a sequence or constellation of perceptions of sufficient interest, felt by the poet intensely enough to demand of him their equivalence in words: he is *brought to speech.* Suppose there's the sight of the sky through a dusty window, birds and clouds and bits of paper flying through the sky, the sound of music from his radio, feelings of anger and love and amusement roused by a letter just received, the memory of some long-past thought or event associated with what's seen or heard or felt, and an idea, a concept, he has been pondering, each qualifying the other; together with what he knows about history; and what he has been dreaming—whether or not he remembers it—working in him. This is only a rough outline of a possible moment in a life. But the condition of being a poet is that periodically such a cross section, or constellation, of experiences (in which one or another element may predominate) demands, or wakes in him this demand: the poem. The beginning of the fulfillment of this demand is to contemplate, to meditate; words which connote a state in which the heat of feeling warms the intellect. "To contemplate" comes from "*templum,* temple, a place, a space for observation, marked out by the augur." It means not simply to observe, to regard, but to do these things in the presence of a god. And to meditate is "to keep the mind in a state of contemplation"; its synonym is "to muse," and to muse comes from a word meaning "to stand with open mouth"—not so comical if we think of "inspiration"—to breathe in.

So—as the poet stands open-mouthed in the temple of life, contemplating his experience, there come to him the first words of the poem: the words which are to be his way in to the poem, if there is to be a poem. The pressure of demand and the meditation on its elements culminate in a moment of vision, of crystallization, in which some inkling of the correspondence between those elements occurs; and it occurs as words. If he forces a beginning before this point, it won't work. These words sometimes remain the first, sometimes in the completed poem their eventual place may be elsewhere, or they may turn out to have been only forerunners, which fulfilled their function in bringing him to the words which are the actual beginning of the poem. It is faithful attention to the experience from the first moment of crystallization that allows those first or those forerunning words to rise to the surface; and with that same fidelity of attention the poet, from that moment of being let in to the possibility of the poem, must follow through, letting the experience lead him through the world of the poem, its unique inscape revealing itself as he goes.

During the writing of a poem the various elements of the poet's being are in communion with each other, and heightened. Ear and eye, intellect and passion, interrelate more subtly than at other times; and the "checking for accuracy," for precision of language, that must take place throughout the writing is not a matter of one element supervising the others but of intuitive interaction between all the elements involved.

In the same way, content and form are in a state of dynamic interaction; the understanding of whether an experience is a linear sequence or a constellation raying out from and into a central focus or axis, for instance, is discoverable only in the work, not before it.

Rhyme, chime, echo, reiteration: they not only serve to knit the elements of an experience but often are the very means, the sole means, by which the density of texture and the returning or circling of perception can be transmuted into language, apperceived. A may lead to E directly through B, C, and D; but if then there is the sharp remembrance or revisioning of A, this return must find its metric counterpart. It could do so by actual repetition of the words that spoke of A the first time (and if this return occurs more than once, one finds oneself with a refrain—not put there because one decided to write something with a refrain at the end of each stanza, but directly because of the demand of the content). Or it may be that since the return to A is now conditioned by the journey through B, C, and D, its words will not be a simple repetition but a variation . . . Again, if B and D are of a complementary nature, then their thought- or feeling-rhyme may find its corresponding word-rhyme. Corresponding images are a kind of non-aural rhyme. It usually happens that within the whole, that is, between the point of crystallization that marks the beginning or onset of a poem and the point at which the intensity of contemplation has ceased, there are distinct units of awareness; and it is—for me anyway—these that indicate the duration of stanzas.

Sometimes these units are of such equal duration that one gets a whole poem of, say, three-line stanzas, a regularity of pattern that looks, but is not, predetermined.

When my son was eight or nine I watched him make a crayon drawing of a tournament. He was not interested in the forms as such, but was grappling with the need to speak in graphic terms, to say "And a great crowd of people were watching the jousting knights." There was a need to show the tiers of seats, all those people sitting in them. And out of the need arose a formal design that was beautiful — composed of the rows of shoulders and heads. It is in very much the same way that there can arise, out of fidelity to instress, a design that is the form of the poem — both its total form, its length and pace and tone, and the form of its parts (for example, the rhythmic relationships of syllables within the line, and of line to line; the sonic relationships of vowels and consonants; the recurrence of images, the play of associations, etc.). "Form follows function" (Louis Sullivan).

Frank Lloyd Wright in his autobiography wrote that the idea of organic architecture is that "the reality of the building lies in the space within it, to be lived in." And he quotes Coleridge: "Such as the life is, such is the form." (Emerson says in his essay "Poetry and Imagination," "Ask the fact for the form.") The *Oxford English Dictionary* quotes Huxley (Thomas, presumably) as stating that he used the word "organic" "almost as an equivalent for the word 'living.' "

In organic poetry the metric movement, the measure, is the direct expression of the movement of perception. And the sounds, acting together with the measure, are a kind of extended onomatopoeia — that is, they imitate not the sounds of an experience (which may well be soundless, or to which sounds contribute only incidentally) — but the feeling of an experience, its emotional tone, its texture. The varying speed and gait of different strands of perception within an experience (I think of strands of seaweed moving within a wave) result in counterpointed measures.

Thinking about how organic poetry differs from free verse, I wrote that "most free verse is failed organic poetry, that is, organic poetry from which the attention of the writer had been switched off too soon, before the intrinsic form of the experience had been revealed." But Robert Duncan pointed out to me that there is a "free verse" of which this is not true, because it is written not with any desire to seek a form, indeed perhaps with the longing to avoid form (if that were possible) and to express inchoate emotion as purely as possible.[1] There is a contradiction here, however, because if, as I suppose, there is an inscape of emotion, of feeling, it is impossible to avoid presenting something of it if the rhythm or tone of the feeling is given voice in the poem. But perhaps the difference is this: that free verse isolates the "rightness" of each line or cadence—if it seems expressive, o.k., never mind the relation of it to the next; while in organic poetry the peculiar rhythms of the parts are in some degree modified, if necessary, in order to discover the rhythm of the whole.

But doesn't the character of the whole depend on, arise out of, the character of the parts? It does, but it is like painting from nature: suppose you absolutely imitate, on the palette, the separate colors of the various objects you are going to paint; yet when they are closely juxtaposed in the actual painting, you may have to lighten, darken, cloud, or sharpen each color in order to produce an effect equivalent to what you see in nature. Air, light, dust, shadow, and distance have to be taken into account.

Or one could put it this way: in organic poetry the form sense, or "traffic sense," as Stefan Wolpe speaks of it, is ever present along with (yes, paradoxically) fidelity to the revelations of meditation. The form sense is a sort of Stanislavsky of the imagination: putting a chair two feet downstage there, thickening a knot of bystanders upstage left, getting this actor to raise his voice a little and that actress to enter more slowly—all in the interest of a total form he intuits. Or it is a sort of helicopter scout flying over the field of the poem, taking aerial photos and reporting on the state of the forest and its creatures—or over the sea to watch for the schools of herring and direct the fishing fleet toward them.

A manifestation of form sense is the sense the poet's ear has of some rhythmic norm peculiar to a particular poem, from which the individual lines depart and to which they return. I heard Henry Cowell tell that the drone in Indian music is known as the horizon note. Al Kresch, the painter, sent me a quotation from Emerson: "The health of the eye demands a horizon." This sense of the beat or pulse underlying the whole I think of as the horizon note of the poem. It interacts with the nuances or forces of feeling which determine emphasis on one word or another, and decides to a great extent what belongs to a given line. It relates the needs of that feeling-force which dominates the cadence to the needs of the surrounding parts and so to the whole.

Duncan also pointed to what is perhaps a variety of organic poetry: the poetry of linguistic impulse. It seems to me that the absorption in language itself, the awareness of the world of multiple meaning revealed in sound, word, syntax, and the entering into this world in the poem, is as much an experience or constellation of perceptions as the instress of nonverbal sensuous and psychic events. What might make the poet of linguistic impetus appear to be on another tack entirely is that the demands of his realization may seem in opposition to truth as we think of it; that is, in terms of sensual logic. But the apparent distortion of experience in such a poem for the sake of verbal effects is actually a precise adherence to truth, since the experience itself was a verbal one.

Form is never more than a *revelation* of content.

"The law—one perception must immediately and directly lead to a further perception." [2] I've always taken this to mean, "no loading of the rifts with ore," because there are to be no rifts. Yet alongside this truth is another truth (that I've learned from Duncan more than from anyone else)—that there must be a place in the poem for rifts too—(never to be stuffed with imported ore). Great gaps between perception and perception which must be leapt across if they are to be crossed at all.

The X-factor, the magic, is when we come to those rifts and make those leaps. A religious devotion to the truth, to the splendor of the authentic, involves the writer in a process rewarding in itself; but when that devotion brings us to undreamed abysses and we find ourselves sailing slowly over them and landing on the other side—that's ecstasy.

(1965)

Notes

1. See, for instance, some of the forgotten poets of the early twenties— also, some of Amy Lowell, Sandburg, John Gould Fletcher. Some imagist poems were written in "free verse" in this sense, but by no means all.

2. Edward Dahlberg, as quoted by Charles Olson in "Projective Verse," *Selected Writings* (New York: New Directions, 1966).

Robert Duncan

Notes on Poetic Form

AT THIS POINT I would distinguish the following kinds of form and their associations with ideas of the universe:

1. Convention — conformation to a model, "plan": the universe and life itself is *really* a mess, a savage bloody wild bore. But rational men by their social agreements (the Constitution as guarantor of correct freedoms) maintain models of garden; household; relationships; language decorum, or grammar; literature; in which sensibilities can replace passions (or compassion replace passion), etc.

2. Ideal — striving to achieve a likeness of eternal pre-existent models, "perfection": the universe and life itself is *really* grounded in an harmonic system. Plato remains the prime statement of this concept of form. Forms here are eternal and ultimate reality. Plato is quite clear that poets (and language) ain't perfectionists. I think that in this second concept of the meaning of form the poet would be mathematician and even more geometer. (And I remain puzzled and excited by how much *ideal* form haunts my imagination as I work in a foreign ground.)

3. Organic form — (a) incorporating in the work birth, youth, maturation, aging, death (Aristotle's beginning, middle, and end): the universe is proceeding from its birth toward its ultimate demise. In the work of art there is a generative seed (think of Henry

James), an energetic productive youth, a maturation, and death: in tragedy, a critical demise; in comedy, a peaceful laying to rest of all elements. Each work is an individual belonging to a species but "complete in itself" (as contemporary life sciences view every individual as the end of a species and the beginning of a species). (b) self-expressive form: here the poem, novel, painting, is thought of as a leaf of the tree; we are concerned with its signature. (We can tell it is a Duncan by shape, structure, function, comparison, etc.) Offshoot of this is what looks at first like an anti-formal idea: the poem or story, etc., is a gesture or e-motion of the author — no longer a creator but a self expanding the range of his feeling in the human community.*

4. Projective — form is happening in the process, "evolution": the universe and life are *energetic*, at work. Form appears as the survival of elements in any area, time, or locality. As in Darwinian evolution by chance significance emerges: i.e. out of multiple "formless" possibilities only one thing "actually" happens. Form lies in the creative activation (recognition) of what happens. In this aspect, the poet is concerned with the activity of forces present in the language in their evolution in the poem. The word, its sounds and meanings, may be "recognized" by the poet, but the word itself initiates all possibilities. In contrast with the Platonic form, where ultimate reality is pre-existent in the ideal, in the projective form the ultimate "reality" is always in process (i.e. no poem can in itself propose its ultimate form, tho every poem comes into being *toward* that form).

5. Chance — "zen." This is so much the rage that I don't bother my mind about it. That ZEN is the appropriate key seems questionable. Cage, Dom Houedard, or early Arp have to do with incorporating our Western recognition of the absoluteness of a thing's happening.

6. Physical or sensitive form — that the artist feels relationships, i.e. weights, measures, durations, correspondences, gravities, propulsions, and cooperates to set them in motion. The physical universe has "laws" of motion and the artist is sensitive to them. Here

* The universe here is ultimately, as in Hindoo world view, "scene" and "seen," a continuation of the person or actors, and readily expresses his mood. "Roses and blood flood the clouds."

language—as well as paint, tones struck from the string—is a "matter" of vibrations; and form has to do with the working in structures of moving parts.

7. I am more and more fascinated by the idea of form as creation or fiction of a universe, as a way of "knowing" the real universe. Form as a mode of participation in the real. It is not only in order to participate in the universe but also to participate in self.

The difficulty here is how to keep this a series of poetics and not to get off into amateur philosophy (I feel the "philosophic" content as a drag as I think here).

(1969)

Seamus Heaney

Feelings into Words

I AM UNEASY about speaking under the general heading of "inno-vation in contemporary literature." Much as I would like to think of myself as breaking new ground, I find on looking at what I have done that it is mostly concerned with reclaiming old ground. My intention here is to retrace some of my paths into that ground, to investigate what William Wordsworth called "the hiding places":

> the hiding places of my power
> Seem open; I approach, and then they close;
> I see glimpses now; when age comes on,
> May scarcely see at all, and I would give,
> While yet we may, as far as words can give,
> A substance and a life to what I feel:
> I would enshrine the spirit of the past
> For future restoration.

Implicit in those lines is a view of poetry which I think is also im-plicit in the few poems I have written that give me any right to be here addressing you: poetry as divination; poetry as revelation of the self to the self, as restoration of the culture to itself; poems as elements of continuity, with the aura and authenticity of archae-ological finds, where the buried shard has an importance that is not obliterated by the buried city; poetry as a dig, a dig for finds, that end up being plants.

"Digging," in fact, was the name of the first poem I wrote where

I thought my feelings got into words, or, to put it more accurately, where I thought my *feel* had got into words. Its rhythms and noises still please me, although there are a couple of lines in it that have the theatricality of the gunslinger rather than the self-absorption of the digger. I wrote it in the summer of 1964, almost two years after I had begun to dabble in verses, and as Patrick Kavanagh said, a man dabbles in verses and finds they are his life. This was the first place where I felt I had done more than make an arrangement of words: I felt that I had let down a shaft into real life. The facts and surfaces of the thing were true, but more important, the excitement that came from naming them gave me a kind of insouciance and a kind of confidence. I didn't care who thought what about it: somehow, it had surprised me by coming out with a stance and an idea that I would stand over:

> The cold smell of potato mould, the squelch and slap
> Of soggy peat, the curt cuts of an edge
> Through living roots awaken in my head.
> But I've no spade to follow men like them.
>
> Between my finger and my thumb
> The squat pen rests.
> I'll dig with it.

As I say, I wrote it down ten years ago; yet perhaps I should say that I dug it up, because I have come to realize that it was laid down in me years before that even. The pen/spade analogy was the simple heart of the matter, and *that* was simply a matter of almost proverbial common sense. People used to ask a child on the road to and from school what class you were in and how many slaps you'd got that day, and invariably they ended up with an exhortation to keep studying because "learning's easy carried" and "the pen's lighter than the spade." And the poem does no more than allow that bud of wisdom to exfoliate, although the significant point in this context is that at the time of writing I was not aware of the proverbial structure at the back of my mind. Nor was I aware that the poem was an enactment of yet another digging metaphor that came back to me years later. This was a rhyme that also had a currency on the road to school, though again we were not fully aware of what we were dealing with:

> "Are your praties dry
> And are they fit for digging?"
> "Put in your spade and try,"
> Says Dirty-Face McGuigan.

Well, digging there becomes a sexual metaphor, an emblem of initiation, like putting your hand into the bush or robbing the nest, one of the various natural analogies for uncovering and touching the hidden thing. I now believe that the "Digging" poem had for me the force of an initiation: the confidence I mentioned arose from a sense that perhaps I could work this poetry thing, too, and having experienced the excitement and release of it once, I was doomed to look for it again and again.

I don't want to overload "Digging" with too much significance. I know as well as you do that it is a big coarse-grained navvy of a poem, but it is interesting as an example—and not just as an example of what one reviewer called "mud-caked fingers in Russell Square," for I don't think that the subject matter has any particular virtue in itself; it is interesting as an example of what we call "finding a voice."

Finding a voice means that you can get your own feeling into your own words and that your words have the feel of you about them; and I believe that it may not even be a metaphor, for a poetic voice is probably very intimately connected with the poet's natural voice, the voice that he hears as the ideal speaker of the lines he is making up. I would like to digress slightly in order to illustrate what I mean more fully.

In his novel *The First Circle*, Solzhenitsyn sets the action in a prison camp on the outskirts of Moscow where the inmates are all highly skilled technicians forced to labor at projects devised by Stalin. The most important of these is an attempt to invent a mechanism to bug a phone. But what is to be special about this particular bugging device is that it will not simply record the voice and the message, but that it will identify the essential sound patterns of the speaker's voice; it will discover, in the words of the narrative, "what it is that makes every human voice unique" so that no matter how he disguises his accent or changes his language, the fundamental structure of his voice will be caught. The idea was that a voice is like a fingerprint, possessing a constant and unique signature that can, like a fingerprint, be recorded and employed for identification.

Now, one of the purposes of a literary education as I experienced it was to turn your ear into a poetic bugging device, so that a piece of verse denuded of name and date could be identified by its diction, tropes, and cadences. And this secret policing of English verse was also based on the idea of a style as a signature. But what I wish to suggest is that there is a connection between the core of a poet's speaking voice and the core of his poetic voice, between his original accent and his discovered style. I think that the discovery of a way of writing that is natural and adequate to your sensibility depends on the recovery of that essential quick which Solzhenitsyn's technicians were trying to pin down. This is the absolute register to which your proper music has to be tuned.

How, then, do you find it? In practice, you hear it coming from somebody else, you hear something in another writer's sounds that flows in through your ear and enters the echo chamber of your head and delights your whole nervous system in such a way that your reaction will be, "Ah, I wish I had said that, in that particular way." This other writer, in fact, has spoken something essential to you, something you recognize instinctively as a true sounding of aspects of yourself and your experience. And your first steps as a writer will be to imitate, consciously or unconsciously, those sounds that flowed in, that in-fluence.

One of the writers who influenced me in this way was Gerard Manley Hopkins. The result of reading Hopkins at school was the desire to write, and when I first put pen to paper at university, what flowed out was what had flowed in, the bumpy alliterating music, the reporting sounds and ricocheting consonants typical of Hopkins' verse. I remember lines from a piece called "October Thought," in which some frail bucolic images foundered under the chain mail of the pastiche:

> Starling thatch-watches, and sudden swallow
> Straight breaks to mud-nest, home-rest rafter
> Up past dry dust-drunk cobwebs, like laughter
> Ghosting the roof of bog-oak, turf-sod and rods of willow . . .

and then there was "heaven-hue, plum-blue and gorse-pricked with gold" and "a trickling tinkle of bells well in the fold."

Well, anyhow, looking back on that stuff by Hopkins out of Heaney, I believe there was a connection, not obvious at the time but, on reflection, real enough, between the heavily accented consonantal noise of Hopkins' poetic voice and the peculiar regional characteristics of a Northern Ireland accent. The late W. R. Rodgers, another poet much lured by alliteration, said that the people from his (and my) part of the world were

> an abrupt people
> who like the spiky consonants of speech
> and think the soft ones cissy; who dig
> the k and t in orchestra, detect sin
> in sinfonia, get a kick out of
> tin-cans, fricatives, fornication, staccato talk,
> anything that gives or takes attack
> like Micks, Teagues, tinker's gets, Vatican.

It is true that the Ulster accent is generally a staccato consonantal one. Our tongue strikes the tangent of the consonant rather more than it rolls the circle of the vowel—Rodgers also spoke of "the round gift of the gab in southern mouths." It is energetic, angular, hard-edged, and it may be because of this affinity between my dialect and Hopkins' oddity that those first verses turned out as they did.

I couldn't say, of course, that I'd found a voice, but I'd found a game. I knew the thing was only word play, and I hadn't even the guts to put my name under it. I called myself *Incertus*, uncertain, a shy soul fretting, and all that. I was in love with words themselves, had no sense of a poem as a whole structure, and no experience of how the successful achievement of a poem could be a stepping stone in your life. Those verses were what we might call "trial pieces," little stiff inept designs in imitation of the master's fluent interlacing patterns, little heavy-handed clues by which the archaeologist can project the whole craft's mystery.

I was getting my first sense of crafting words, and for one reason or another, words as bearers of history and mystery began to invite me. Maybe it began very early, when my mother used to recite lists of affixes and suffixes, and Latin roots with their English meanings, rhymes that formed part of her schooling in the early part of the century. Maybe it began with the exotic listing on the wireless dial: Stuttgart, Leipzig, Oslo, Hilversun. Maybe it was stirred by the beautiful sprung rhythms of the old BBC weather forecast: Dogger, Rockall, Malin, Shetland, Faroes, Finisterre; or with the gorgeous and inane phraseology of the catechism, such as "the solemnization of marriage within forbidden degrees of kindred"; or with the litany of the Blessed Virgin that was part of the enforced poetry in our household: "Tower of Gold, Ark of the Covenant, Gate of Heaven, Morning Star, Health of the Sick, Refuge of Sinners, Comforter of the Afflicted." None of these things was consciously savored at the time, but I think the fact that I still recall them with ease, and can delight in them as verbal music, means that they were bedding the foundation of my ear with a kind of linguistic hard core that could be built on someday.

That was the unconscious bedding, but poetry involves a conscious centering on words also. This came by way of reading poetry itself, and being required to learn pieces by heart, phrases even, like Keats's, from "Lamia":

> and his vessel now
> Grated the quaystone with her brazen prow . . .

or Wordsworth's

> All shod with steel,
> We hiss'd along the polished ice . . .

or Tennyson's

> Old yew, which graspest at the stones
>   That name the underlying dead,
>   Thy fibres net the dreamless head,
> Thy roots are wrapped about the bones.

These were picked up in my last years at school, touchstones of sorts, where the language could give you a kind of aural gooseflesh. At the university I was delighted in the first weeks to meet the moody energies of John Webster—"I'll make Italian cutworks in their guts/ If ever I return"—and later on to encounter the pointed masonry of Anglo-Saxon verse and to learn about the rich stratifications of the English language itself. Words alone were certain good. I even went so far as to write these "Lines to myself":

> In poetry I wish you would
> Avoid the lilting platitude.
> Give us poems humped and strong,
> Laced tight with thongs of song,
> Poems that explode in silence
> Without forcing, without violence.
> Whose music is strong and clear and good
> Like a saw zooming in seasoned wood.
> You should attempt concrete expression,
> Half-guessing, half-expression.

Ah, well. Behind that was "Ars Poetica," MacLeish's and Verlaine's, and Eliot's "objective correlative" (half-understood), and several critical essays (by myself and others) about "concrete realization." At the university I kept the whole thing at arm's length, read poetry for the noise and wrote about half a dozen pieces for the literary magazine. But nothing happened inside me. No experience. No epiphany. All craft—and not much of that—and no technique.

I think technique is different from craft. Craft is what you can learn from other verse. Craft is the skill of making. It wins competitions in *The New Statesman*. It can be deployed without reference to the feelings or the self. It knows how to keep up a capable verbal athletic display; it can be content to be *vox et praeterea nihil*—all voice and nothing else, but not voice as in "finding a voice." Learning the craft is learning to turn the windlass at the well of poetry. Usually you begin by dropping the bucket halfway down the shaft and winding up a taking of air. You are miming the real thing until one day the chain draws unexpectedly tight, and you have dipped into waters that will continue to entice you back. You'll have broken the skin on the pool of yourself. Your praties will be "fit for digging."

At that point it becomes appropriate to speak of technique rather than craft. Technique, as I would define it, involves not only a poet's way with words, his management of meter, rhythm, and verbal texture; it involves also a definition of his stance toward life, a definition of his own reality. It involves the discovery of ways to go out of his normal cognitive bounds and raid the inarticulate: a dynamic alertness that mediates between the origins of feeling in memory and experience and the formal ploys that express these in a work of art. Technique entails the watermarking of your essential patterns of perception, voice, and thought into the touch and texture of your lines; it is that whole creative effort of the mind's and body's resources to bring the meaning of experience within the jurisdiction of form. Technique is what turns, in Yeats's phrase, "the bundle of accident and incoherence that sits down to breakfast" into "an idea, something intended, complete."

It is indeed conceivable that a poet could have a real technique and a wobbly craft—I think this was true of Alun Lewis and Patrick Kavanagh—but more often it's a case of sure-enough craft and a failure of technique. And if I were asked for a figure who represents pure technique, I would say a water diviner. You can't learn the craft of dousing or divining—it's a gift for being in touch with what is there, hidden and real, a gift for mediating between the latent resource and the community that wants it current and released. If I might be permitted a sleight of quote, as it were, I would draw your attention to Sir Philip Sidney's animadversion in his *Apologie for Poetrie*: "Among the Romans a Poet was called *Vates*, which is as much as a Diviner..." And I am pleased to say I came upon the coincidence myself, again unconsciously, by that somnambulist process of search and surrender that is perhaps the one big pleasure of poetry that the reader of it misses.

The poem was written simply to allay an excitement and to name an experience, and at the same time to give the excitement and the experience a small *perpetuum mobile* in language itself. I quote it here, not for its own technique, but for the image of technique contained in it. The diviner resembles the poet in his function of making contact with what lies hidden, and in his ability to make palpable what was sensed or raised.

THE DIVINER

Cut from the green hedge a forked hazel stick
That he held tight by the arms of the V:
Circling the terrain, hunting the pluck
Of water, nervous, but professionally

Unfussed. The pluck came sharp as a sting.
The rod jerked with precise convulsions,
Spring water suddenly broadcasting
Through a green hazel its secret stations.

The bystanders would ask to have a try.
He handed them the rod without a word.
It lay dead in their grasp till nonchalantly
He gripped expectant wrists. The hazel stirred.

What I had taken as matter of fact as a youngster became a matter of wonder in memory. I'm pleased when I look at the thing now that it ends with a verb "stirred," the heart of the mystery; and I'm also glad that "stirred" chimes with "word," bringing the two functions of *vates* into the one sound.

I suppose technique is what allows that first stirring of the mind round a word or an image or a memory to grow toward articulation, articulation not necessarily in terms of argument or explication but in terms of its own potential for harmonious self-reproduction. The seminal excitement has to be granted conditions in which, in Hopkins' words, it "selves, goes itself . . . crying What I do is me, for that I came." Technique ensures that the first gleam attains its proper effulgence. And I don't just mean a felicity in the choice of words to flesh the theme — that is a problem also, but it is not so critical. A poem can survive stylistic blemishes, but it cannot survive a stillbirth. The crucial action is pre-verbal: to be able to allow the first alertness or come-hither, sensed in a blurred or incomplete way, to dilate and approach as a thought or a theme or a phrase. Frost put it this way: "A poem begins as a lump in the throat, a homesickness, a lovesickness. It finds the thought and the thought finds the words." As far as I'm concerned, technique is more vitally and sensitively connected with that first activity where the "lump in throat" finds "the thought" than with "the thought" finding "the words." That first epiphany involves the divining, vatic, oracular function; the second, the making, crafting function. To say, as Auden did, that a poem is a "verbal contraption" is to keep one or two tricks up your sleeve.

Traditionally, an oracle speaks in riddles, yielding its truths in disguise, offering its insights cunningly. And in the practice of poetry, there is a corresponding occasion of disguise, a protean, chameleon moment when the lump in the throat takes protective coloring in the new element of thought. One of the best documented occasions in the canon of English poetry, as far as this process is concerned, is a poem that survived in spite of its blemish. In fact, the blemish has earned it a peculiar fame.

> High on a mountain's highest ridge,
> Where oft the stormy winter gale
> Cuts like a scythe, while through the clouds
> It sweeps from vale to vale;
> Not five yards from the mountain path,
> This thorn you on your left espy;
> And to the left, three yards beyond,
> You see a little muddy pond
> Of water never dry;
> I've measured it from side to side:
> 'Tis three feet long and two feet wide.

That final couplet was probably more ridiculed than any other lines in *The Lyrical Ballads*, yet Wordsworth maintained "they ought to be liked." That was in 1815, seventeen years after the poem had been composed; but five years later, he changed the lines to "Though but of compass small, and bare/ To thirsting suns and parching air." Craft, in more senses than one.

Yet far more important than the revision, for the purposes of this discussion, is Wordsworth's account of the poem's genesis. " 'The Thorn,' " he wrote in a letter of 1843, "arose out of my observing on the ridge of Quantock Hills, on a stormy day, a thorn which I had often passed in calm and bright weather without noticing it. I said to myself, 'Cannot I by some invention do as much to make this thorn permanently an impressive object, as the storm has made it to my eyes at this moment?' I began the poem accordingly, and composed it with great rapidity." The storm, in other words, was nature's technique for granting the thorn its epiphany, awakening in Wordsworth that engendering, heightened state which he describes at the beginning of "The Prelude," again in relation to the inspiring influence of wind.

> For I, methought, while the sweet breath of Heaven
> Was blowing on my body, felt within
> A corresponding, mild, creative breeze,

A vital breeze which travell'd gently on
O'er things which it had made, and is become
A tempest, a redundant energy
Vexing its own creation.

This is exactly the kind of mood in which he would have "composed with great rapidity"; the measured recollection of the letter where he makes the poem sound as if it were written to the thesis propounded (retrospectively) in the revised preface of 1802 — "Cannot I by some invention make this thorn permanently an impressive object?" — probably tones down an instinctive, instantaneous recognition into a rational procedure. The technical triumph was to discover a means of allowing his slightly abnormal, slightly numinous vision of the thorn to "deal out its being."

What he did to turn "the bundle of accident and incoherence" of that moment into "something intended, complete" was to find, again in Yeats's language, a mask. The poem as we have it is a ballad in which the speaker is a garrulous, superstitious man, a sea captain, according to Wordsworth, who connects the thorn with murder and distress. For Wordsworth's own apprehension of the tree, he instinctively recognized, was basically superstitious: it was a standing-over, a survival in his own sensibility of a magical way of responding to the natural world, of reading phenomena as signs, occurrences requiring divination. And in order to dramatize this, to transpose the awakened appetites in his consciousness into the satisfactions of a finished thing, he needed his "objective correlative," which was, I suppose, what they called a mask in St. Louis. To make the thorn "permanently an impressive object," images and ideas from different parts of his conscious and unconscious mind were attracted by almost magnetic power. The thorn in its new, wind-tossed aspect had become a field of force.

Into this field were drawn memories of what the ballads call "the cruel mother," who murders her own baby.

She leaned her back against a thorn
All around the loney-o
And there her little babe was born
Down by the greenwood side-o

is how a surviving version runs in Ireland. But there have always been variations on this pattern of the woman who kills her baby and buries it. And the ballads are also full of conclusions where briars and roses and thorns grow out of graves in symbolic token of the life and death of the buried one. So in Wordsworth's imagination the thorn grew into a symbol of tragic, feverish death, and to voice this, the ballad mode came naturally; he donned the traditional mask of the tale-teller, legitimately credulous, entering and enacting a convention. The poem itself is a rapid and strange foray where Wordsworth discovered a way of turning the "lump in the throat" into a "thought," discovered a set of images, cadences, and sounds that amplified his original visionary excitement into "a redundant energy/ Vexing its own creation":

> And some had sworn an oath that she
> Should be to public justice brought;
> And for the little infant's bones
> With spades they would have sought.
> But then the beauteous hill of moss
> Before their eyes began to stir;
> And for full fifty yards around
> The grass it shook upon the ground.

I have spent this time on "The Thorn" because it is a nicely documented example of feeling getting into words, in ways that parallel much in my own experience; although I must say that it is hard to discriminate between feeling getting into words and words turning into feeling, and it is only on posthumous occasions like this that the distinction arises. Moreover, it is generally conceded that it may be dangerous for a writer to become too self-conscious about his own processes: to name them too definitively may have the effect of confining them to what is named. A poem always has elements of accident about it, which can be made the subject of inquest afterward, but there is always a risk in conducting your own inquest: you might begin to believe the coroner in yourself rather than put your trust in the man in you who is capable of the accident. Robert Graves's "Dance of Words" puts this delightfully:

> To make them move, you should start from lightning
> And not forecast the rhythm: rely on chance
> Or so-called chance for its bright emergence
> Once lightning interpenetrates the dance.

Grant them their own traditional steps and postures
But see they dance it out again and again
Until only lightning is left to puzzle over —
The choreography plain and the theme plain.

What we are engaged upon here is a way of seeing that turns the lightning into "the visible discharge of electricity between cloud and cloud or between cloud and ground" rather than its own puzzling, brilliant self. There is nearly always an element of the bolt from the blue about a poem's origin.

When I called my second book *Door into the Dark*, I intended to gesture toward this idea of poetry as a point of entry into the buried life of the feelings or as a point of exit for it. Words themselves are doors; Janus is to a certain extent their deity, looking back to a ramification of roots and associations and forward to a clarification of sense and meaning. And just as Wordsworth sensed a secret asking for release in the thorn, so in *Door into the Dark* there are a number of poems that arise out of the almost unnamable energies that, for me, hovered over certain bits of language and landscape. The poem "Undine," for example.

It was the dark pool of the sound of the word that first took me: if our auditory imaginations were sufficiently attuned to plumb and sound a vowel, to unite the most primitive and civilized associations, the word "undine" would probably suffice as a poem in itself. *Unda*, a wave; *undine*, a water-woman — a litany of undines would have ebb and flow, water and woman, wave and tide, fulfillment and exhaustion in its very rhythms. But old two-faced vocable that it is, I discovered a more precise definition once, by accident, in a dictionary. An undine is a water sprite who has to marry a human being and have a child by him before she can become human. With that definition, the lump in the throat, or rather the thump in the ear, *undine*, became a thought, a field of force that called up other images. One of these was an orphaned memory, without a context, obviously a very early one, of watching a man clearing out an old spongy growth from a drain between two fields, focusing in particular on the way the water, in the cleared-out place, as soon as the shovelfuls of sludge had been removed, the way the water began to run free, rinse itself clean of the soluble mud, and make its own little channels and currents. And this image was gathered into a more conscious reading of the myth as being about the liberating, humanizing effect of sexual encounter. Undine was a cold girl who got what the dictionary called a soul through the experience of physical love. So the poem uttered itself out of that nexus—more short-winded than "The Thorn," with less red*undant* energy, but still escaping, I hope, from my incoherence into the voice of the undine herself.

> He slashed the briars, shovelled up grey silt
> To give me right of way in my own drains
> And I ran quick for him, cleaned out my rust.
>
> He halted, saw me finally disrobed,
> Running clear, with apparent unconcern.
> Then he walked by me. I rippled and I churned
>
> Where ditches intersected near the river
> Until he dug a spade deep in my flank
> And took me to him. I swallowed his trench
>
> Gratefully, dispersing myself for love
> Down in his roots, climbing his brassy grain —
> But once he knew my welcome, I alone
>
> Could give him subtle increase and reflection.
> He explored me so completely, each limb
> Lost its cold freedom. Human, warmed to him.

When I read it once in a convent school, I said it was a myth about agriculture, about the way water is tamed and humanized when streams become irrigation canals, when water becomes involved with seed. And maybe that's as good an explanation as any. I like the paraphrasable extensions of a poem to be as protean as possible, and yet I like its elements to be as firm as possible. Words can allow you that two-faced approach, also. They stand smiling at the audience's way of reading them and winking back at the poet's way of using them.

Behind this, of course, there is a good bit of symbolist theory. Not that I am in any way consciously directed by symbolist prescriptions in my approach to the composition of poems, but I am sympathetic to a whole amalgam of commonplaces that might vaguely deserve that label, from Rimbaud's notion of vowels as colors and poetry as an alchemy of sounds, to Yeats's notion of the work of art as a "masterful image." And the stylistic tenets of imagism as well as the aesthetics of symbolism I find attractive: to present an image, "an intellectual and emotional complex in a moment of time." I suppose all this was inevitable, given a conventional course in English literature that culminated with Eliot and Yeats.

In practice, however, you proceed by your own experience of what it is to write what you consider a successful poem. You survive in your own esteem not by the corroboration of theory but by the trust in certain moments of satisfaction that you know intuitively are moments of extension. You are confirmed by the visitation of the last poem and threatened by the elusiveness of the next one, and the best moments are those when your mind seems to implode and words and images rush of their own accord into the vortex. Which happened to me once when the line "We have no prairies" drifted into my head at bedtime and loosened a fall of images that constitute the poem "Bogland," the last one in *Door into the Dark*.

I had been vaguely wishing to write a poem about bogland, chiefly because it is a landscape that has a strange assuaging effect on me, one with associations reaching back into early childhood. We used to hear about bog-butter, butter kept fresh for a great number of years under the peat. Then when I was at school the skeleton of an elk had been taken out of a bog nearby, and a few of our neighbors had got their photographs in the paper, peering out across its antlers. So I began to get an idea of bog as the memory of the landscape, or as a landscape that remembered everything that happened in and to it. In fact, if you go round the National Museum in Dublin, you will realize that a great proportion of the most cherished material heritage of Ireland was "found in a bog." Moreover, since memory was the faculty that supplied me with the first quickening of my own poetry, I had a tentative unrealized need to make a congruence between memory and bogland and, for the want of a better word, our national consciousness. And it all released itself after "We have no prairies . . ."—but we have bogs.

At that time I was teaching modern literature in Queen's University, Belfast, and had been reading about the frontier and the West as an important myth in the American consciousness, so I set up—or, rather, laid down—the bog as an answering Irish myth. I wrote it quickly the next morning, having slept on my excitement, and revised it on the hoof, from line to line, as it came.

We have no prairies
To slice a big sun at evening—
Everywhere the eye concedes to
Encroaching horizon,

Is wooed into the cyclops' eye
Of a tarn. Our unfenced country
Is bog that keeps crusting
Between the sights of the sun.

They've taken the skeleton
Of the Great Irish Elk
Out of the peat, set it up
An astounding crate full of air.

Butter sunk under
More than a hundred years
Was recovered salty and white.
The ground itself is kind, black butter

Melting and opening underfoot,
Missing its last definition
By millions of years.
They'll never dig coal here,

Only the waterlogged trunks
Of great firs, soft as pulp.
Our pioneers keep striking
Inwards and downwards,

Every layer they strip
Seems camped on before.
The bogholes might be Atlantic seepage.
The wet centre is bottomless.

Again, as in the case of "Digging," the seminal impulse had
been unconscious. I believe what generated the poem about mem-
ory was something lying beneath the very floor of memory, some-
thing I connected with the poem only months after it was written,
which was a warning that older people would give us about going
into the bog. They were afraid we might fall into the pools in the
old workings, so they put it about (and we believed them) that
there was no bottom in the bogholes. Little did they—or I—
know that I would filch it for the last line of a book.

There was also in that book a poem called "Requiem for the Croppies," which was written in 1966 when most poets in Ireland were straining to celebrate the anniversary of the 1916 Rising. Typically, I suppose I went farther back. Nineteen sixteen was the harvest of seeds sown in 1798, when revolutionary republican ideals and national feeling coalesced in the doctrines of Irish republicanism and in the rebellion of 1798 itself — unsuccessful and savagely put down. The poem was born of and ended with an image of resurrection based on the fact that some time after the rebels were buried in common graves, these graves began to sprout with young barley, growing up from barley corn the "croppies" had carried in their pockets to eat while on the march. The oblique implication was that the seeds of violent resistance sowed in the Year of Liberty had flowered in what Yeats called "the right rose tree" of 1916. I did not realize at the time that the original heraldic murderous encounter between Protestant yeoman and Catholic rebel was to be initiated again in the summer of 1969, in Belfast, two months after the book was published.

From that moment, the problems of poetry moved from being simply a matter of achieving the satisfactory verbal icon to being a search for images and symbols adequate to our predicament. I do not mean liberal lamentation that citizens should feel compelled to murder one another or deploy their different military arms over the matter of nomenclatures, such as British or Irish. I do not mean public celebrations or execrations of resistance or atrocity — although there is nothing necessarily unpoetic about such celebration, if one thinks of "Easter 1916." I mean that I felt it imperative to discover a field of force in which, without abandoning fidelity to the processes and experience of poetry as I have outlined them, it would be possible to encompass the perspectives of a humane reason and, at the same time, to grant the religious intensity of the violence its deplorable authenticity and complexity. And when I say religious, I am not thinking simply of the sectarian division. To some extent the enmity can be viewed as a struggle between the cults and devotees of a god and a goddess. There is an indigenous territorial numen, a tutelar of the whole island — call her Mother Ireland, Kathleen Ni Houlihan, the poor old woman, the Shan Van Vocht, whatever — and her sovereignty has been temporarily usurped or infringed by a new male cult whose founding fathers were Cromwell, William of Orange, and Edward Carson, and whose godhead is incarnate in a rex or caesar resident in a palace in London. What we have is the tail end of a struggle in a province between territorial piety and imperial power.

Now, I realize that this idiom is remote from the agnostic world of economic interest whose iron hand operates in the velvet glove of "talks between elected representatives," and remote from the political maneuvers of power-sharing; but it is not remote from the psychology of the Irishmen and Ulstermen who do the killing, and not remote from the bankrupt psychology and mythologies implicit in the terms Irish Catholic and Ulster Protestant. The question, as ever, is "How with this rage shall beauty hold a plea?" And my answer is, by offering "befitting emblems of adversity."

Some of those emblems I found in a book that was published here, appositely, the year the killing started, in 1969. And again appositely, it was entitled *The Bog People*. It was chiefly concerned with preserved bodies of men and women found in the bogs of Jutland, naked, strangled, or with their throats cut, disposed under the peat since early Iron Age times. The author, P. V. Glob, argues convincingly that a number of these, and, in particular, the Tollund Man, whose head is now preserved near Aarhus in the museum at Silkeborg, were ritual sacrifices to the Mother Goddess, the goddess of the ground who needed new bridegrooms each winter to bed with her in her sacred place, in the bog, to ensure the renewal and fertility of the territory in the spring. Taken in relation to the tradition of Irish political martyrdom for the cause whose icon is Kathleen Ni Houlihan, this is more than an archaic barbarous rite; it is an archetypal pattern. And the unforgettable photographs of these victims blended in my mind with photographs of atrocities, past and present, in the long rites of Irish political and religious struggles. When I wrote this poem, I had a completely new sensation: one of fear. It is a vow to go on pilgrimage, and I felt as it came to me — and again it came quickly — that unless I was deeply in earnest about what I was saying, I was simply invoking dangers for myself. It is called "The Tollund Man."

I

Some day I will go to Aarhus
To see his peat-brown head,
The mild pods of his eye-lids,
His pointed skin cap.

In the flat country nearby
Where they dug him out,
His last gruel of winter seeds
Caked in his stomach,

Naked except for
The cap, noose and girdle,
I will stand a long time.
Bridegroom to the goddess,

She tightened her torc on him
And opened her fen,
Those dark juices working
Him to a saint's kept body,

Trove of the turfcutters'
Honeycombed workings.
Now his stained face
Reposes at Aarhus.

II

I could risk blasphemy,
Consecrate the cauldron bog
Our holy ground and pray
Him to make germinate

The scattered, ambushed
Flesh of labourers,
Stockinged corpses
Laid out in the farmyards,

Tell-tale skin and teeth
Flecking the sleepers
Of four young brothers, trailed
For miles along the lines.

III

Something of his sad freedom
As he rode the tumbril
Should come to me, driving,
Saying the names

Tollund, Grauballe, Nebelgard,
Watching the pointing hands
Of country people,
Not knowing their tongue.

Out there in Jutland
In the old man-killing parishes
I will feel lost,
Unhappy and at home.

And just how persistent the barbaric attitudes are, not only in
the slaughter but in the psyche, I discovered, again when the fris-
son of the poem itself had passed, and indeed after I had fulfilled
the vow and gone to Jutland, "the holy blisful martyr for to seeke."
I read the following in a chapter on "The Religion of the Pagan
Celts" by the Celtic scholar Anne Ross:

> Moving from sanctuaries and shrines . . . we come now to con-
> sider the nature of the actual deities . . . But before going on to
> look at the nature of some of the individual deities and their
> cults, one can perhaps bridge the gap as it were by considering a
> symbol which, in its way, sums up the whole of Celtic pagan relig-
> ion and is as representative of it as is, for example, the sign of the
> cross in Christian contexts. This is the symbol of the severed hu-
> man head; in all its various modes of iconographic representation
> and verbal presentation, one may find the hard core of Celtic re-
> ligion. It is indeed . . . a kind of shorthand symbol for the entire
> religious outlook of the pagan Celts.

My sense of occasion and almost awe as I vowed to go to pray to
the Tollund Man and assist at his enshrined head had a longer an-
cestry than I had at the time realized.

I began by suggesting that my point of view involved poetry as
divination, as a restoration of the culture to itself. In Ireland in
this century it has involved for Yeats and many others an attempt
to define and interpret the present by bringing it into significant
relationship with the past, and I believe that effort in our present
circumstances has to be urgently renewed. But here we stray from
the realm of technique into the realm of tradition; to forge a poem
is one thing, to forge the uncreated conscience of the race, as Ste-
phen Dedalus put it, is quite another, and places daunting pres-
sures and responsibilities on anyone who would risk the name of
poet.

(1974)

Gary Snyder

The Real Work (Excerpts from an Interview)

INTERVIEWER: For you personally, what is the attraction of the rural life?

SNYDER: Well, apart from arguments about poetry, and *city* or *country*, it's obvious that city life has become difficult. It's *quite* obvious. And it's only natural that people should look for other ways to live. There is an implicit satisfaction in rural life, and in back-country life—at least for some people. The pleasures are numerous and the work is hard, and one is literally less alienated from one's water, one's fuel, one's vegetables, and so forth. Those are fundamentals, those are ancient human fundamentals.

And it wouldn't be going too far to say that human creativity and all of the arts will begin to wither if they are pulled too far away from fundamentals of how people really should and have had to live, over millennia. We are, after all, an animal that was brought into being on this biosphere by these processes of sun and water and leaf. And if we depart too far from them, we're departing too far from the mother, from our own heritage. But I've written some of my best poems working in the engine room of a tanker for months at a time where I didn't see a green leaf, or even a fly. That's not the problem. The problem is, where do you put your feet down, where do you raise your children, what do you do with your hands. Now, working in a tanker with my body and with my hands in the engine room of a ship is in some ways less alienated than it would be to sit and look at this beautiful view, talking constantly on a telephone, and typing on a typewriter and never *touching* it. It's the use of the *body* and the involvement of all the senses that is important at that point . . .

INTERVIEWER: You mentioned Eliot—don't you find Eliot . . . a *heady* poet?

SNYDER: What's really fun about Eliot is his intelligence, and his highly selective and charming use of Occidental symbols which point you in a certain direction. I read *From Ritual to Romance,* and went on to read *Prolegomena to Greek Religion,* Jane Ellen Harrison, and it just kept pushing me back. It takes you all the way back to the cave at Trois Frères in France, ultimately. If you follow anything that has any meat to it it'll take you back there. And so Eliot, without maybe even consciously being aware of it, points us in some profound directions. *Four Quartets* is my favorite Eliot work, and I think that it is a major work. He had the sense of the roots. He had the sense of the roots more deeply than Pound did, actually. Pound was never able to get back to—you know, he could get back to the Early Bronze Age and his imagination couldn't go back any further than that. Olson at least gets to the Neolithic.

INTERVIEWER: What do you mean when you say modern poets can get back to the Neolithic?

SNYDER: I mean their imagination is able to encompass it, that they feel that it's part of their lives, that they feel comradeship in connection with it, that they feel that there is humanity in that that speaks to them. This is part of our history . . .

INTERVIEWER: In the genesis of the poem as you write it: Do you take notes, or do these things just come to you? How does it arrive and what do you do first?

SNYDER: I listen to my own interior mind-music closely, and most of the time there's nothing particularly interesting happening. But once in a while I hear something which I recognize as belonging to the sphere of poetry. I listen very closely to that.

INTERVIEWER: Inside?

SNYDER: Inside. But it's coming from outside, if you like. Maybe I have a radio receiver planted in my spinal cord.

INTERVIEWER: Are you talking about voices or ideas that are being directed at you? For example, your son might mention something about the creek that might trigger something—

SNYDER: I might hear that too, that's true. Prior to the writing of the poems I tend to have a sense of key areas that I'm watching that are beginning to evolve as points I must know about, that are beginning to evolve in my life. And poems will flow out of those in time. Now here's the list of things I want to watch right now. [He opens a file drawer and takes out several cards.] These three cards. That's how I identify things, by those little phrases. Part of my psychological and spiritual evolution is tied up with that. Out of that more precise language and symbol ultimately will come—more precise *music* will come. I tend to nourish poems in the mind for a long time before I actually sing them and write them down. So that when they're born they're generally about the right term, and they don't have to be corrected or re-tuned too much.

INTERVIEWER: You don't do much revising, then?

SNYDER: Don't have to because I do it in my mind. I give them lots of time before they come out. That's short poems. On long poems, like "Mountains and Rivers Without End," which I'm working on now, I have to be more organized. Because I'm doing a number of long poems simultaneously, writing them all simultaneously. [He opens the various file cabinets and explains the use of the many folders, cards, and catalogues to the ongoing work of composing poetry.] So what I'm saying, I use a system of organization to keep on top of it . . .

INTERVIEWER: Can you conceive of a person being a good teacher of poetry?

SNYDER: I like the apprentice relation as a way to go for that. I think that young people who want to have a teacher should not look at a university as a university, but look for the teacher. If the teacher happens to be a professor in the university, that's all right. But if not, not. In either case you go to that person directly, not to the administration building, and you say, "I want to be your student. What do I have to do?" And in doing that you expand the relationship into something more *personal*, more *menial*, more *direct*.

The model for that, for me, is the Japanese potters who take apprentices. And the thing that the apprentice first learns how to do is mix clay. Or Japanese carpentry apprentices who will spend months learning how to sharpen chisels and planes before they ever touch the tools to do work.

INTERVIEWER: And for poets: Is it to see, or to sharpen the language?

SNYDER: Depends on what they're studying at that time and what the teacher is. The teacher could be a car repair man. You could learn as much from a good mechanic and how parts go together, and how you move and what goes in what order—you learn craft from a craftsman, it doesn't matter which. You learn how to use your mind in the act of handling parts and working. You learn how to work. You learn how things go together.

INTERVIEWER: You're making an analogy here.

SNYDER: But it's a *true* analogy. A master is a master. If you saw a man who was a master mechanic you'd do better—say you wanted to be a poet, and you saw a man that you recognized is a master mechanic or a great cook. You would do better, for yourself as a poet, to study under that man than to study under another poet who was not a master, that you didn't recognize as a master.

INTERVIEWER: Who was not a true poet?

SNYDER: Not only a true poet but a master—a *real* craftsman. There are true poets who can't teach because they're hooked onto inspiration, spontaneity, voice, language—they do it but they're not grounded in details. They don't *really* know the materials. A carpenter, a builder knows what Ponderosa pine can do, what Douglas fir can do, what Incense cedar can do and builds accordingly. You can build some very elegant houses without knowing that, but some of them aren't going to work, ultimately.

And so, I'm saying that behind the scenes there is the structural and the fundamental knowledge of materials in poetry, and learning from a master mechanic would give you some of those fundamentals as well as studying from an academician, say.

INTERVIEWER: It sounds as if you're talking more about an Oriental or an eastern kind of mechanic, someone who is more sensitive, or *sensitized.*

SNYDER: No. I use the term "master mechanic" because I know a master mechanic. Whenever I spend any time with him, I learn something from him.

INTERVIEWER: About?

SNYDER: About *everything*. But I see it in terms of my craft as a poet. I learn about my craft as a poet. I learn about what it really takes to be a craftsman, what it really means to be committed, what it really means to work. What it means to be *serious* about your craft and no bullshit . . . Not backing off any of the challenges that are offered to you. You know, like not being willing to read books, for Christ's sake. You run into people who want to write poetry who don't want to read anything in the tradition. That's like wanting to be a builder but not finding out what different kinds of wood you use.

INTERVIEWER: When a person teaches poetry, ought he to talk about inspiration?

SNYDER: Inspiration is something that can be talked about, but can't be taught in the university context. What you *can* point out is that inspire has the word "spirit" in it, and is related to *ex*pire, *re*spire, and *con*spire. And point out a few other connections like that. I would say, offhand, if you want inspiration, the two simplest and best ways to get it are to go on a long walking trip by yourself, or take a sweat bath. This will inspire you for poetry. Sweat baths, especially . . .

INTERVIEWER: Kerouac talks a lot about the idea of spontaneity: the "spontaneous get with it," the "spontaneous recall of the unconscious." Do you also feel that way about composing poetry?

SNYDER: It's only part of it. The spontaneity is beautiful, and Jack's *haiku*, in *Mexico City Blues*, are some of the prettiest poems in the English language. But to complete the work of poetry as I see it in our time, here, I'd like to see some instantly apprehended because so-well-digested larger loopings of loic. Now, if you haven't digested it and it hasn't become part of you, then you are looking things up in your library books. Or, as Philip Whalen says, in your Handbook of Comparative Mythology—to look for the symbols to put in. That, of course, is wrong. But if you've absorbed and apprehended and digested it, why your apprehensive, prehensive mass that you can draw on is very large and very beautiful. This is part of the training you come in there with. Your spontaneity, in other words, can be very rich.

INTERVIEWER: But it's a prior experience that makes it rich?

SNYDER: That's right. That's really what we mean by learning and by being cultured — that the time process really does enrich and deepen what you have at hand at any time. And there's a point where you have enough at hand at any time and you're so comfortable with it that you can really turn some very rich thing out. That's what a great potter is . . .

INTERVIEWER: Do you feel the university has a function beyond what Allen Ginsberg feels is its importance — cataloguing?

SNYDER: Well, that's a great value of it. But in fact the university also has the function of reassessing our tradition, our body of lore, every generation. And in the process sometimes discovering things that were missed before and bringing them back to our attention — as Blake was brought to us, or as Melville's poetry was brought to us — that might have been lost otherwise. So the English department is a cardboard box that everybody throws every poetry magazine that comes in the mail into and says, "Well, we'll look at that later. I haven't got time to read it now." So it's a backward function in time. Like some kinds of academic and intellectual pursuits are forward-looking — most of the sciences are looking for new breakthroughs, new discoveries. An English department is looking backward in time, trying to understand what happened as they go — you know, looping backward as they go, and trying to connect.

So they're establishing the tradition and that is their value. And I respect that. I have great respect for that. I don't think that they *understand* their function enough to have enough pride or enough pleasure in their work, though. And that's what makes me sad. They don't have a *tribal* sense of their own work, and it is a truly tribal work.

INTERVIEWER: What would you suggest to them?

SNYDER: I suggest that they get an anthropological and a prehistoric perspective on these things and then they'll see where what they're doing fits into the picture. And how the professors in the English department are like *kiva* priests, priests of the *kiva* that we have to go to from time to time to say "Now why was it that there are three lines painted at the top of this eagle feather, with a little bit of red fluff on it. Now what was the reason for doing that?" Somebody who keeps that in mind for us.

It doesn't mean that they have to care a lot about it. But they do have to care about their role, about their function. And their function is maybe to tell some young guy who's going to be a beautiful poet or a beautiful dancer, to give him that one little extra bit of information to deepen what he's doing.

Because, you know, they carry the lore, they bear it. And they bear it for the benefit of the dancers who get inspired out there in the plaza.

In earlier times the English professor would have also been the *raconteur*, the storyteller who would, to a small select audience of students after the storytelling was over and the audience had gone home, tell them some of the *inner* meanings, some of the *background*, some of the *professional secrets* of what he had just recited. He doesn't have to be the poet who made it up necessarily, see? . . .

INTERVIEWER: Some people would say to a young poet, "Poetry is self-expression. Sit down and write what you can whenever you can." Would you say that?

SNYDER: No, I wouldn't say that. I don't think that's true. I think that poetry is a social and traditional art that is linked to its past and particularly its language, that *loops* and draws on its past and that serves as a vehicle for contact with the depths of our own unconscious—and that it gets better by practicing. And that the expression of self, although it's a nice kind of energy to start with, would not make any expression of poetry *per se.*

We all know that the power of a great poem is not that we felt that person expressed himself well. We don't think that. What we think is "How deeply *I* am touched." That's our level of response. And so a great poet does not express his or her self; he expresses *all* of our selves. And to express *all* of our selves you have to go beyond your own self. As Dogen, the Zen master, said, "We study the self to forget the self. And when you forget the self, you become *one* with all things." And that's why poetry's not self-expression in those small self terms.

INTERVIEWER: Japan plays a considerable role in your poetry. Would you say to a young poet, "Go to Japan"?

SNYDER: Good heavens, no. What Japan as advice implies is: if there's a spiritual path that you feel is important to you, go out and study it, no matter where it leads. And the other thing that implies is: if you have the will and the energy and the opportunity, go live in an alien culture for a while. It really does, as they say, "broaden" you. [He laughs.]

INTERVIEWER: So a poet then, like a novelist, has to know human nature?

SNYDER: Well, I like the way Jack Spicer saw it where all pure and true poetry is ultimately inspired in origin. It comes to us as a voice from outside. To even say that it comes from within is to mislead yourself. So we are the vehicle of that voice. However, if we are people who can hear that voice, then we should strive to be the best possible vehicle of that voice we can. Which means to learn other languages, to become as broadly human and as well informed and aware as we can because that will give strength to our handling and expressing the power of the voice. I think that's just right on the money.

INTERVIEWER: Including translations?

SNYDER: Yeah, including translations. Reading. Learning how to *do* translations.

INTERVIEWER: Wallace Stevens said that the translator is a parasite. Do you agree with that?

SNYDER: We need everyone who can do it. Any good translator is a great help to all of us . . . A translator's no more a parasite than an interpreter standing at the edge of the creek helping a group of Crow and a group of Hunkpapa Sioux do some trading is a parasite—it's a valuable function. A translator is a valuable switch in an energy-exchange flow . . .

You ask me what is the function of poetry so I think, "What is the function of poetry since forty thousand years ago?" In all cultures of the world—total planetary overview. And in that sense the function of poetry is not only the intensification and clarification of the implicit potentials of the language, which we can hope means a sharpening, a bringing of more delight to the normal functions of language and making maybe language even work better since communication is what it's about. But on another level, poetry is intimately linked to any culture's fundamental world view, body of lore, which is its myth-base, its symbol-base, and the source of much of its values—that myth-lore foundation that underlies any society. That foundation is most commonly expressed and transmitted in the culture by poems, which is to say *by songs.* By songs that are linked to a dramatic or ritual performance much of the time.

INTERVIEWER: Then it doesn't have to be poetry *per se* — it could be through the drama or novels —

SNYDER: But we haven't had novels for forty thousand years. We have had poems.

INTERVIEWER: No, but we've had tales. We've had *Gilgamesh,* and that sort of thing.

SNYDER: All right. But those were in the oral tradition. What we're talking about there is the epic, and that is a variety of poetry because it is sung or chanted. The oral tradition almost always puts its transmission into a form of measured language, which is easier to remember and can be chanted. Much of the world's lore has been transmitted, in one form or another, via poetic forms, measured language or sung language.

INTERVIEWER: In terms of today's society, particularly the American, what forms would you see that might develop back into, or *forward* to, the mythic or oral tradition?

SNYDER: Well, we don't necessarily have to transmit a body of myth lore in only an oral mode. A key line of Occidental poetic transmission is the one that runs through Homer, Virgil, Dante, Goethe, Milton, James Joyce, and William Blake. Now, each one of those major poets has attempted in his own time, through a process of vision and meditation, so to speak, to assimilate, absorb and re-speak the fundamental myth-archetypal, world-view images of that whole world that they were in — to compress it and compact it and bring it back again into its own time. That's the ongoing work of major poets; to restate the society's whole body of world-view lore periodically. And, with the exception of Homer, all of the poets I've just mentioned were in writing. . . .

INTERVIEWER: W. H. Auden said about poetry that it won't change anything. Is that how you see poetry?

SNYDER: Ezra Pound said, to quote an oft-quoted line, that artists are the antennae of the race. How that probably functions in practice is that some people's sensibilities, as well as maybe their lifestyles, are out at the very edge of the unraveling cause-and-effect network of a society in time. And also are, by virtue of the nature of their sensibilities, tuned into other voices than simply the social or human voice. So they are like an early-warning system that hears the trees and the air and the clouds and the watersheds beginning to groan and complain a little bit. And so they try to send a little bit of a warning back, although they themselves may not know what it is they're hearing. They also can hear the stresses and the fault block slippage creaking in the social batholith and also begin to give out warnings.

What proceeds on that is, for the poet in particular, a sense of the need to look at the key archetype image and symbol blocks and see if the blocks are working. Poetry effects change by fiddling with the archetypes and getting at people's dreams about a century before it actually effects historical change.

INTERVIEWER: I'm not too clear on the idea of the archetype blocks.

SNYDER: What I'm saying is we change the values of a society.

INTERVIEWER: Then the poet is essentially a pioneer?

SNYDER: No, I wouldn't say a pioneer. A pioneer clear-cuts an ecosystem and sets the succession phase back to zero again. A poet would be, in terms of the ecology of symbols, noting the main structural connections and seeing which parts of the symbol system are no longer useful or applicable, though everyone is giving them credence. And out of his own vision and hearing of voices he seeks for new paths for the mind energy to flow, which would be literally more creative directions, but directions which change politics. Poets are more like mushrooms or fungi — they can digest the symbol detritus . . .

The value and function of poetry can be said in a very few words. One side of it is *in time*, the other is *out of time*. The in-time side of it is to tune us in to *mother* nature and *human* nature so that we live *in time*, in our societies in a way and on a path in which all things can come to fruition equally, and together in harmony. A path of beauty. And the out-of-time function of poetry is to return us to our own true original nature at this instant forever. And those two things happen, sometimes together, sometimes not, here and there all over the world, and always have.

Now whether or not that particular pattern of processes has had any great or small effects on the major flow of human social evolution is not something I can say. And yet if you look at a society that *sings* and that *dances* as a regular thing, it's not that it has an effect on their life — it *is* their life. It is their life: the lore of the culture is carried in the songs. And so poetry *is* our life. It's not that poetry has an effect on it, or a function in it, or a value for it. It *is* our life as much as eating and speaking is our life. It's like asking, "Well, what's the function of eating? What's the value of speaking?" . . .

INTERVIEWER: On a personal level, is the individual poet important? Does he need recognition?

SNYDER: Some do, some don't. I think for a lot of poets recognition from their peers is essentially what they need. You know, architects seldom get a lot of recognition from the public — the public doesn't see what's going on. An architect is pleased to have a fellow architect say, "I saw what you did there — that's really something." That's what you need, for the most part. People who crave recognition beyond that I tend to suspect a little bit as wanting some food for their ego, which won't do them any good. Excessive recognition — it does no harm to have lots of money, to be sure. That's not entirely true. But we can hope it doesn't do much harm to have lots of money. It may even be helpful. But *recognition* can really be detrimental to somebody who's interested in getting his or her work done and not in collecting Karma Cookies at testimonial dinners.

Even so young and little-known a poet as myself could fritter away a great deal of time going to testimonial dinners, so to speak, which would not write any more poems or give me any time to do all the work I want to do. So I need a certain level of anonymity, and I *am* that level of anonymity — I don't need it, I *make* it. I *live* that level of anonymity because I'm not interested in gaining social fruits from being a poet. I'm interested in writing my poems and finishing out the work that I envision for myself . . .

INTERVIEWER: In your poem "The Real Work" you mention that the "real work" is

> washing and sighing,
> sliding by.

What exactly is "the real work"?

SNYDER: I've used that phrase, "the real work," a few times before. I used that term, "the real work," and then I asked myself a lot:

What is the real work? I think it's important, first of all, because it's good to work — I love work; work and play are one. And that all of us will come back again to hoe in the ground, or gather wild potato bulbs with digging sticks, or hand-adze a beam, or skin a pole, or scrape a hive — we're never going to get away from that. We've been living a dream that we're going to get away from it, that we won't have to do it again. Put that out of our minds. We'll always do that work. That work is always going to be there. It might be stapling papers, it might be typing in the office. But we're never going to get away from that work, on one level or another. So that's real. The real work is what we really do. And what our lives are. And if we can live the work we have to do, knowing that we are real, and it's real, and that the world is real, then it becomes right. And that's the *real work*: to make the world as real as it is, and to find ourselves as real as we are within it.

I used that phrase again at the end of the poem "The Maverick Bar," where we go back out of that bar in Farmington, New Mexico, out onto the highway

> under the tough old stars . . .
> To the real work, to
> What is to be done.

The *real work* is to be the warriors that we have to be, to find the heart of the monster and kill it, whether we have any hope of actually winning or not. That's part of it. To take the struggle on without the *least* hope of doing any good. To check the destruction of the interesting and necessary diversity of life on the planet so that the dance can go on a little better for a little longer. The other part of it is that it is always here,

> washing and sighing,
> sliding by.

That was the wash of the waves on the island out in San Francisco Bay with the sea birds, and the feeding and schooling of the little fish — that's going on. The *real work* is eating each other, I suppose . . .

(Interviewed by Paul Geneson, 1977)

A Very Selective Reading List

Notes on the Poets and
Selections

A Very Selective Reading List

Note: Additional works by poets included in this volume are mentioned in the Notes on the Poets and Selections.

I. Interviews, questionnaires, collections of essays.

A. Of historical importance.

Hoffman, Daniel G., ed. *American Poetry and Poetics: Poems and Critical Documents from the Puritans to Robert Frost.* Garden City, N.Y.: Doubleday Anchor Books, 1962. Essays by Cotton Mather, Bryant, Poe, Emerson, Whitman, and others.

Norman, Charles, ed. *Poets on Poetry.* New York: Collier Books, 1962. Essays by Sidney, Jonson, Dryden, Johnson, Wordsworth, Coleridge, Shelley, Bryant, Emerson, Poe, Arnold, Pound, Eliot, Tate, Stevens, Cummings.

Rhys, Ernest, ed. *The Prelude to Poetry: The English Poets in Defence and Praise of Their Own Art.* New York: Dutton, Everyman Series, no 789, 1970. Essays by poets from Chaucer to C. Day Lewis, including Sidney's *Apologie,* Jonson, Wordsworth, Coleridge, Landor, Yeats, Pound, and others.

B. Twentieth-century poets.

Allen, Donald, and Tallman, Warren, eds. *The Poetics of the New American Poetry.* New York: Grove Press, 1973. Essays by D. H. Lawrence, Williams, Creeley, Ginsberg, Imamu Amiri Baraka, and others.

Gross, Harvey, ed. *The Structure of Verse: Modern Essays on Prosody,* revised edition. New York: Ecco Press, 1978. Technical essays by Pound, Eliot, Graves, Roethke, Kunitz, and others.

Heyen, William, ed. *American Poets in 1976*. Indianapolis: Bobbs-Merrill, 1977. Poets writing about their own poems and sources. Includes Bly, Brinnin, Creeley, Hugo, Ignatow, Meredith, Oates, Peck, Plumly, Rich, Sexton, Simpson, Stafford, James Wright, and others.

Nemerov, Howard, ed. *Poets on Poetry*. New York: Basic Books, 1966. Essays in which each poet responds to a questionnaire about his or her methods: Aiken, Moore, Eberhart, Cunningham, Belitt, Howes, Brinnin, Berryman, Gilbert, Miller, Duncan, Swenson, Wilbur, Corso, Smith, Whittemore, Weiss, Dickey, Nemerov.

Packard, William, ed. *The Craft of Poetry: Interviews from the New York Quarterly*. New York: Doubleday, 1974.

The Paris Review *Writers at Work* series, ed. by Malcolm Cowley and others. New York: Viking, 1958, 1963, 1967, 1976.

Scully, James, ed. *Modern Poets on Poetry*. London: Fontana, 1966. Essays by Yeats, Pound, Eliot, Frost, Williams, Hopkins, Ransom, Moore, Cummings, Stevens, Crane, Auden, Thomas, Jones, Lowell.

Turner, Alberta, ed. *Fifty Contemporary Poets: The Creative Process*. New York: David McKay/Longman, 1977. Poets answer a questionnaire taking as example one of their own poems.

II. Books by poets.

Benn, Gottfried. *Primal Vision: Selected Writings*, ed., E. B. Ashton. New York: New Directions, 1960.

Berryman, John. *The Freedom of the Poet*. New York: Farrar, Straus & Giroux, 1976.

Bly, Robert. *Leaping Poetry*. Boston: Beacon, 1975.

Creeley, Robert. *A Quick Graph: Collected Notes and Essays*. San Francisco: Four Seasons Foundation, 1970.

Cunningham, J. V. *The Collected Essays of J. V. Cunningham*. Chicago: Swallow, 1976.

Davie, Donald. *Articulate Energy*. London and Boston: Routledge and Kegan Paul, 1976.

Eliot, T. S. *On Poetry and Poets*. New York: Noonday Press, 1957.

———. *The Sacred Wood*. New York: Barnes and Noble, 1964.

Robert Frost on Writing, ed., Elaine Barry. New Brunswick, New Jersey: Rutgers University Press, 1973.

Jacob, Max. *Advice to a Young Poet*, trans., John Adlard. London: Menard Press, 1976.

Jones, David. *Epoch and Artist*. London: Faber, 1959.

Kunitz, Stanley. *A Kind of Order, A Kind of Folly*. Boston: Little, Brown, 1975.

MacNeice, Louis. *Modern Poetry: A Personal Essay*. Oxford: The Clarendon Press, 1968.

Olson, Charles. *Selected Writings*. New York: New Directions, 1966.

Mayakovsky, Vladimir. *How Are Verses Made?*, trans. G. M. Hyde. London: Jonathan Cape, 1970.

Nemerov, Howard. *Reflexions on Poetry and Poetics*. New Brunswick, New Jersey: Rutgers University Press, 1972.

Paz, Octavio. *The Bow and the Lyre*, trans. Ruth L. C. Simms. New York: McGraw-Hill, 1973.

Ponge, Francis. *The Voice of Things*, trans. Beth Archer. New York: McGraw-Hill, 1974.

Pound, Ezra. *ABC of Reading*. New York: New Directions, 1960.

_____. *Literary Essays*. New York: New Directions, 1968.

Rilke, Rainer Maria. *Letters to a Young Poet*, trans. M. D. Herder Norton. New York: Norton, 1962.

Roethke, Theodore. *On the Poet and His Craft*. Seattle: University of Washington Press, 1965.

Tate, Allen. *Essays of Four Decades*. Chicago: Swallow, 1968.

_____. *Memoirs and Opinions 1926–1974*. Chicago: Swallow, 1974.

Warren, Robert Penn. *Democracy and Poetry*. Cambridge, Mass.: Harvard University Press, 1975.

Wilbur, Richard. *Responses: Prose Pieces 1948–1974*. New York: Harcourt Brace Jovanovich, 1976.

Wright, Judith. *Because I Was Invited*. Melbourne: Oxford University Press, 1975.

Yeats, W. B. *Essays and Introductions*. New York: Macmillan, 1968.

Zukovsky, Louis. *Prepositions: The Collected Critical Essays*. London: Rapp and Carroll, 1967.

III. Secondary books.

Alain. *The Gods*, trans. Richard Pevear. New York: New Directions, 1974.

Barfield, Owen. *Poetic Diction*. Middletown, Connecticut: Wesleyan University Press, 1973.

Fussell, Paul. *Poetic Meter and Poetic Form* (revised edition). New York: Random House, 1979.

Hamburger, Michael. *The Truth of Poetry: Tensions in Modern Poetry from Baudelaire to the 1960s*. New York: Harcourt Brace Jovanovich, 1969, and London: Penguin, 1972.

Mandelstam, Nadezhda. *Hope Against Hope*, trans. Max Hayward. New York: Atheneum, 1970.

IV. Magazines and book series.

Antaeus, Numbers 30/31 (Spring 1978) is a special issue on poetry and poetics, including essays by Kunitz, Fussell, Miller, Williams, Justice, Plumly, Hass, Strand, Simic, Montale.

Field (Oberlin, Ohio) continues to publish essays by contemporary poets on their craft; consult all back issues.

University of Michigan Press (Ann Arbor, Michigan) is publishing a series of books by poets, under the editorship of Donald Hall. Future volumes will be by Robert Bly, Donald Davie, Maxine Kumin, Diane Wakoski, and others. Those published to date are:

Hall, Donald. *Goatfoot, Milktongue, Twinbird*. 1978.

Kinnell, Galway. *Walking Down the Stairs: Selections from Interviews*. 1978.

Stafford, William. *Writing the Australian Crawl*. 1978.

Notes on the Poets
and Selections

(see copyright page for sources
of the selections included in this volume)

W. H. AUDEN (1907–1973), "Writing." This piece, from *The Dyer's Hand*, has a companion essay, "Reading." Auden's prose is collected in several volumes, and his poems in *Collected Poems*, ed. by Edward Mendelson (New York: Random House, 1976).

WENDELL BERRY (1934–   ), "The Specialization of Poetry." In all his work, Berry strives to give poetry power and precedence as a critique of culture. See especially *Openings* (New York: Harcourt Brace and World, 1968) and *Clearing* (New York: Harcourt Brace Jovanovich, 1977). For more of Berry's prose, see *A Continuous Harmony* (New York: Harcourt Brace Jovanovich, 1972).

LOUISE BOGAN (1897–1970), "The Pleasures of Formal Poetry." Bogan's work combines great technical control with a sense of powerful, uncontrolled emotion. See *The Blue Estuaries: Poems 1923–1968* (New York: Ecco Press, 1977) and *Achievement in American Poetry* (South Bend, Indiana: Gateway Editions, Ltd., 1950).

LUIS CERNUDA (1902–1963), "Words Before a Reading." Cernuda's first major collection of poems was published the year following this reading. For poems in English, see *Selected Poems of Luis Cernuda*, trans. by Reginald Gibbons (University of California Press, 1978).

RENÉ CHAR (1907–   ), from "The Formal Share." Much of Char's work is in the form of the prose poem, to which these paragraphs about poetry bear some resemblance. See *Poems of René Char*, trans. by Mary Anne Caws and Jonathan Griffin (Princeton University Press, 1976).

HART CRANE (1899–1932), "General Aims and Theories." A poet of compression and metaphorical vigor, Crane wrote comparatively few essays, but his letters contain many technical asides about his art. See *The Letters of Hart Crane*, ed. by Brom Weber (University of California Press, 1965).

ROBERT DUNCAN (1919–   ), "Poetic Form." Associated with the aesthetic principles of the Black Mountain group of poets, Duncan has published many books; for poems, see especially *The Opening of the Field* and *Roots and Branches* (New York: New Directions, 1960 and 1968), and, for prose, *The Truth and Life of Myth: An Essay in Essential Autobiography* (Fremont, Michigan: The Sumac Press, 1968).

FEDERICO GARCÍA LORCA (1898–1936), "The Duende: Theory and Divertissement." Lorca's ability to fuse the learned and popular traditions of Spanish poetry came from his having given both strains great study; the vernacular is evident especially in his plays, but also see "The Poetic Image in Don Luis de Góngora" (trans. by Ben Belitt), *Quarterly Review of Literature*, Thirtieth Anniversary Criticism Retrospective (vol. XX, nos. 3–4, 1977).

SEAMUS HEANEY (1939–   ), "Feelings into Words." This lecture was delivered to the Royal Society of Literature on October 17, 1974. Heaney's several volumes of poetry include *Death of a Naturalist* (London: Faber, 1966) and *North* (New York: Oxford University Press, 1976).

A. D. HOPE (1907–   ), "The Three Faces of Love." An Australian poet, Hope has preferred the traditional forms of poetry while treating very modern material. See *Collected Poems* (Penguin, 1968).

RANDALL JARRELL (1914–1965), "The Woman at the Washington Zoo." See *Complete Poems* (New York: Farrar, Straus and Giroux, 1969) and Jarrell's remarkable criticism, collected in *The Third Book of Criticism* and *Poetry and the Age* (New York: Farrar, Straus and Giroux, 1969 and 1972).

GÜNTER KUNERT (1929–   ), "Why Write." Kunert, who lives in East Berlin, is a poet whose work has been influenced by Kafka, Brecht, and Marx. He has not yet been translated into English.

DENISE LEVERTOV (1923–   ), "Some Notes on Organic Form." Here, Levertov takes up nomenclature established by Coleridge, and endeavors to explain its accuracy with regard to her own work, which is characteristically meditative and precise. In the volume from which this piece is drawn, *The Poet in the World* (New York: New Directions, 1973), see also "Work and Inspiration: Inviting the Muse." Among her many volumes of poems, see especially *The Jacob's Ladder* and *O Taste and See* (New York: New Directions, 1962 and 1964).

HUGH MACDIARMID (Christopher Murray Grieve) (1892–1978), "Poetry and Science." The most important Scottish poet of our century, MacDiarmid published scores of books and almost self-handedly determined the course of modern Scottish poetry, for he resurrected and half-created the modern dialect poetry of Scotland. All the while, he tried to bring the economic and scientific dimensions of modern life into poetry. "On a Raised Beach" is a great example of his success. See *Collected Poems* (New York: Macmillan, 1962), *More Collected Poems* (London: MacGibbon and Kee, 1970), and *Selected Poems* (Penguin, 1970).

ANTONIO MACHADO (1875–1939), from "Notes on Poetry." Machado's poetry rejected the florid phrasing and diction of the nineteenth century in favor of a conversational meditativeness on daily life. As he says in another context, "Poetry is the word in time," that is, in a temporal dimension—not an art of static images but of dramatic unfolding. See other writings on poetry in *Juan de Mairena: Epigrams, Maxims, Memoranda and Memoirs of an Apocryphal Professor*, trans. by Ben Belitt (University of California Press, 1963).

OSIP MANDELSTAM (1891–1938), "The Word and Culture." Mandelstam's prose is rich and allusive; there are many perceptive and original remarks about writing in the long essay "Talking About Dante," in the *Selected Essays*, ed. by Sidney Monas. For poems, see versions in Clarence Brown, *Mandelstam* (Cambridge: Cambridge University Press, 1973) and also in several translated collections.

CZESLAW MILOSZ (1911–   ), "Ars Poetica?" A Polish poet now living in the United States, Milosz exemplifies the powerful, unadorned poetics of many writers in eastern Europe. English versions of his poems are published in *Selected Poems* (New York: Seabury Press, 1973) and *Bells in Winter* (New York: Ecco Press, 1978); his literary essays are translated in *Emperor of the Earth: Modes of Eccentric Vision* (University of California Press, 1977).

EUGENIO MONTALE (1896–   ), from "Intentions (Imaginary Interview)." Montale has drawn many of his poems from the landscape of Liguria, as he has explored the relationship between emotion and place. For poems, see *Selected Poems* (New York: New Directions, 1965), *The Storm and Other Poems*, trans. by Charles Wright (Oberlin, Ohio: Field

Translation Series, Number 1, 1978), and other volumes. His selected essays, translated by Jonathan Galassi, are forthcoming from the Ecco Press.

MARIANNE MOORE (1887–1972), "Idiosyncrasy and Technique." One of the most original and painstaking of American poets, Moore developed very early a poetic method based on precise observation and description. Also a witty translator of the fables of La Fontaine, she insisted on the close relationship of poetry to speech. See *A Marianne Moore Reader* (New York: Viking, 1965).

BORIS PASTERNAK (1890–1960), "Some Statements." Both poet and novelist, Pasternak moved from the dense, rather elevated, poetic diction of his early poems to a more direct, though no less luminous, manner, retaining a sense of poetry as a mysterious and powerful medium, mostly elegiac. See *The Poems of Doctor Zhivago*, trans. by Donald Davie (New York: Barnes and Noble, 1965).

FERNANDO PESSOA (1888–1935), "Toward Explaining Heteronymy." Pessoa wrote poetry under his own name and also under that of his three "heteronyms": Alberto Caeiro, Ricardo Reis, and Alvaro de Campos — each quite distinct as a poet. Pessoa's work was largely unknown until after his death, when its discovery established him as the most powerful Portuguese poet of his time. This essay comes from a posthumously published volume of self-analytical prose. In English, see *Selected Poems*, ed. and trans. by Peter Rickard (Austin: University of Texas Press, 1971) and *Selected Poems of Fernando Pessoa*, trans. by Jonathan Griffin (Penguin, 1974).

DELMORE SCHWARTZ (1913 1966), "The Vocation of the Poet in the Modern World." Schwartz's own career, which took him erratically from brilliant early work through periods of no writing at all, was the material he pondered in writing about "the poet in the world," to use Levertov's phrase. See *Selected Poems: Summer Knowledge* (New York: New Directions, 1967) and his stories, *In Dreams Begin Responsibilities* (New York: New Directions, 1978).

GEORGE SEFERIS (1900–   ), "from *A Poet's Journal*." Translator of Yeats, Eliot, and Pound, Seferis united the international literary sensibility of these poets with the luminous landscapes and history of Greece. His continual prodding of himself, in his journals, to work harder and to let up at the same time, allowing the peculiar processes of poetic composition to begin, is highly instructive. See *Collected Poems*, trans. by Edmund Keeley and Philip Sherrard (Princeton: Princeton University Press, 1967).

KARL SHAPIRO (1913–   ), "What Is Not Poetry?". Shapiro has been a poet-polemicist of considerable penetration, and his poetic work has been matched by the energy and seriousness of his essays. In addition to *In Defense of Reason*, see *To Abolish Children* (Chicago: Quadrangle Books, 1968) and *Collected Poems* (New York: Random House, 1978).

GARY SNYDER (1930–   ), "The Real Work" (Excerpts from an Interview). This interview appeared in full in *The Ohio Review*. Known for bringing Oriental aesthetics to his poetry, Snyder has concentrated mostly on the poetic treatment of the natural world; however, as these excerpts show, it would be wrong to think of him as a poet with no concern for the poetic tradition. For poems, see especially *The Back Country* and *Regarding Wave* (New York: New Directions, 1967 and 1970).

WALLACE STEVENS (1879–1955), "The Irrational Element in Poetry." Many of Stevens' poems address the question of the nature of poetry, and of all acts of the imagination. More of his prose is collected in *The Necessary Angel* (New York: Vintage, 1965).

DYLAN THOMAS (1914–1953), "Poetic Manifesto." Thomas wrote little on the subject of his own writing. His expansive personal manner, with which he virtually invented the modern American practice of reading poetry to public audiences, belied his solitary dedication to writing. See *Collected Poems* (New York: New Directions, 1971).

PAUL VALÉRY (1871–1945), "A Poet's Notebook." Valéry gave considerable thought to the creative process, and wrote several important essays, especially "Poetry and Abstract Thought" in *The Art of Poetry*, introduction by T. S. Eliot (New York: Vintage, 1961). See, in addition to the *Selected Writings* (New York: New Directions, 1964), the many volumes of his work published in translation by the Bollingen Foundation (Princeton University Press).

WILLIAM CARLOS WILLIAMS (1883–1963), "Projective Verse" and "The Practice." These chapters from Williams' autobiography show how important it was for him to encourage a poet's understanding of the local, concrete reality around him, including the historical associations hidden there. For more of Olson's prose, see the reading list above. For more Williams, see *Selected Essays* (New York: New Directions, 1969).